Voices of a New Chicana/o History

Voices of a New Chicana/o History

Refugio I. Rochín and Dennis N. Valdés, editors

Michigan State University Press
East Lansing

∞ The paper used in this publication meets the minimum requirements of ANSI/NISO Z39.48–1992 (R 1997) (Permanence of Paper).

Michigan State University Press
East Lansing, Michigan 48823-5202

05 04 03 02 01 00 1 2 3 4 5 6

Library of Congress Cataloging-in-Publication Data

Voices of a new Chicana/o history / Refugio I. Rochín and Dennis Nodín Valdés, editors.
p. cm.
Essays originally presented at a conference, "Towards a New Chicana/o History," held at Michigan State University, 22–23 April 1996.
Includes Bibliographical references.
ISBN 0-87013-523-6 (alk. paper)
1. Mexican American women—History—Congresses. I. Rochín, Refugio I. II. Valdés, Dennis Nodín.
E184.M5 V65 2000
305.48'86872073—dc21

00-008064

Cover design by Ariana Grabec-Dingman
Book design by Michael J. Brooks

Visit Michigan State University Press on the World Wide Web at:
http://www.msu.edu/unit/msupress

CONTENTS

New and Divergent Histories

Historiographies: Surveys of the Field

History and the Chicano Movement

PREFACE

THE FRUITLESS SEARCH FOR A CHICANA/O PARADIGM

Dennis N. Valdés and Refugio I. Rochín

THE ESSAYS IN THIS COLLECTION are inspired by an event sponsored at Michigan State University, "Toward a New Chicana/o History," the largest conference dedicated solely to this field since its birth more than a generation ago. As conference co-coordinators, our goal was to examine the collective state of Chicana/o history—past, present, and future—according to several of its creators, other established historians, and younger scholars. As editors of this book, our aim is not to seek a definition for Chicana/o history or determine its content, but rather to examine leading strands of thought that have evolved since the 1960s. We purposely sought out a broad range of approaches and viewpoints. The authors are united by a personal commitment to enhancing understanding about Mexicans in the United States.

A question of long-standing interest among practitioners in Chicana/o studies is examined at least implicitly in all of the essays in this collection: namely, what is unique to the field, other than its focus on Chicana/os? The Chicana and Chicano scholars who address this question represent different generations, enjoy expertise in a wide range of historical subfields, and are conscious of the transdisciplinary nature of Chicana/o studies. Some were trained in history and the social sciences, others in literature and anthropology. A common interest among them, however, is the critical link between scholarship and activism as addressed in the formation of the field of Chicana/o studies. The authors express their concerns about activism and scholarship in many ways, and the different views suggest their awareness of the complexity of the issue. They also address the links between theory and practice on a number of topics, including Chicana/o origins, gender, race, class, and geography, and the impact each has had on understanding and shaping Chicana/o history.

The essays in this collection provide further evidence that from its turbulent beginning in the late 1960s, there has been no dominant approach to Chicana/o history. The field has become more varied and complex over time, reflecting in part the involvement of an increasing number of historians, their widely differing training, and the introduction of new theoretical approaches. It also reflects conscious efforts by practitioners to broaden the chronology and geography of the field, leading to an increasing awareness of the complexity of subject populations, past and present.

While there are some differences in viewpoints among the different generations of scholars, as discussed by José Cuello in the introduction to this volume, different historical perspectives that cross generations are more noteworthy. Most historians of Chicana/o history are comfortable with and apply more than one approach in their writings. They are simultaneously aware of both the strengths and the weaknesses of any single theoretical application.

Among individuals trained in the history of the United States, several models strongly influenced by modernism have been popular. Cultural pluralism, perhaps most influential among students of ethnic studies and ethnic populations in dominant scholarship, has been adopted by some individual students of Chicana/o history, including those identified by Rámon Gutiérrez in his chapter as "conservative labor historians." Most historians, modernist and postmodernist alike, find serious theoretical and practical pitfalls in applying cultural pluralism to the history of Chicanas/os. As an alternative, Marxism has influenced several Chicana/o historians, particularly in its approaches to inequality, despite its limitations. One limitation, as noted by Dennis Valdés, is that Marx had little regard for Mexico or the capacities of Mexicans. Nonetheless, Marx is credited by his successors as the inspiration for current world-systems analysis, a framework that influences many students of Chicana/o history, for whom Marxism provides an understanding of networks and an international framework for Chicana/o history that bridges the United States and Latin America. It also permits a more systematic approach to inequality than internal colonial models, which had been very influential in early writings on Chicana/o history.

Some Chicana/o historians recently have turned to postmodernism to overcome the unitary, dominant, male voice in modernist approaches, and to permit space for the "other." Postmodernism offers a valuable framework for understanding contradictions, complexity, and hybridity. Postmodernism does not, however, adequately address a critical dilemma among Chicana/o studies scholars, namely the linking of academia and activism beyond the written text. This weakness is well demonstrated in the recent work of leading postmodernist author Jacques Derrida, *Spectres of Marx*.[1] Derrida's work demonstrates that the deconstruction of language and the texts created by language are less problematic than the construction of political agendas on behalf of the oppressed.

Cognizant of weaknesses inherent in accepting imported models, a number of scholars have engaged in a quest for a distinct Chicana/o paradigm.[2] Yet the practitioners in this volume would agree with Rudy Acuña that, "a single paradigm will not solve the riddle (of history) nor result in justice." In other words, given the wide range of interests and the growing heterogeneity of Chicana/o populations, any search for a single paradigm will be fruitless.

A great strength of writings on the history of Chicanas and Chicanos has been its breadth. As the readings presented here suggest, its students have borrowed widely and engage theory on a number of levels simultaneously. They also cast a wide geographical net, not confined to the narrow strip of territory north of the political border between Mexico and the United States. The collective writings in the field have expanded our understanding of a myriad of concerns facing academics and practitioners beyond Chicana/o studies. The greatest strength of the field has been its capacity to transcend disciplines, theoretical approaches and historical subfields among individuals interested in the United States, Mexico, Latin America, and international relations. Given the need to understand a number of literatures and simultaneously cognizant of social action in research, it is necessary to create a dialogue that transcends the respective fields from which practitioners of Chicana and Chicano history have borrowed. Ours is necessarily global history, and it has been that way for five centuries. The complex and multi-faceted study of Chicanas and Chicanos past and present will continue to stimulate debate, a multiplicity of approaches, and a rich scholarship in the coming generation.

Notes

1. Jacques Derrida, *Spectres of Marx: The State of the Debt, the Work of Mourning, and the New International* (New York: Routledge, 1994).
2. See, e.g., Alfredo Mirandé, *The Chicano Experience* (Notre Dame: University of Notre Dame Press, 1985); Carlos Muñoz, "The Quest for Paradigm: The Development of Chicano Studies," in *Latinos and Education: A Critical Reader*, ed. Antonia Darder, Rodolfo D. Torres and Henry Gutiérrez (New York: Routledge, 1997) 439–53; Rodolfo F. Acuña, *Sometimes There is No Other Side: Chicanos and the Myth of Equality* (Notre Dame: University of Notre Dame Press, 1998); and *Chicana Critical Issues,* ed. Norma Alarcón, Rafaela Castro, Emma Pérez, Beatriz Pesquera, Adaljiza Sosa Riddell, and Patricia Zavella (Berkeley, Calif.: Third Woman Press, 1993).

INTRODUCTION: CHICANA/O HISTORY AS A SOCIAL MOVEMENT

José Cuello

The Movement Penetrates Academia

IT HAS BECOME APPARENT to many scholars of Chicana/o History that the explosive growth and diversification in research and interpretation now requires the community to pause and evaluate where the field has been, and where it might go in the future.[1] Thus, the conference "Towards a New Chicana/o History," held at Michigan State University, 22–23 April 1996, was organized at a timely juncture, and at a particularly exciting moment in terms of observing Chicana/o History. As a relatively new field—established less than two generations ago—Chicana/o History constitutes a living laboratory dedicated to the formation of a new academic discipline, born out of a social and political movement with which it remains closely intertwined. For historians who are interested in the writing of history and the forces that affect it—that which we call historiography—the evolution of Chicana/o History offers the opportunity to observe in the making a process of intellectualization that historiographers traditionally have had to extract from documents after the fact, after the writers of a particular history are dead.

Many of the issues that stimulated the conference on a new Chicana/o History have been lived, and are being lived, by the participants in the conference, people who have contributed to the debate on the character and future of the field. Historians expressing their views at the conference included some of the original activists in the Chicana/o political movement, and others who lived through the movement's early years in the 1960s. The new generation of Chicana/o historians who took part in the conference debate, but were born after 1960, are also living the history of the movement.

It must be remembered that Chicana/o History and Chicana/o studies together embody a movement that represents the penetration of societal concerns into academia. Thus, the initial questions that defined Chicana/o History using temporal, spatial, and thematic parameters are now being augmented and redefined by newer questions centered in gender, generation, class, sexual orientation, religion, changing regionalities, and other social issues. As conference participant Lorena Oropeza observed, other new fields which have emerged from social movements—women's, African-American, Native American, and gay-lesbian history—are undergoing similar experiences. Within the discipline of history, these new fields represent multifaceted intellectual/cultural engagements which are shifting the paradigm through which "mainstream" history is studied and interpreted. At the same time, internal priorities and hierarchies are being challenged within each of the new fields as they all undergo rapid evolutionary changes in their conceptual growth. [2]

The trajectory of Chicana/o History as a cultural construct is part of a larger experience that extends across all academic disciplines. Some might say that it is a scholar's truism to assert that the cultural formation of the scholar shapes her perception of her field.[3] Truism or not, the statement is made especially relevant today by the fact that so many "other voices" have risen up to reclaim and rewrite a history previously constructed from an overwhelmingly male, Euro-American perspective. Political consciousness and the drive for self-empowerment have encouraged many social groups to seize control of their own histories and recontextualize the images of their national, ethnic, or gender past from within their own communities. The internal questions circulating within the field of Chicana/o History are therefore part of a multilayered questioning of assumptions occurring at all levels of scholarly endeavor which interrogate the relationship of the discipline to life outside the university. Often criticized for having political agendas, the new fields of study have exposed the invisible naturalized politics of established historiographies, and have raised our shared consciousness that all writing, including the consciously "objective," is political.

In order to understand the variety of perspectives expressed at the conference and format them conceptually, it is important for the reader to understand that the mission objectives of Chicana/o History, as part of Chicana/o studies, have been reformulated and reprioritized as advances in the political/academic agenda have been made over the last three decades. As a shared political and academic enterprise, Chicana/o History has been charged with implementing the following complex and logistically daunting agenda:

1. Serve the political movement by producing new knowledge and refining the ideological foundations of the movement;
2. Increase the number of Chicana/os in university faculties and student bodies. Initially, the fastest and most effective way of accomplishing this was through the establishment of Chicana/o studies programs and departments;
3. Convert historians and scholars in other fields to the study of Chicana/o history and train new ones in the field;
4. Produce the knowledge and interpretations, not just to provide the intellectual resources for the political movement, but also to correct the actual imbalances and distortions in the historiography;
5. Establish a competitive field of study within an elitist and hostile intellectual and political academic environment. This required the invention of a new field of activity with rationalized temporal, spatial, and thematic parameters, and effective research methodologies;
6. Integrate and transform mainstream fields of research by shifting their paradigms to include Chicana/o history;
7. Integrate university faculties, administrations, and student bodies beyond the segregated islands of representation in Chicana/o studies programs and departments. The transformation of the larger society and university environments requires Chicana/o scholars researching and teaching in mainstream academic departments, with a good number of them specializing in non-Chicana/o topics;
8. Integrate mainstream curricula and redefine and enrich them through the inclusion of Chicana/o History and Chicana/o perspectives;
9. Refine and redefine Chicana/o History itself by expanding its knowledge base and reworking its interpretations. This includes the conceptual adjustment to the great diversity of Chicana/o historical experiences that challenges the myth of a homogenous community. It also means the application of methodologies imported from other fields and the analytical comparison of Chicana/o historical experiences with those of other groups;

10. Diversify Chicana/o faculties through the inclusion of women and other scholars whose perspectives and interests are different from those of the more established members in the field;
11. Explore and define the conceptual and historical bases for alliances with other Latina/o groups, both in academia and outside of it. This includes negotiating the conceptual and political relations with Latina/o History, which is perceived by some Chicana/o scholars as a threat that will dilute and weaken Chicana/o History;
12. Preserve the gains made in all of these areas through institutionalized programs, networks, and pipelines;
13. Maintain open perspectives to new opportunities, challenges, and changes.

The Debate Over the Mission of Chicana/o Studies

This complex set of mission objectives has led to real and perceived conflicts among scholars and activists who have differed over priorities and strategies in the face of resource shortages and external threats to Chicana/o studies and the Chicana/o movement. The reader will best understand the simultaneous conflict and harmony apparent in the following essays as resulting from the creative tension between two evolutionary stages. The founding stage, invented to challenge mainstream U.S. historiography, was confrontational by nature. The developmental stage, transitional in nature, retains the traditional belief that Chicana/o History is marginalized by the mainstream field. However, younger Chicana/o scholars, rather than take a confrontational approach, are finding increasing common ground thematically and methodologically with mainstream scholars, especially within the new cultural history that has arisen over the last generation. Scholars of the developmental stage often define the newer stage in contrast to the founding stage, even while acknowledging that the previous tradition actually enabled the latter. Thus, scholars of the founding generation tend to believe integration will lead to the destruction of Chicana/o History, while younger scholars are much more likely to see integration as opportunity rather than crisis. The ensuing debate concerning how, and on what terms, Chicana/o History should relate to the mainstream historiography of the United States is consequently reflected in this collection of essays.

To stimulate thought and discussion about the state of the field, participants were sent an essay by Ignacio García in advance of the conference.[4] A scholar of the founding stage of Chicana/o studies, García believes that the field is in crisis because its practitioners and beneficiaries have lost the militancy of the original generation and forgotten the purpose for which Chicana/o studies programs were originally established—to serve the community. According to García, Chicana/o studies is being fatally weakened by scholars who, for various reasons, have either lost or never had an "ideological connection with the original premises of Chicano studies." Among these scholars are: (1) those seeking to integrate themselves and their programs into the general curriculum of the university; (2) older scholars who have become concerned more with advancing their individual careers than with strengthening Chicana/o studies; (3) younger scholars who have no depth of connections to the movement or the historiography, and do their work in a vacuum; and (4) female scholars who create internal ruptures in Chicana/o studies by promoting either a feminist agenda or a lesbian agenda at the expense of ethnic solidarity. García perceives two other threats to the survival and prosperity of Chicana/o studies: (1) lack of student involvement, which was once a pillar of support; and (2) the rise of Latina/o studies which dilutes the purpose of Chicana/o studies.

García advocates for a recommitment to Chicana/o studies and its revival. He believes a search for new paradigms will reenergize the field the way that the internal colony paradigm energized it in the founding generation. This search would be complemented by a new "master plan" for educating and politicizing Mexican-American students, carried out by yet-to-be-formed regional associations. García does not underestimate the difficulty of implementing such an agenda, but asserts that the alternative will be the further decline of Chicana/o studies.

The Broader Purpose of the Conference

The essay had the desired effect of stimulating comment and debate, but the participants did not limit themselves to the issues raised by García. Each participating scholar was asked to address one of the following four broad themes:

Connections: The synergy between Chicana/o and Mexican History;
Directions: The evolution and future path of Chicana/o History;

Variations: A comparison of thematic and methodological variations, especially between the Southwest and Midwest;
Positions: Different perspectives on Chicana/o and ethnic studies.

The result was a set of essays that range from sweeping interpretations of the field's evolution to the analysis of specific trends and historical problems. Some essays serve the purpose of providing important background information on the field, while others show how specific areas of the field have developed, and what topics need to be pursued in the future. The theme and format of the conference encouraged the interlacing of personal experiences with the abstract conceptualization of the field and the politics of academia in the presentations and discussions.

The Historical Background and Evolution of Chicana/o History

Two presenters provide analytical overviews of the background on which Chicana/o studies and History rose to prominence. In "Asymmetry: A Thematic Handbook," Ramón Eduardo Ruiz gives us an overview of the complex relationships along the U.S.-Mexico border stemming from the unequal power of the two nations. In a tour de force that can only come from deep study and personal knowledge of the border states, Ruiz explains the economic basis of the asymmetry, the different geographies (economic, ecological, and social) of the border regions, the inequalities in wealth of their populations, the urbanization of the border, the stifling effect of political centralization on Mexican border development, the *agromaquila* industry, the dynamics of sister city economics, and the varied histories of the border cities. The overview sets the historical and international context against which Chicana/o history has taken place. While Ruiz does not explicitly relate the complexities of the border to Chicana/o history, his discussion of border inequalities, distortions, and hybridizations in economics, demographics, and culture contributes significantly to making Chicana/o history more comprehensible. The historical and conceptual intertwinings between United States-Mexican relations and Chicana/o history are further pursued by other contributors, including Roberto Rodríguez, Louise Año Nuevo Kerr, Steven Pitti, Zaragosa Vargas, and Ramón Gutiérrez.

Rodríguez's synthesis of "The Origins and History of the Chicano Movement" firmly contextualizes Chicana/o studies within the historical, political movement, and provides essential background for understanding the evolution of Chicana/o History and the issues that converge around the field. Specifically, Rodríguez reminds us that the modern political Chicana/o movement began as a struggle for civil rights, dignity, and respect that coincided with the Black Power movement of the 1960s. Its mass national character and strong student base differentiated it from earlier Mexican-American civil rights movements that were necessarily more conservative out of fear of the frequent political attacks on immigrants, with whom Mexican Americans were often confused in the public and political mind. Rodríguez explains that a key element of the 1960s movement was a change in attitude wherein Chicana/os no longer saw themselves as foreigners, but as natives. Furthermore, the national "movement" was really composed of many smaller movements in different parts of the country, often with different aims. Collectively, these smaller movements spawned hundreds of organizations and laid the foundation for other Chicana/o and Latina/o civil rights organizations and campaigns in the areas of gender, higher education, immigration, and the arts.

Rodríguez describes the genesis of Chicana/o studies within the larger sociopolitical movement. Before the 1960s, Mexican Americans were not represented in higher education in the same way that African Americans were represented by their own black colleges (and in the national dialogue on race centered on white/black relations). In the 1960s, however, new educational opportunities drew enough Chicana/o students to the nation's campuses, particularly those in California, to make the universities centers of Chicana/o social protest. Chicana/o studies programs are a product of the movement and particularly of an extension of the movement into academia. Thus a heavy expectation materialized—that the new academic programs would fill the role of advocates for social causes at the same time that they were being pressed to fit into the traditional mold of academia. Rodríguez believes that the attacks on affirmative action and the death of Cesar Chávez have stimulated a resurgence of the Chicana/o movement that is reenergizing the activism of Chicana/o studies and Chicana/o History. Although the dilemma of Chicana/o studies that Rodríguez identifies and that Chicana/o scholars at the conference actively debated arises from the circumstances of its origins, it is similar to two other persistent tensions in academia: one is the seemingly inherent competition between theoretical and applied research; the other is the stress between the research objectives and the urban outreach missions experienced by city-based universities.[5]

Two scholars provide straightforward overviews of the development of the field of Chicana/o History. Alberto Camarillo, in "Reflections on the Growth of Chicana/o History," underlines the origins of the field in the baseline monographs of the 1970s and early 1980s and its transformation into what he consider to be a dynamic subfield of U.S. history that is interacting with the "new" subfields of U.S. social, cultural, women's, labor, urban and western histories. The first specialists in Chicana/o history, trained in the 1970s and 1980s, laid the foundations of the field by recovering and reconstructing a neglected history. A second generation of Chicana/o scholars are building on these foundations with provocative research on (1) urban communities and subregions; (2) urban and rural workers; (3) women; and (4) political and institutional history, often combining two or more of these themes.

In "State of the Discipline: Chicano History," Louise Año Nuevo Kerr reviews the past twenty years of Chicana/o History noting that Chicana/o studies was born out of a negation by the established disciplines that subsequently encouraged Chicana/o scholars to produce works on Chicana/o immigration, urbanization, and rural and industrial labor, and to begin to look at the role of women. Kerr provides alternative explanations for why Chicana/o studies is in transition, including weakened institutional support in California, national foundations less predisposed to fund Chicana/o programs and research, and massive attacks on affirmative action by political forces outside of the university. On a more positive note, Kerr also points out that support is improving in the Midwest, and that the number of Chicana/o historians is growing, while libraries and other institutions are paying more serious attention to collecting Chicana/o documentation.

While recognizing the importance of new trends in cultural studies, Kerr's agenda for future research emphasizes the need to continue the development of established paths of investigation. Calling for additional community studies to facilitate a new synthesis, Kerr recommends the following areas for future study: Mexican immigration since 1960 and its impact on established communities in the context of economic globalization; the additional impact of Central and South American immigration on established Mexican communities in the United States; transnational cultural change; leadership and community development in different circumstances; the impact of the Chicana/o movement on the political life of communities; institutional and social change in local schools; the rise of Chicana/o and Latina/o professional organizations; changes in social rituals like the *quinceañera* and pathways of social mobility, such as the military; individual biographies and family histories; and comparative experiences across time and space. To "facilitate the making of the new history," she recommends a continued effort to raise consciousness and facilitate collaboration with organizations like the Midwest Consortium for Latino Research in order to improve support for scholars. She also advocates the creation of research teams for interdisciplinary and comparative projects. While not antagonistic to the choices made by research-oriented scholars, Kerr reiterates her conviction that the purpose of Chicana/o studies is not just to create knowledge, but to advance the community.

Two writers analyze the regional patterns in the rise and development of Chicana/o historiography in the Southwest and Midwest respectively. Antonio Ríos-Bustamante in "A General Survey of Chicana/o Historiography," an essay that was solicited by the editors to complement the conference papers, gives us a multifaceted view of the main historiographical body centered in the Southwest from a variety of angles. He attributes the late development of a field of Mexican-American history to the racist attitudes held by the white male scholars who dominated the mainstream field of U.S. History. It was only with access to higher education made possible by the G.I. Bill that a generation of Mexican-American scholars rose to write the history of their own people and contribute to the creation of Chicana/o History as a field of study. Prior to the creation of this new field, the study of Mexican Americans and of Mexican immigrants in the United States was carried out by isolated individuals within the framework of other fields of history, and other disciplines that did not give primacy to these populations. The first generation of scholars in Chicana/o History received their degrees in the 1970s in 1980s. The rise and development of the field was powered by a convergence of progressive, liberal, and radical ideologies which produced a new social history beginning in the 1960s that focused on the recovery and validation of the histories of populations previously marginalized by mainstream historians. Ríos-Bustamante illustrates the tremendous explosion in production and diversity of perspectives applied to the study of Chicana/o History in less than two generations, identifying four major historical paradigms and twenty thematic approaches in the field.

Dennis Valdés illustrates that Chicana/o history cannot be accurately conceived as taking place only in the Southwest and California in his essay entitled, "Region, Nation, and World-System: Perspectives on Midwestern Chicana/o History." He points out that Mexican settlements in the Midwest date only from the beginning of the twentieth century. Since Mexicans in this region have a stronger immigrant experience, they do not identify themselves with the Chicana/o movement as strongly as Chicana/os in the Southwest, who see themselves as "natives of the land." Valdés examines the interpretive perspectives from which scholars have studied Mexicans and Chicana/os in the Midwest. He finds that non-Mexican sociologists, anthropologists, social workers, and economists writing in the 1920s and 1930s tended to take a paternalistic view toward Mexicans, even when they were sympathetic to their subjects of study. In the worst cases, they adopted Eugenics and Social Darwinist theories that typecast Mexicans as culturally and biologically deficient. In the best cases, they saw Mexicans as the last of the immigrant groups with the potential for assimilation into American society. Following the national pattern, writers of Mexican descent began to challenge the racial and cultural stereotypes after the Second World War. Valdés credits Mexican-American writers of the postwar, pre-Chicana/o era with a greater degree of social activism than is generally attributed to them by other Chicana/o scholars. Valdés finds that about eighty percent of the published historical literature on Mexicans in the Midwest focuses on the period between 1900 and 1933. He also shows that a World System approach to the interpretation of the Midwest Chicana/o experience is more appropriate than theories arising out of the Southwestern Chicana/o experience.

Competing Visions of Chicana/o History

Two participants, Ramón Gutiérrez and Rudy Acuña, analyze Chicana/o History by examining the paradigms—the conceptual frameworks and perspectives—applied by historians to the interpretation of Chicana/o historical experiences. Gutiérrez, in "Chicano History: Paradigm Shifts and Shifting Boundaries," shows that, despite the continued marginalization of Chicana/o History by scholars dominating the construction and dissemination of U.S. History, the approaches used by most writers of Chicana/o History actually fit within the traditional, post-Enlightenment paradigm used by mainstream scholars to discuss and understand human "progress."

While they vary in terms of applying bourgeois, Marxist, antiquarian, and other interpretations to the field, Chicana/o writers still have much in common with writers of the established national historiography, with the notable exception that they write about Chicana/os, and that they do it from Chicana/o perspectives. For Gutiérrez and for many of the young scholars who participated in the conference, the applications of race, class, gender, and gay/lesbian analyses are enriching the field of Chicana/o History by revealing its diversity and complexity, while at the same time bringing it closer into a mutually beneficial relationship with mainstream national history. Gutiérrez observes that the questioning of established paradigms and the assumption of linear progress underlying them has taken the study of history into a post-modern era wherein previously unexplored or underdeveloped perspectives abound.

Acuña takes a less sanguine view of the field's evolution in "Truth and Objectivity in Chicana/o History." Drawing on the work of Thomas Kuhn,[6] Acuña explores the nature of traditional and revolutionary paradigms, their indispensable role in human thought, and the way they selectively gather and interpret information, as well as resist being replaced by new paradigms. Acuña's understanding of structures of power and empowerment as paradigmatic is the basis for his argument that Chicana/o historians must construct paradigms that challenge and confront the Eurocentric, Cold War mentality of mainstream U.S. historiography. His own book, *Occupied America: A History of Chicanos*, is the most widely known adaptation of the internal colony model from Third World and African-American studies to the interpretation of the condition of Chicana/os in the United States.[7]

Acuña sees the absence of new paradigms as a failure of Chicana/o studies scholars to challenge the Eurocentric character of the historiography. He believes the use of gender, class, and racial analyses by Chicana/o scholars reflects the outdated, mechanical application of imported methodologies from other disciplines. While some scholars look to the integration of Chicana/o and mainstream historiography, believing the former tradition has the potential to transform the latter, Acuña sees this process as intellectual co-optation.[8] In analyzing the patterns of Chicana/o historiography, Gutiérrez characterizes Acuña's perspective as radical Chicana/o nationalism occupying a position further left than the more familiar liberatory perspectives advancing ideas like class struggle, assimilation, and civil rights activism.

While Acuña does not agree with all of Ignacio García's statements, it is not surprising that he best represented at the conference García's position on the decline, even betrayal, of Chicana/o studies. For Acuña, the intellectual co-optation is linked to social and occupational co-optation within the political arena of the historical profession. Acuña, like García, holds the position that Chicana/o History is inherently confrontational and directed to serving the needs of the political movement and the community. He believes many Chicana/o scholars have been co-opted by the system of rewards and punishments in academia. Acuña has an answer to the charge that service to the Chicana/o social movement corrupts the scientific objectivity of Chicana/o History, which its critics believe should strive to be more professionally academic. Acuña cites the work of Peter Novick who documents the racism of Anglo-Saxon scholars against Jewish scholars as revealed in the private correspondence of the former at the time when the latter were entering the historical profession.[9] Acuña believes that Chicana/o scholars who naively seek to integrate themselves into mainstream academia are cooperating with a racist and fascist establishment that will destroy Chicana/o studies and its sociopolitical mission. Acuña thus considers the research agenda of the Chicana/o scholar as both a moral choice and a social act.

Two Applications of the Term "Chicano"

In order to better understand the debates at the conference and the responses of younger historians to the positions taken by García and Acuña, it is important to first note that the term *Chicano* has come to have various meanings and contextual applications—at least two major ones—that need to be distinguished from one another in order to avoid confusion and miscommunication. In its strictest sense—and leaving aside the gender issue that troubles it—the term *Chicano* and its derivatives apply to the political movement that erupted in the late 1960s and declined in the early 1970s. This application of the term can be extended to individuals who have voluntarily taken up the political ideology and social agenda of the movement and have continued to champion them into the present despite the disappearance of a national or even regional movement. However, Chicana/o History and studies programs and departments are caught between this very specific and politically-charged definition, and a second much broader definition which, ironically, they have been a major force in shaping and promoting.

In this broader application, the term *Chicano* replaces the term *Mexican-American*, and is used to refer to the population of Mexican descent in the United States, and its history, and to its antecedents in both the pre-Anglo American Southwest and in Mexico. In this second usage, the term has a much more diffuse political charge, comparable to the sequential replacement of terms from "Negro" and "Colored" to "Afro-American," "black," and "African-American" in reference to the population of African descent in the United States. In this admittedly "politically correct" usage, the term is extended to populations who do not share the political convictions of the Chicana/o movement and it adherents. It is also extended rhetorically to historical populations who existed before the Chicana/o movement. In their broader usage of the term, scholars and activists have to be careful not to project inappropriately a political mentality where and when it did not exist as a form of self-identification. Many scholars still use the terms *Mexican-American* and *Mexican* to avoid the political colorization of non-Chicana/o populations. For activists who believe they represent the interest of a whole people, the difference between the two meaning of *Chicano* is often blurred.[10]

Reinventing Chicana/o History

Three young scholars, María E. Montoya in "Beyond Internal Colonialism: Class, Gender, and Culture as Challenges to Chicano Identity," Lorena Oropeza in "Making History: The Chicano Movement," and Stephen J. Pitti in "Ernesto Galarza Remembered: A Reflection on Graduate Studies in Chicano History," answer García and Acuña's challenge by arguing for expanded definitions of the Chicana/o identity and Chicana/o History. They particularly challenge the assumptions that Chicana/os are working-class barrio dwellers, and that only they constitute "the community." Montoya grew up in a hostile white environment in a Denver suburb and was not raised with either Spanish or Catholicism. She nevertheless claims a role in the shaping of the field of Chicana/o History. Oropeza responds to being characterized by García as one of the young scholars from middle-class backgrounds who do not identify with the community. Pitti draws on the lessons in the life of Ernesto Galarza, who earned a doctorate from Columbia University but spent his life challenging academia as an activist in agricultural labor while, at the same time, maintaining a broad and international vision of the historical stage on which Chicana/os have acted out their lives. Taken in combination, these historians highlight the different fronts along which Chicana/o History must face its crisis to reinvent and strengthen itself.

It is not surprising that young scholars would take up the issue of generational differences. They freely recognize that Chicana/o History is now being remade by scholars without a personal memory of the movement's or the field's beginnings. They credit the first and second generations with doing their job too well in opening the doors for younger scholars who otherwise would not be occupying positions that once did not exist. However, they turn the argument around and believe the founding fathers should investigate why the newer generation is not as radical as its predecessor—or, perhaps, how the younger scholars are radical in their own way. Rather than trying to turn the clock back to what they consider a static notion of Chicana/o History, Montoya, Oropeza, and Pitti throw themselves unreservedly into the intellectual embrace of all the forces that García sees as threats to the field.

The newer scholars advocate opening up the conceptualization of the physical space in which Chicana/o History takes place. Every nation creates its myths of origins and a homeland. The Chicana/o movement, while not a nation in the way we understand the term at this historical moment, nevertheless, exhibited a number of characteristics of nation building. Most prominent was the idea that the mythical homeland of the Aztecs, Aztlán, was located in the U.S. Southwest, in the territory taken by conquest from Mexico. Chicana/os, therefore, have the deepest claim to the land on which they live—equal to that of any other Native American group. The modern-day actualization of Aztlán, as an occupied or colonized Chicana/o homeland, is the barrio, the Chicana/o ghetto, which was converted ideologically into a fortress within whose walls Chicana/o culture replicates itself. This is a logical and ideological invention because the Chicana/o movement was, in fact, a class-based movement for greater political and material equality. Young scholars, however, now find this construct to be more a prison than a homeland. They point to the histories of Chicana/os in multiple places, not just outside of the barrio, but also outside of the city and the Southwest.

Inseparable from the need to expand the definition of Chicana/o History beyond the barrio is the call to expand it to include economic classes not found in the inner city of the working and jobless poor. One can almost palpably feel the tension between the politically charged definition of *Chicano* and its broader inclusive application. The young scholars feel constricted by the model of the internal colony that worked so well in the early days of the struggle and that García uses as an example to be replicated in order to avoid what Acuña sees as a blind aping of mainstream academia. For the younger scholars, the model suppresses the perception and study of the class differences that separate Mexican Americans and discourages, even condemns, the study of the middle class along with scholars who have the questionable misfortune of not being born or not wanting to live in the barrio. Against the ideological grain of the political movement, young scholars who identify themselves as Chicana/os are willing to expand Chicana/o History to include the study of persons and groups of Mexican descent in the United States who are not, or who never had the chance to be, self-identified political Chicana/os. For them, the study of class differences and class struggles among Chicana/os enriches, rather than weakens, Chicana/o History, and opens up the field to the examination of forms of adaptation other than victimization and resistance.

No other force has had a deeper or wider impact on Chicana/o studies and History than the women's movement. Again, the complex interplay between real lives and the writing of history is evident in the works produced for this volume. As a gay historian, Ramón Gutiérrez, has been particularly sensitive to issues of gender. He notes in his essay in this collection that the feminist critique of male-dominated Chicana/o historiography began with the attack on male chauvinism in the Chicana/o political movement. His voice at the conference was joined by those of Montoya, Oropeza, and Pitti in observing that most scholars who have written about the Chicana/o movement have been male participants in the movement. Montoya adds that, with a few prominent exceptions, male Chicana/o historians have failed to incorporate gender as a method of analysis in their work. For Montoya, Chicana/o studies has also created a gendered division of labor in which women do women's history and men do everything else.

If Chicano male scholars feel embattled, Montoya observes that Chicana female scholars do not have it any easier. While they are busy championing the importance of gender within Chicana/o studies, and are accused of causing divisions within the ranks, they have to reverse roles in their dialogue with mainstream women's studies historians who downplay the importance of class and ethnicity. If Chicanas are breaking down the sexism they face both in their professional lives and in the writing of history, they are also using history to link the oppression of Chicanas at work and their oppression at home, further opening up the possibilities for liberation in both domains. In giving voices to the previously mute, Chicanas are helping to merge Chicana/o History thematically and methodologically with other fields of study.

This merging or joining is something that is not happening by accident. While young scholars call for an expansion of the boundaries of Chicana/o History to include the diversity within the Chicana/o experience, they also advocate for a deliberate contextualization and comparison of the field with other areas of research. Pitti reminds us that while Ernesto Galarza was an activist who belonged to a previous generation, he nevertheless advocated studying the Chicana/o experience in the broadest possible contexts. This included U.S.-Mexican international economic interdependency and comparisons with the experiences of other hyphenated Americans. Rather than look for themes, methodologies, and concepts that separate Chicana/o History from mainstream areas of study, the young scholars call for the deliberate pursuit of linkages with U.S., Mexican, and Latin American histories as well as with Latina/o studies that include the experiences of Cubans, Puerto Ricans, and other Latin American groups. Pitti cautions against the tendency of recent scholars in Chicana/o History to move away from the study of Latin-American history. Rather than defend the fortress of Chicana/o History for the political education of Chicana/o students, Montoya believes Chicana/o scholars must reconceptualize U.S. history by integrating Chicana/o history into it, and educate non-Chicana/o students in a new world of multiculturalism, race, and ethnic requirements in college curriculums.

To those who would accuse them of betraying a commitment to the community, the young scholars respond that scholarship *is* activism and that even the "Plan de Santa Bárbara" recognized that knowledge produces social change. They cite Rudy Acuña's own *Occupied America* as an example of scholarship that has had an impact beyond the boundaries of academia. Acuña and García would not quarrel with this. What the younger scholars are saying, however, is that activism and service to the community can be defined much more broadly than implied by the measures of physical contact with the barrio or even other Chicana/o communities. Entering and excelling in new fields of scholarship and competing in the academic marketplace is as important to furthering the cause of the community as going back to it personally. Breaking stereotypes held by non-Chicana/os clears a path for other Chicana/os, just as the first generation of scholars provided the beachhead for today's young scholars.

Research Redefines Chicana/o History

Conference participants also addressed other issues related to the definition of Chicana/o History as a field of study in its temporal, methodological, and thematic aspects. Much of the research and work reported on at the conference illustrates three of the most basic tasks facing Chicana/o scholars: (1) establishing links between modern Chicana/o cultures and those of past eras; (2) overcoming stereotypes of an inferior people without a history; and (3) reconstructing truer histories of the various Chicana/o peoples and communities in the United States. These three themes were almost invariably intertwined in each of the studies to follow.

Two individuals comment on Chicana/o literary and cultural history in their essays. Contrary to the established view of scholars and non-scholars that Mexican Americans have no literary history in the United States, Luis Leal, in "Chicano Literary History: Origin and Development," shows that Mexican-American scholars since the beginning of the century have documented a strong folkloric tradition dating back to the Spanish colonial period. Leal himself makes an argument that the antecedents of Chicana/o literature go back to the colonial chronicles of New Mexico and the future Southwest. The early writings laid the basis for Chicana/o culture and were further developed during the periods of Mexican and U.S. ownership of the Southwest. Gutiérrez concludes that, in defining itself within Chicana/o History, the feminist perspective has also contributed to the projection of Chicana/o history back in time. The perspective crossed the border and pushed back the temporal boundaries of Chicana/o History from 1848 to 1519 by reinterpreting Mexican history and rehabilitating the image of La Malinche (the mythologized, native woman who collaborated with Cortés) from a traitor to her race to the mother of *mestizaje* and *mexicanidad.*

Zaragosa Vargas, in "Citizen, Immigrant, and Foreign Wage Workers: The Chicana/o Labor Refrain in U.S. Labor Historiography," complements the essay by Ramón Ruiz and addresses part of the international context called for by Stephen Pitti by showing how recent works on Chicana/o labor have given us a view of the international character of labor utilization in Texas, California, and the Midwest. A major theme in the new historical literature is the commodification of Mexican labor in the United States from the early-nineteenth century to the present and the reshaping of the labor force consisting of Chicana/o and Mexican workers by economic trends and technological changes. Another theme is that of union organization based on fraternal and mutual aid societies influenced by radical political organizations on both sides of the border (the anarcho-syndicalist Partido Liberal Mexicano, the Texas Socialist Party, the Industrial Workers of the World, and the Western Federation of Miners). The history of international bonding in resistance to exploitation has carried forward to recent and present times with the organization of the United Farm Workers (UFW) in the Southwest and the Farm Labor Organizing Committee (FLOC) in the Midwest. Veteran organizers Ernesto Galarza and Bert Corona, who had an impact on the formation of Chicana/o studies, emerge as leaders in the struggle to unionize and secure workers' rights. Today, in the 1990s, labor strikes and alternative labor unions in manufacturing and service sectors in California are being led by Chicana/o and Mexican janitors, garment workers, carpenters, and high-tech workers while the UFW experiences a revival. The set of themes is rounded out by a discussion of the role of the federal government in assisting employers in the exploitation of Chicana/o and Mexican workers and withholding protection from abuse.[11]

Martha Menchaca, in "History and Anthropology: Conducting Chicano Research," addresses two topics. One is the continued domination of anthropology by white males who are attempting to let the "other" speak, but who do not train minority and third-world scholars so that they can voice the "other's" view. She believes this is a problem that Chicana/o History has overcome through the training of Chicana/o scholars. As an example of the obstacles that have been faced in anthropology, she cites the case of William Madsen's interpretation of South Texas Mexican-American culture as dysfunctional that had to be challenged by Octavio Romano. The second topic is her own work in documenting the discrimination against Mexican Americans in Santa Paula, an agricultural community in Ventura County, California, where whites have been able to maintain power despite the end of legal segregation. Her new study in progress will focus on how Indians in Texas were forced to adopt a Mexican cultural identity after 1848 or be placed on Indian reservations.

Lorena Oropeza, in "Making History: The Chicana/o Movement," analyzes the origins of the National Chicano Moratorium March Against the War in Vietnam on 29 August 1970. She explains how the National Chicano Moratorium Committee Against the War in Vietnam was able to turn traditional Mexican-American pride in military service into an antiwar demonstration by tapping into powerful ethnic group notions of legitimacy, soldiering, and citizenship. The high casualty rates in Vietnam did not become a factor in overcoming the pride of older Mexican Americans and the GI Forum (the national organization for Mexican-American veterans) in their military service to their country until they were asked why Chicana/os were dying abroad in disproportionately high numbers when their rights had not been secured at home. The value of machismo usually associated with bravery in war thus became equated with the bravery required to oppose the war. Oropeza observes that mainstream historians who have written about the antiwar movement have very little to say about the Chicano Moratorium because (as Acuña would agree) their cultural biases and backgrounds selected for the central actors who were relevant to their own cultural makeup. She recommends further research to place the Chicana/o movement within the larger contexts of the experiences of the Mexican-American population as a whole and the national antiwar movement. The Chicana/o movement should also be studied from a variety of perspectives and viewpoints, and the Chicano Moratorium is one of these.

Creative Crisis as a Constructive Experience

The conference on a New Chicana/o History captured vividly the depth and complexity of the creative crisis being experienced by Chicana/o History and Chicana/o studies, both in the responses of conference participants to the challenges issued by García and Acuña and in the research agendas they present as their own or as those of other scholars.

García and Acuña raise issues that impact on professional identities, research priorities, and even personal identities. These issues underscore the extent to which Chicana/o History is still very much anchored in contemporary politics and social concerns. Gender, class, and the definition of service to the community are all intertwined in the issues being debated. The varying research agendas also indicate that Chicana/o History is still in a developmental stage of bringing to light and interpreting a multidimensional history that would otherwise be lost. Many of the mission objectives previously identified as imposed on Chicana/o History by the social movement that created it and by the university environment in which it must function are still being worked out by the scholars who write it and live it. Almost everyone involved has a personal stake in the formation of Chicana/o History and, therefore, experiences a passion for the process that, in the best profiles, is coupled with an earnest search for truth.

Notes

1. The rise of women's studies and a feminist perspective in all disciplines and fields of study has called into question many assumptions and practices that take for granted (or operate from) a male-centered perspective. The fields formally known as "Chicano" and "Latino" studies are no exception. In fact, they suffer from a particular problem centered in the historical evolution of the Spanish language. The English language has gender-neutral terms like "American" to refer to both genders. This is not the case with Spanish, wherein the male version of a noun like "Español," "Mexicano," "Latino," or "Chicano" is used to refer to both genders. Feminist scholars and activists have insisted on equal billing in the naming of the fields and programs and in any reference to both genders simultaneously. Given the absence of a gender-neutral alternative, the result has been the institutionalization of slashed terminology: "Chicana/o," "Chicana/Chicano," "Latina/o," and "Latina/Latino." Modern political correctness (or, in hindsight, the initial political incorrectness of the male shapers of the Spanish language) has created a grammatically awkward construction in both written and oral forms. I believe the slash-and-paste usage must evolve into something less artificial and emblematic of the gender clash that currently characterizes academic politics. I suggest that, until a linguist comes up with a better solution, we remove the slash and coin new terms that incorporate both genders like "Chicanao" and "Latinao." Conference participant Lorena Oropeza deals with the problem in the following way: "I try to avoid the inherent sexism of Romance language by using [such] gender neutral

terms as 'movement participants' and 'activists' with frequency. When I use the plural 'Chicanos,' I usually refer to men and women. I also [use] the word 'Chicano' as a general adjective, as in 'Chicano moratorium.'" see Oropeza's chapter, "Making History: The Chicano Movement," endnote 7. I believe this is a formula that would not be well received from a male writer, considering the risk of sounding sexist.

I also use the term "Chicana/o History" with a capital "H" to refer to the organized study of "Chicana/o history" with a small "h." The latter refers to the actual life experiences of the diverse human groups that are the subjects of study.

2. For examples of the rapidly changing perspectives in various fields, see the discussions in Florencia E. Mallon's "Dialogues Among the Fragments: Retrospect and Prospect" in *Confronting Historical Paradigms: Peasants, Labor and the Capitalist World System in Africa and Latin America,* ed., Frederick Cooper, Allen Isaacman, William Roseberry, and Steve J. Stern (Madison: University of Wisconsin Press, 1993), 371–401; Teresa Mead, Steve, J. Stern, Judith Stacey, Linda Gordon, Allen Hunter, Temma Kaplan, and Pamela Haag, "Forum: What Comes After Patriarchy? Comparative Reflections on Gender and Power in the 'Post Patriarchal' Age," *Radical History Review* 71 (Spring 1998), 52–95; and *Selected Subaltern Studies,* ed., Ranajit Guha and Gayatri Chakravotry Spivak (New York: Oxford University Press, 1988). Teresa Cordóva reviews the writings of Chicana scholars in the 1990s as they reflect the interrelationship of personal identities and professional scholarship in "Anti-Colonial Chicana Feminism" in *Latino Social Movements: Historical and Theoretical Perspectives,* ed., Rodolfo D. Torres and George Katsiaficas (New York: Routledge, 1999), 11–41. See "A General Survey of Chicana/o Historiography" by Antonio Ríos-Bustamante in this volume for the numerous perspectives that have been applied to Chicana/o History.
3. In deference to our sensitized collective consciousness on the use of gendered pronouns, I use "she" rather than "he" when referring to the single reader or actor whose sex is unspecified. The alternative use of "she/he" is too grammatically cumbersome.
4. Ignacio M. García, "Juncture in the Road: Chicano Studies Since 'El Plan de Santa Bárbara,'" ed. David R. Maciel and Isidro D. Ortiz, *Chicanas/Chicanos at the Crossroads: Social, Economic, and Political Change* (Tucson: University of Arizona Press, 1996), 181–203.
5. See Carlos Muñoz Jr., *Youth, Identity, Power: The Chicano Movement* (Verso: New York, 1989) for a finely nuanced book-length interpretation of the Chicana/o student movement and its complex intertwining with the Chicana/o political movement. Frances R. Aparicio addresses the problematic relationships of Latina/o and Chicana/o studies to each other and to the multiple realities they attempt to define in "Reading the 'Latino' in Latino

Studies: Towards Re-imagining our Academic Locations," paper presented at the conference on "Constructing Latina/Latino Studies: Location and Dislocation," University of Illinois, Urbana-Champaign, 2–3 April 1998.

6. Thomas Kuhn, *The Structure of Scientific Revolutions*, 2d ed., enl. (Chicago: University of Chicago Press, 1970).
7. Rodolfo F. Acuña, *Occupied America: A History of Chicanos,* 3d ed. (New York: Harper & Row, 1988). Originally published in 1972. See chapter by Ramón Gutiérrez in this volume for a more detailed depiction of the conceptual transfer.
8. In his revised essay, Acuña makes a point of drawing a distinction between his views and those of Ignacio García. Acuña does not see women's and gay/lesbian studies or ethnic studies as a threat, and he differs on the organizational options for regenerating Chicana/o studies.
9. Peter Novick, *That Noble Dream: The "Objectivity Question" and the American Historical Profession* (Cambridge: Cambridge University Press, 1988).
10. Lorena Oropeza, in "Making History: The Chicano Movement," endnote 7, for example resolves the problem in the following manner: "I tend to reserve the words 'Chicano,' 'Chicana,' and their respective plurals to describe participants in the movement and use 'Mexican American' as a more general ethnic group label." Muñoz, *Youth, Identity, Power*, 1–8, 15–16, limits the application of the term *Chicano* to the social-political movement of the 1960s and the early 1970s.
11. Among the books reviewed by Vargas are David Montejano, *Anglos and Mexicans in the Making of Texas* (Austin: University of Texas Press, 1987); Emilio Zamora, *The World of the Mexican Worker in Texas* (College Station: Texas A & M University Press, 1993); Cletus Daniel, *Chicano Workers and the Politics of Fairness* (Austin: University of Texas Press, 1991); Kitty Calavita, *Inside the State: The Bracero Program, Immigration, and the I.N.S.* (New York: Routledge, Chapman and Hall, 1992); and Dennis Valdés, *Al Norte: Agricultural Workers in the Great Lakes Region, 1917–1970* (Austin: University of Texas Press, 1991).

CHAPTER 1

TRUTH AND OBJECTIVITY IN CHICANO HISTORY

Rodolfo F. Acuña

Introduction

THIS CHAPTER IS ABOUT MY perception of my own research as it relates to truth and objectivity. My remarks are in great part conditioned by personal experiences in academe, as well as my own life as an activist scholar. To start with, my own education is a bit unconventional. For instance, I received my bachelor's degree at a time when there was still considerable controversy regarding the degree in social studies, which I received in order to become a schoolteacher. I pursued a graduate degree in history, although my advisor told me that Mexicans generally did not go into history, and that I would be better off with an M.A. in education. Nevertheless, I earned a master's degree in history, and three of my four areas of study were in U.S. history. Fortune would have it that I wandered into a Ph.D. program in Latin-American studies, where three of my six areas of study were in history. Over the next five years, I taught full time, was active in the community, continued to raise a family, and successfully pursued my studies. The experience imbued me with a sort of elitism that I would carry with me for the next three decades: I was bitter at seeing Euro-Americans get awards that they did not financially need or academically earn. Bitter at being excluded from these awards on the basis of my surname, but at the same time, I felt a sort of superiority that I was a night school Ph.D., making it on my own.

In the 1960s, any kind of area study program, whether Latin-American, American, or Asian studies, was dismissed by academe. Scholars disapproved of the mixing of disparate disciplines. Furthermore, although most of my training was in history (some seventy of my ninety-some graduate credits were in history), history departments let me know that they were doing me a favor to even interview me because I had my degree in a studies program. In part, today's antipathy toward ethnic studies programs is a legacy of this past.

The methodological eclecticism of most ethnic and women's studies research often offends purists, who view these emerging disciplines as lacking a consistent theoretical framework. They see the act of borrowing from other fields as empiricism, opportunism and worst of all—journalism. What offends them most is that these fields often do not accept the paradigms and the canons of the mainstream disciplines, daring to challenge accepted knowledge. For the mainstream scholar, research is the process of deduction from "accepted knowledge," acquired through established methods. In many ways this chapter is the other side of the coin.

Despite my obvious skepticism, I believe that it is possible to write good history and that a measure of truth can be approached. In my opinion, history is supposed to be an understandable narrative based on documents. Good history reduces everything to its lowest common denominator in order for the historian to determine what facts are most reliable in his or her narrative. In sum, good history is driven by the facts—and it tells a good story.

Don Ramón Ruiz recommended to me an excellent little book by Edward Hallett Carr, *What Is History?* In the book, Carr readily admits that there is no "objective" historical truth. He makes it clear that history represents a point of view. He criticizes the historian's icon Leopold Von Ranke and his mechanical retelling of the past, and the positivist claim that history is a science. Carr calls for a "commonsense" view of history. "History consists of a corpus of ascertained facts," he says, which in itself is a chore, since "The historian is necessarily selective." (Carr 1961, 10) The historian's life experiences play a determined role in the selection of the facts, which may prevent him or her from understanding the truths of others.

Not all historians are as candid as Carr, however. For instance, I recently reread Oscar Handlin's pretentious *Truth in History*. As a student I admired Handlin. However, years later Handlin struck me as a somewhat pompous fraud. In his preface, titled "The Abuses of History," he writes: "Historians, like other scholars in the United States, long occupied themselves in self-justification" (Handlin 1979, vii), which sounds objective, but Handlin, throughout his professional life, does what he accuses others of doing: making "judgment and objectives by ideology or other sectarian factors."

Handlin admits to the inability of scholars to escape the limitations of their culture, but he himself does not recognize his own limitations, displaying an arrogance that irritates me most about Euro-American scholars. Handlin, a cold war warrior from start to finish, launches a vicious attack on so-called revisionists like William Appleman Williams, implying that they manufactured their facts and that they were pro-Communist (Handlin 1979, 145–61). Handlin also displays an antipathy toward minority scholars. He writes: "I was surprised in 1968 at the request that I recommend teachers not according to ability but according to race and political orientation"(Handlin 1979, 6). He describes this as a dissolution of the sense of community of academe, as if it ever existed.

What is Good History?

The problem, in my view, is how to write a history that is more like that of Carr and less like that of the pretentious Handlin. In my opinion, in order for Chicano/a studies to just tell its story, there must be a community called a department where the different disciplines come together and organically interrelate. Without a department, you have scholars studying Chicana/os from the vantage of disparate disciplines. The result is that Chicana/o historians or sociologists, simply by virtue of their ethnicity, become "Chicano/a studies specialists." This is different than Chicano/a studies. In mainstream departments, knowledge is accumulated and refined by scholars in disciplines with very little communication with one another. The lack of a department results in competition within the field Chicana/o studies, with the different disciplines intellectually encroaching upon each other instead of interacting and mixing, forming a new field of study. Chicana/o studies history necessarily differs from history written by a historian in a traditional department. My own feeling is that Chicano history as we know it today is an area of study within the discipline of history. It is not part of Chicana/o studies, which involves the integration of other disciplines. It is my own feeling that every discipline forms its own culture, which is forged by the interactions of the members of a community of scholars. Unfortunately, Chicano/a studies, unlike women's studies, is not forging that culture—either intellectually or spatially. Indeed, few Chicano/a studies departments exist in the United States (see Acuña 1998).

Chicano studies history is and should be unabashedly political in the tradition of African-American and feminist studies. Objectivity is a weapon used by those in power to control the "other." The aim of Chicano studies history is not to reinvent another reality, but to seek facts that challenge Eurocentric interests. By its very nature, Chicana/o studies history is oppositional.

The problem that then arises is whether one can be oppositional and still be objective, still seek the truth? I posit that truth and objectivity are based on facts, on knowledge, rather than emanating from a disciplined methodology. Indeed, definitions among traditional scholars vary. Take the definition of University of California, Santa Barbara, historian Jeffrey Russell, who testified the role of the scholar is the search for the truth, but that "absolute truth is whatever would exist in the mind of God, to which we have no access…we cannot even hope to get close to it [absolute truth]." In a 7 March 1991 lecture, Russell said, "The purpose of the University is to proclaim the intricate mystery and glory of God…" Although Russell is a respected historian, I wonder how objective he is, and how much his definition differs from that of the scientists in history.

Even though the discourse regarding truth and objectivity is a ruse, it is important to establish standards. A lack of guidelines results in the weakest becoming victims to the whims of those in power. Moreover, just because one has been the victim of distortions, this does not give one the license to invent or manipulate the facts. Above all, I believe that there is right and wrong, and that a lack of standards disadvantages the poor more than the rich. For example, I always had problems with Ivan Illich and his *Deschooling Society,* which advocated the dissolution of schools. In my perception, Illich wanted to do away with schools when he already had his doctorates. I have the same problem with some postmodernists, who reduce everything to the imagination and consider everything relative. Given, I do not fully understand the movement, but it strikes me as escapist, somewhat like the euphemistic movements that obscured language to avoid direct indictment.

It is humanly impossible to be totally objective or to identify completely the truth. However, it is possible to establish a coherent record. One of the tasks of the Chicana/o studies historian is to help the public to overcome the presumption that scholars are objective and that they tell the truth. Institutions of higher learning are pillars of the state, which consequently must be unmasked.

I concede that many scholars try to be objective. The problem is that they are prisoners of their profession and culture who are tightly controlled by a system of rewards and punishment. Historians, like other members of the academy, are controlled by the academic review process, which allows the academy to socially control its members by defining the truth. This definition establishes its own moral authority by predetermining the entire discourse. In the end, like culture, it operates to control scholars (and public alike), who from an early age are conditioned to believe prescribed definitions of truth and objectivity. As Feminist philosopher Sandra Harding so aptly puts it in *The Science Question in Feminism*, "[T]he story stresses epistemological determinism—a form of idealism: the scientific conception of nature and inquiry and the information that science produces have been the prime progressive movers in modern social history" (Harding 1986, 230).

The question is, should Chicana/o studies historians start with the established truth, the paradigm that is accepted by the profession? In response to government officials and others who wanted to minimize the Holocaust by saying that the stories had not been proven and that all sides had to be given before the stories could be confirmed, the legendary journalist Edward R. Murrow replied, "Sometimes there is no other side" ("Historical Account of Buchenwald Liberation Replayed," National Public Radio, Transcript # 1119–18, 15 April 1995). Murrow later recalled that even during World War II, news organizations ignored or diminished reports about the death camps, saying that the independent stories (those of the survivors) had not confirmed what happened, or that the "statistics were imprecise, [and] one-sided." At the time, the German government denied the stories; the Allies said they were exaggerated. We only had the word of the survivors.

Murrow was one of the first journalists to report the horrors and liberation of Buchenwald. Murrow, along with other journalists and soldiers, was shocked when German civilians in the neat, prosperous villages surrounding the camps said that they had seen nothing, heard nothing, and smelled nothing from the ovens that burned human flesh and housed the living dead, and where bodies were "stacked up like cord wood." Murrow simply held that the Germans were lying and that the survivors were telling the truth—"Sometimes there is no other side."

In Los Angeles, we have crisscrossing freeways that take Angelenos to work and then back to their homes, to the malls and back to their homes, and to the music center and back to their homes. Angelenos of different class and racial backgrounds see each other only on the freeways. Similarly, most scholars divide their worlds between the campus and their homes. Societal tensions are learned through local newspapers—and occasionally through television. Even minority scholars need atlases to find their way to surrounding ghettoes or barrios. The academics' world is what is on their campuses, on their freeways, and in their homes. Their life experiences are their friends, their colleagues, and their graduate students. While some are sympathetic to minorities, their noninclusion in society is an abstraction. They see nothing. They hear nothing. They smell nothing. It never occurs to them to look around their campus and to ask why they see no scholars of color. They see no obligation to take the lead in integrating their university or their departments—although the majority will support resolutions supporting affirmative action (which is not working anyway).

Most scholars would admit that scholarship is not free of political and cultural biases. Yet, they will insist that "knowledge" is constantly revised through a process of peer criticism and review that keeps its distance from the world. It never occurs to them that, by excluding other knowledge, the result is tainted.

Like other institutions, the university has a life of its own—a culture that has developed over centuries. Scholars in research institutions are very well paid and rewarded. They maintain autonomy over what is taught, by reflecting the institutional culture, and are rewarded by government and the industrial complex for supporting this culture. Like federal judges, they have lifetime appointments called tenure. They bolster their claims for promotion by building in review processes to justify merit increases to the point where many full professors at the University of California make in excess of $100,000 yearly. Reviews take place at almost every step of the way, as academics rise from a lowly assistant professor to majestic full professor rank (some twenty steps in all), which occur about every two years at the University of California. The university says that this review process insures that scholarly integrity is maintained. Does it?

There's another way of looking at the university review process. Because it is so closely linked to the rewarding of faculty, it often promotes conformity, opportunism, and intellectual incest. Down the line you know you are going to be reviewed, so it is to your advantage to be "collegial"—a "good citizen," as some reviewers like to say—especially as you approach the upper limits of the professorial ranks.

Many professors also live in university towns in close proximity to each other. They socialize with one another and intellectually banter with one another at social events. They eat at the faculty club, and their children date. They recycle each other's ideas, biases, and—even worse—tolerate each other's prejudices. These intellectual incestuous affairs often cross over class, race, and even gender lines, with faculties becoming institutionalized and professionalized. In other words, the professors bond.

Within the halls of academe, scholarship thus becomes a political weapon. The universities are neo-liberal. In recent years, as the faculties have gotten older, these communities have also gotten more conservative. Indeed, a goodly number of 1960s historians who opposed the Vietnam War and bled for minorities are today's nativists, defending Western civilization. The overwhelming majority of these professors are white, male, and come from middle- and upper-middle-class families. Most have been educated in U.S. or European academies. They look at the world through the same lens; their knowledge is derived through common sources. It thus seems consistent to them to have a text on "World Literature," with 90 percent of its selections from Europe, or to have a Spanish Department staffed entirely by Spaniards. You might say, then, that they look at societal themes through a Eurocentric prism.

What I would like to see is for Chicano scholars to strive not for impartiality, but for a form of fairness, to apply knowledge for the benefit of those who are studied—that is Chicanos and other Latinos. Hopefully, we would thus recognize injustice to any group. Unfortunately, in the United States truth and objectivity are tied to tests such as patriotism. This makes the study of history very difficult, since criticism of America's past is unpatriotic and consequently unobjective and untruthful.

My own historical narratives are not designed to prove that the Mexicans in the United States are right—or that they have a monopoly on the truth. They are at most imperfect narratives of Mexican Americans. They critique the dominant society—raising questions of possible biases and flaws in the Euro-American culture that contribute to the failures of Mexicans. Like the works of other critics, my narratives are severely criticized. American universities are not the Eden constructed by conservative scholars; they are not forums of free and open discourse. The Academy has always been the dominion of upper-class scholars, who can afford the luxury of an advanced education. World civilization courses reflect what these ruling classes have always required students to know. The rejection of mine and other works by the Academy is thus natural, since we are outside the paradigm.

The American Paradigm and Chicana/o Studies

I have always questioned the old historian's tale that a function of history is to understand the present more deeply. While it is true that the historian accomplishes this task first by seeking to identify the distinctive "essence" of past events, it is just as true that it is impossible for a historian or other social scientist to understand the past without knowing the present. Part of the craft is to know people, especially those that we are studying. I am a firm advocate of having a grasp of qualitative knowledge—there is no substitute for facts. Many historians, however, say that it is essential to trace the evidence of the essence in history. In part, I agree. By employing concepts such as "paradigm analysis" and "paradigm shift," which were popularized by Thomas Kuhn, an American philosopher of science, in his book *The Structure of Scientific Revolutions,* we can better understand why academe is so resistant to Chicana/o studies.

Kuhn, at the height of his popularity in the 1960s and again in the 1970s, popularized "paradigms," the theory that in every field of study the established order sets structural guidelines that influence the thinking and actions of its scientists and social scientists. The concept holds that in this context, existing paradigms restrict the growth and expansion of new and competing models.

Kuhn defines a paradigm as a set of theories, standards, methods, and beliefs, which are accepted as the norm by most scientists in a particular field of study. Through the use of the scientific method, scientists deduce the truth or the essence of it. Change is therefore difficult, since inductive reasoning is discouraged and often severely criticized and even rejected. Accordingly, change takes place only through "paradigm shifts," which occur in times of extreme agitation. They require a fundamental shift in mind-sets of practitioners at all levels of an organization. Complete changes in attitudes are difficult because many leaders do not fully understand the complexities of the concept of paradigms or the sort of qualitative change needed.

Kuhn and his followers posit that human beings cannot think abstractly without paradigms. Intellectual and scientific advancement is possible only if and when a paradigm has become incapable of explaining newly discovered facts. The old paradigm is thus displaced by yet another paradigm to interpret facts. For example, students of international relations may be incapable of interpreting international affairs using "the cold war paradigm," or, for that matter, to think of the variables of race, gender, and even class in present-day society with the time-worn paradigm. A case in point are Chicano/as, who were not part of the race equation three decades ago, so it is difficult to conceive of them as a majority in places like California.

Logically, a paradigm is necessary in order to search out and understand developments in U.S. society since World War II. The "clash of cultures" taking place in society, for example, cannot be reduced to an understanding of family values. In this context, ethnic and women's studies models advance paradigms for understanding and carrying on relations within a culturally diverse society. The United States is not the same now as it was in 1900 or 1950. In this scheme, the various ethnic paradigms compete with the prevailing paradigm and with each other to deconstruct culture as a static concept and reality. However, this can take place only if the discourse is vigorous and a substantial number of minority scholars agree.

Chicano/a studies is not responding to the challenges implicit in this paradigmatic methodology in our changing society. Chicano/a scholars mechanically apply variables such as gender, class, and race, using the outdated methodologies of their individual disciplines. At most, Chicano/a studies has kept pace with the semantic shift from a society that used a monoracial, noncultural model. By the very nature of change these dormant and ethnic cultures and ideas are destined to clash. History will show that the old model is incapable of interpreting this new reality. The new rationality and the role of Chicanos and other Latinos can only be interpreted through an understanding of the paradigm shift.

It is plain dumb for social scientists to pretend that civilization has stood still since 1950. It cannot be presumed that white, middle- and upper-class males are the only ones capable of interpreting society. Cultural stresses and strains are better understood through the inclusion of new knowledge and a new model for interpreting that knowledge. In other words, there is no monolithic U.S. society. There is no such thing as being color-blind. The different realities of the multiple citizens in the United States demand a construct to match them, and to explain how these citizens think and see other populations and cultures. Only in this way can we interpret how these emerging forces and tensions are impacting political and cultural systems. Diverse cultural norms, values, and ideas are clashing today. How do the clashes affect American values and the interests of the diverse peoples?

The cultural and ideological war that is consuming the United States and the rest of the world has to be dated, chronicled, and assessed. Some would surely argue that this cannot be done with the dominant paradigm. If it was adequate, society would have already found solutions to its problems. Instead we are a society that is stuck in 1945, both domestically and internationally. The construct of the "other" is ever present, with the controlling ideology determining paradigms that defend Western civilization.

Whether Americans want to admit it or not, we are dealing with a permanent and fundamental clash of cultures in the United States. This will not get better. It is a problem that will not go away. Ideas are important to the peaceful solution of this culture war. In order to arrive at solutions, the inclusion of other knowledge and ways of looking at things is absolutely necessary. As in the case of foreign affairs, U.S. society has historical baggage that it must deal with. The collapse in 1989 of the Soviet economy did not erase a history of colonialism by the West. The growing gap between rich and poor, white, black, and brown in this country also confirms many historical accounts of racism in the United States, witness recent assaults on affirmative action. Self-evident is that the United States, even with the changes produced by the civil rights movement, is not committed to a class- and race-proof society. There are fault lines separating ethnically and racially diverse peoples.

How should the Chicano/a scholar explain this long-standing American reluctance to understand other cultures? A gap in knowledge and intelligence exists, which explains why American universities so vehemently reject foreign paradigms and knowledge. Anything not known by the dominant "cold war" scholars is rejected as nonscholarly or polemical. (Polemics are fundamental to the interaction of ideas that results in the paradigm shift.) It is this intellectual rigidity that is making a future clash highly probable.

For the Chicano/a scholar the need for a "paradigm shift" or cultural revolution is elementary. New disciplines or "discourses" continually emerge and establish themselves. The parameters that we construct in our minds, the use of language and statistics in Chicano/a studies must be made more inclusive. A single paradigm will not solve the riddle or result in justice—this can be accomplished only by a better understanding of social interactions. Definitions must be debated in order to fully understand what is happening.

Culture war will intensify as diverse cultures, with diverse languages and diverse types of discourse, clamor for attention, sometimes peacefully and sometimes confrontationally. This makes the necessity for communication and common definitions critical. The solution goes beyond tolerance, beyond the present multicultural solutions.

Traditionalists claim that "identity politics" or multiculturalism divide the nation into antagonistic and irreconcilable fragments. They worry that multiculturalism denies the possibility of assimilation and erodes our national sense as Americans. From the beginning, the question for Chicano/as has been what the parameters of assimilation are and what the word itself means. Togetherness has its pitfalls, especially when everyone is not equal. The paradigm that produced a so-called equality and collective identity for the American colonists in 1776 is not functional today.

The present culture war is connected to the cold war. American intellectual thought was tainted and corrupted by the cold war, which demanded patriotism. Today we are engendered by the same rigidities. Ironically, this rigidity is propelling historians and other social scientists toward the postmodernism that they so dread.

This resistance of academe to new paradigms is not an aberration. University of Chicago historian Peter Novick's book, *That Noble Dream: the "Objectivity Question and the American Historical Profession"* is a synthesis or history of American historiography centered around the idea of objectivity. Novick points out that it was not until the 1880s that scholars claimed professional status for historians. Gradually they claimed to be scientists, using a scientific method that was objective, and producing truth. The founding fathers of the profession, who held the field under sway for many years, guarded the canons of the profession. They resisted new ideas and changes called for by younger scholars.

Novick deconstructs the assumption that there is truth, and documents the lives and works of historians, showing how fluctuations impacted the teaching and the writing of historians, as well as their conduct toward each other. According to Novick, the professional history was an Anglo-Saxon enterprise, with members largely coming from this race. These members determined that institutions and ideas of value were of Anglo-Saxon origin. He shows that biases among the early historians were "near unanimous." Members of the profession were slow to accept changes in the cultures and minority scholars, and they resisted the entrance of Jews into the profession. Indeed, many made casual slurs about them. Novick cites overt anti-Semitism in the correspondence of leading historians.

After World War I, historians still claimed to be scientists. The foremost challengers of "that noble dream" of historical objectivity were Carl L. Becker and Charles A. Beard in the 1930s, as well as William Appleman Williams in the 1950s. These men held that historical interpretation was, and always had been, relative to the historian's time, place, views, prejudices, interests, and circumstances. For their heresy, they were called "relativists" by their scientific critics.

According to Novick, after World War II the cold war strengthened the defenders of objectivity, as did the optimism generated by the history boom in the universities. Many historians joined the cold war purge. Beard became a casualty to patriotism during and after World War II. Distinguished members of the profession unfairly associated him with fascism because he opposed American intervention in World War II. Lewis Mumford, Allan Nevins, and Samuel Eliot Morrison were among those who reproved him. Beard, a former American Historical Association president, was jeered at its meetings. Oscar Handlin, a contemporary of Beard, pompously pronounced that Beard "had no students," and that his "influence upon subsequent scholarship was slight." An illogical link was drawn between Beard and his relativism. All the while, historians cheerfully celebrated the objectivity of their own work.

Changes were, however, taking place. The expansion of the economy brought job opportunities not only for Jews, but for other underrepresented ethnic groups as well. A considerable number had unorthodox views, which were temporarily permitted. According to Novick, unlike the early Jewish historians, who were integrationists and usually assimilationists, many of the Jewish historians of the 1960s, as well as the young black historians of this period, were separatists, nationalists of some sort, who were scornful of assimilation. They organized on the basis of ethnicity or race, or in the case of white women, as feminists. They claimed distinctive styles of perception and thought.

For a brief period in the 1960s, the consensus of American historians was shaken by a sway toward the left in political culture. The stress of the baby boomers on the infrastructure and increased cynicism about truth and objectivity vis-à-vis the Vietnam War shook the confidence in the profession of history. This crisis in objectivity spread to all of the disciplines in the Academy. This included the sciences which had been provoked by Thomas Kuhn's notion of paradigms. The defense of objectivity most often came from the right, while criticism of it came from the left. Objectivity is most frequently associated with the status quo.

From my vantage point, the value of Novick's work is that he documents the reactions of the champions of objectivity to those deviating from their paradigm. After attending his first meeting of the AHA in 1936, Harvard University historian Oscar Handlin wrote in reverential tones about the profession. Unknown to him, the year before, his adviser, Arthur Schlesinger Sr. had noted in a letter of recommendation for Handlin, a Jew, that he had "none of the offensive traits which some people associate with his race" (Novick 1988, 172–73). Schlesinger's colleague, Roger Merriman, recommended Daniel Boorstin in similar terms, as "a Jew though not the kind to which one takes exception" (Novick 1988, 173). Even non-Jewish historians with Jewish sounding names required "protection." In a letter recommending Wallace Notestein for a post at Yale, Charles Hull of Cornell wrote that "his family are Presbyterians, very much so, except Wallace himself, who is a somewhat straying sheep" (Novick 1988, 173). Novick simply argues that there is no such thing as "truth in history." Historical objectivity is an "incoherent" and "dubious" goal. Novick writes, "Most historians generally write about their colleagues the way Arthur Schlesinger Jr., writes about the Kennedys" (Novick 1988, 15). They ignore their flaws and their racism and ultrapatriotism. Novick uncontrovertedly shows the professional, political, psychological, and cultural pressures that influence and even determine the epistemological interpretation of historians. He also shows how they got their knowledge and their philosophical and professional biases.

It is important to establish that purges by historians in this country are nothing new. Take the case of revisionist historian William Appleman Williams, author of *The Tragedy of American Diplomacy*

(1962) and *The Contours of American History* (1973). From the University of Wisconsin, Williams dared to question the objectivity of the cold war historians. Williams feared the irresponsible nation-state and the triumph of an American corporate liberal state intent on economic growth as a way of life. This pursuit justified expansion through an open-door imperialism.

Williams challenged the liberal apologetic that allowed hysterical anticommunism to justify acts of Realpolitik. Williams was a leader among the revisionists and was accused by Arthur Schlesinger Sr. of being a "pro-Communist scholar." Williams was harassed by the House Committee on Un-American Activities, which demanded to see the manuscript of *Contours*. Historians charged that the *New Left Review*, led by Williams, was politicizing the discipline of history.

In my opinion, the works of Kuhn, Novick, and Williams shake the epistemological foundations of the profession through a critique of the objectivity question. There is no truth without a complete reappraisal of the current knowledge. The search for truth is itself the central Western illusion that determines the rules. Truth is socially constructed, not discovered. Strip away the political and cultural coverings that pass as "truth" in each society and the power of hegemonic interests are exposed.

Skepticism is today reaching the point at which all defenses of objectivity and impartiality, even as ideals, are exposed as naive and self-serving, if not ridiculous. As Novick points out, claims to objectivity have been used to exclude the other from full participation in the nation's public life and professions. Chicano/a scholars are left with the choice of accepting or living the lie, ignoring the lie (as Handlin ignored anti-Semitism), or deconstructing the present canons.

What Is Moral Authority?

According to sociologist Fred Katz in his study *Ordinary People and Extraordinary Evil*, ordinary people are capable of making every day choices that result in serious wrongdoing, "even horrendous acts like those of the Nazi Holocaust and the My Lai massacre" (cited in Robinson 1995). Ordinary people also have choices, which are not as monumental. They are judged to be credible or incredible, good or evil, by these choices. Their life is framed by these choices, and through a pattern of choices, they define themselves. Chicano/a scholars themselves are part of this universe, and the kinds of choices they make, such as the kind of research they undertake or the kind of research that they will not do, define them.

"Moral credibility" and "moral authority" are often used interchangeably—but they are different. By moral credibility, I mean the stature of the individual scholar, and the degree of importance that the particular scholar accords the truth. Measured within this definition is the amount of prestige that the scholar has in a specific community or communities. Moral authority is stronger. The definition carries with it the ability to influence. It includes the contributions of the individual. The term can therefore be generalized to include institutions. Both moral credibility and moral authority involve a reputation for fairness and credibility. Are the individuals or even institutions perceived as just? Do they promote the interests of a particular community?

The concept of moral authority has been explored in the field of the criminal justice system. Criminologists ask whether a law has moral authority. Many criminologists believe that the decline of moral authority has contributed to the breakdown in respect for the law and the rise in crime. In the case of Latina/os, there is a marked decline in the moral authority of the law. With the popular use of prisons as a solution, and with more and more families having family members who have gone through the prison system, moral disapproval is becoming more difficult within the Latina/o community. It is difficult to view convicts as social deviants when they are members of your family.

Moral authority or even moral credibility greatly depends on a particular universe. Ronald Reagan, for instance, enjoyed immense moral credibility and moral authority in the United States, but suffered from the lack of both in other parts of the world. In the case of the Chicano/a scholar, he or she can have moral credibility and moral authority in academe but lack it in the Chicano community, or vice versa. Ultimately, authority of any sort depends on how well you serve the interests of a particular universe, how that universe perceives you, and the ability of that universe to reward or punish you.

In the case of the Academy, its moral authority rests on its control of scholars based on their acceptance of the controlling paradigm. In the case of the Chicano/a community, moral authority is based on its ability to honestly interpret not only the community's interests, but also factors that prevent the Latino/a community from growing and prospering. What kind of research the scholar does is a social act, often at odds with the interests of traditional scholars and their culture. The ability of the Chicano/a scholar to resist the social control of the institution over his or her research determines his or her moral authority in the Chicano/a community.

Like society, the Academy is responsible for defining who are "good citizens" and how they are rewarded. Moral judgments are made as part of the institutional culture, which acts as an enforcer of social control, which is based not only on monetary rewards, but also on ideas. The need to receive recognition from our peers, from those whom we respect, is inherent in all of us. We fear and care about the judgments of those whom we respect.

One example of moral authority is our obedience or disobedience of the law. Our respect for the law goes beyond the threat of punishment. We often obey it because we know that it protects us, that it is necessary. We want to be "good citizens," or at least be thought of as "good citizens." This self-control does not break down until the idea is challenged by moral judgments. In the case of scholars, these factors operate in addition to the factor of self-interest. Scholars more often seek the path of least resistance. Like the law, the reality is that the Academy has the ability to reward or punish scholars. It is a power that the Chicano/a community does not have. In academic, as in the rest of society, scholars respond to reward and punishment. The factor that the community can use to influence scholars to do right or wrong vis-à-vis its interests is the common ethnicity of its members. In other words, scholars must care about the judgments made about them by the community for it to have any influence.

In the spring of 1969, Chicano/as met at the University of California, Santa Barbara, and wrote the "Plan of Santa Barbara," reputedly a plan to implement Chicano/a studies nationally. Aside from obvious omissions from the plan, such as the failure to adequately address the women's question, the framers seriously underestimated the co-opting power of the Academy. They believed that Chicano/a scholars were sufficiently bonded to their community to act in its interests. They believed that Chicana/o scholars would play an advocacy role for the interests of the Mexican-American community simply because they were Chicanos.

Obviously, the framers of the plan were naive. As stated earlier, the ability of Chicano/a scholars to resist the social control of the Academy when the latter's interests conflict with those of the community is small. Ultimately, the university wins out. Class and racial differences make the survival of the moral authority of the community very difficult. Good citizenship in these universes has different definitions. Part of the problem when speaking about Chicana/os and other Latina/os is the lack of a political infrastructure to influence the superstructure. The Latina/o community does not have the moral authority to protect its interests within academe because the Chicana/o or Latino scholar must depend on the approval of the majority in order to have moral authority among scholars. Within academe itself, it is almost impossible for the lone Chicano/a scholar in a sea of white male scholars to have any moral authority—to affect a quantitative or qualitative shift, or to distinguish truth from myth. He or she is thus easily controlled.

There are exceptions. My colleagues and students remind me that I have always been independent and have spoken my mind without fear of retribution by the institution or the community. I remind them, however, that I am in a unique situation. First, I teach at a teaching university, that attracted many excellent researchers who were refugees from research institutions in the 1960s. This has given me political space. Most important, I was a full professor at the age of thirty-six, and founding chair of a Department of Chicano/a Studies which today has twenty-two positions. The latter has given me a considerable degree of independence, and I could afford to develop an oppositional paradigm, and thus earn moral authority within the outside Mexican-American community.

Not all Chicano/a scholars achieve this degree of independence. Independence hinges on the material conditions that allow this freedom. Moreover, personal ambition shapes their judgments, and they often take the path of least resistance and make choices based on circumstances that promote self-interest. It is easy to rationalize that they have to get tenure or be promoted in order to be independent. Other compromises are made, to the point that scholars are often not conscious of the fact that they are making negative choices. Ironically, the scholars are frustrated when their credibility and then moral authority suffer within the Chicano community. They sincerely believe that they have made sacrifices in order to receive a Ph.D., and that they should be appreciated, and they do not understand when they are not. By the time they receive their doctorates, most Chicano/a scholars have spent more time in academe than they have with their families or childhood friends. Professors and colleagues become surrogate family members during their school years. They are their role models, an image of what they will become in the future. Once they enter the profession, it is natural that they turn to this community for approval. They are further conditioned in mainstream departments. The prevailing ideas, traditions, and culture influence what they think in a manner that goes beyond the threat of rewards and punishment. Scholars choose to live by certain sets of rules because they fear the disapproval of their social group. They see themselves as moral beings who want to do the right thing as they perceive it.

It is a catch-22 situation: paradigm shifts, whether defined in quantitative or in qualitative terms, cannot take place without the sufficient moral authority of the Chicano/a studies paradigm or community of scholars to challenge the existing truth. Within the Chicano/a community there has never been sufficient moral cohesiveness, let alone authority, to force this change. This conflict has tested the moral authority of many of us.

Conclusion

This chapter began with a brief discussion of truth and objectivity. It examined the bias of mainstream disciplines toward area studies programs in general, and how this prejudice has influenced their perception of Chicana/o studies and other ethnic studies programs. My criticism of the mainstream disciplines is based not so much on the disciplines themselves as on the community of scholars within these communities. Because most of my academic training is in the field of history, my analysis centered on that discipline, although I readily admit that most disciplines are infected by the same flaws.

In the discussion of whether the historian can be objective or approach a semblance of the truth, I discussed British historian Edward Hallett Carr and U.S. historian Oscar Handlin. For me they represent two opposite polls of the discourse, not so much based on what each says about the subject, but based on the roles that they played within the debate itself. Handlin, for me, represents the arrogance of the profession itself, which prides itself in a marketplace of ideas and, in reality, constructs a paradigm where truth can be reached only through knowledge accepted by a consensus of Anglo-Saxon scholars, or those assimilated into that academic community.

Within this context, Chicana/o studies have largely floated. Outside of a few isolated programs, no community of scholars exists that is capable of establishing a research field of study. (This is not to say that a teaching field does not exist.) Therefore, what we have are areas within the various disciplines, in which Chicana/o history develops as part of the discipline of history. As such, Chicana/o scholars are forced to adhere to the canons and paradigm of the discipline that dictates accepted methodologies and knowledge, making it impossible to shift a paradigm, which like the cold war vision of society, does not adequately include the auslander.

Central to the relationship of Chicana/o studies to the American paradigm is the question of truth and objectivity. What I have tried to convey in this discussion is that, although mainstream historians readily admit that truth is an ideal, to some—such as Jeffrey Russell—the ultimate truth is in the mind of God. While the vast majority of traditional Euroamerican scholars are not as unscientific as Russell, they still feel that their truth is closer to the truth than that of other beings. Their methods are just superior to those of others. Their American nationality seems to somehow give them the right to be more true, and the right to define the accepted truth gives them the power to be arrogant.

I posit that objectivity is based on how well the scholar adheres to the accepted paradigm. In the case of historians, patriotism appears to be a guiding principle for objectivity.

Despite my criticism of the manipulation of truth and objectivity as tests that demand conformity to the canons of the profession, I believe that guidelines and even scientific tests are necessary. Without criteria, minorities are at the mercy of the professional class. My answer is that we must emphasize the fact that truth is socially constructed and that objectivity depends on the prism of the scholar. Academe has a culture that we must penetrate, and knowledge of the other must become part of the equation that describes society. In doing so, we must keep in mind that there will be a persistent rejection of these ideas.

I reinforce these conclusions by including a discussion of Thomas Kuhn's work on paradigms. It is the clearest example of how our society is controlled by a positivist rationality. American society is based on authority: in academe, of prominent members of the academy, and in the courts, of the judges. In the field of history the norm is set by prominent members of the American Historical Association and the network of professional organizations and journals that delineate what is accepted knowledge. Paradigm shifts occur only when this mind-set changes and new knowledge is accepted. Kuhn points out that this is very difficult since the approved methodology of the "scientists" is deductive. Ironically, most paradigm shifts have occurred by way of knowledge obtained through inductive reasoning.

I also discuss Peter Novick's groundbreaking history of the American historical profession. It proves that the current struggles of minorities and women are not aberrations. From the beginning the historical profession has demanded conformity to its paradigm and patriotism as requisites for "good citizenship." Those deviating from these principles have been severely criticized and even castigated. Essentially, the profession has remained Anglo-Saxon, with minority scholars such as Handlin assimilating, some becoming more Anglo-Saxon than their predecessors.

Finally, I address the question of moral authority as it pertains to Chicana and Chicano scholars. Basically, what I say is that it is difficult to serve two masters. Academe socializes the scholar, and it mentors the scholar during his or her formative intellectual years. It also has the power to reward or punish the scholar by hiring, promoting, or accepting his or her works. As an individual, no one can force a paradigm shift. Consequently, without a change in the cold war paradigm, which sees minorities as the other, society will remain unprepared to solve current societal problems.

References

Acuña, Rodolfo F. *Anything But Mexican: Chicanos in Contemporary Los Angeles.* London: Verso, 1996.

———. *Occupied America: The Chicano Struggle for Liberation.* San Francisco: Canfield Press, 1972.

———. *Occupied America: The History of the Chicano*, 2d edition. New York: Harper & Row, 1981.

———. *Occupied America: The History of the Chicano,* 3d edition. New York: Harper & Row, 1988.

———. *Sometimes There Is No Other Side: Chicanos and the Myth of Equality.* Notre Dame: University of Notre Dame Press, 1998.

Adams, Guy B. "Culture, Technical Rationality, and Organizational Culture." *American Review of Public Administration* 20, no. 4 (December 1990): 285ff.

Adams, Noah. "Author Charles Murray Defends His Theories." All Things Considered (NPR), 28 October 1994, Transcript # 1649–6.

Ali, Derek. "Confidence, Blacks Told; Speakers Stress Self Worth." *Dayton (Ohio) Daily News,* 27 February 1994.

Allen, Henry. "The Epistemology, Philosophy, History, Psychology, Anthropology, Aesthetics and General Absolute Necessity of Making Lists." *Washington Post,* 12 June 1977.

Amin, Samir. "1492: Columbus and the New World Order 1492–1992." *Monthly Review* 44, no. 3 (July 1992): 10ff.

Anderson, Charles H. *White Protestant Americans.* Englewood Cliffs, N.J.: Prentice-Hall, 1970.

Appleby, Joyce, Lynn Hunt, and Margaret Jacob. *Telling the Truth About History.* New York: W.W. Norton, 1994.

Asante, Molefi Kete. "Point of View; Afrocentric Education." *Washington Post,* 7 April 1991.

Atkinson, Dorothy. "Understanding the Soviets: The Development of U.S. Expertise on the USSR." *Washington Quarterly* 10, no. 3 (summer 1987): 183ff.

Barzun, Jacques. "Scholarship Versus Culture." *Atlantic* 254 (November 1984): 93ff.

Bennett, David H. *From Nativist Movements to the New Right in American History.* Chapel Hill: University of North Carolina Press, 1988.

Bolvin, Jean. "The Status of Academic Relations as an Academic Discipline Within Canadian Universities." *Industrial Relations* 47, no. 2 (22 March 1992): 220ff.

Bozeman, Adda B. "Culture Clash and Liberal Democracy: Toward a New World Order." *Current* no. 367 (November 1994): 24ff.

Brodsky, Joseph. "Profile of Clio: What is History? An Argument for Nomadism." *New Republic* 208, no. 5 (1 February 1993): 60.

Brody, David, "Labor History, Industrial Relations, and the Crisis of American Labor; Labor History and Industrial Relations: a Symposium." *Industrial and Labor Relations Review* 43, no. 1 (October 1989): 7ff.

Brown, Raymond E. "The Narratives of Jesus' Passion and Anti-Judaism." *America* 172, no. 11 (1 April 1995): 8ff.

"Campus Life: U.C.L.A.; Upgraded Status Urged For Chicano Studies." *New York Times,* 10 February 1991.

Carr, Edward Hallett. *What Is History?* New York: Vintage Books, 1961.

Chabram, Angie. "Chicana/o Studies As Oppositional Ethnography." *Cultural Studies* 4, no. 3 (October 1990): 228–47.

Chabran, Richard. "The Emergence of Neoconservatism in Chicano/Latino Discourses." *Cultural Studies* 4, no. 3 (October 1990): 217–27.

Chambon, Adrienne, and Donald F. Bellamy. "Ethnic Identity, Intergroup Relations and Welfare Police in the Canadian Context: A Comparative Discourse Analysis." *Journal of Sociology and Social Welfare* 22, no. 1 (1995): 121–47.

Chapnick, Philip. "Knowledge and Its Representations; Approaches to Knowledge Representation: An Introduction; Conceptual Structures: Information Processing in Mind and Machine; Knowledge Representation: An AI Perspective; and Representations of Common Sense Knowledge; Book Store." *AI Expert* 6, no. 6 (June 1991): 27ff.

Cheney, Lynne. "Humanities Controlled by Fringe." *St. Louis Post-Dispatch,* 17 March 1995.

———. "Mocking America; Reality of Arts and Humanities." *Phoenix Gazette,* 15 March 1995.

———. "Testimony January 24, 1995, Lynne V. Cheney Member American Enterprise Institute House Appropriations Interior Reducing Federal Spending." *Federal Document Clearing House Congressional Testimony,* 24 January 1995.

Clark, Thomas. "Culture and Objectivity." *Humanist* 54, no. 5 (September 1994): 38ff.

Cole, Jonathan R. "Balancing Acts: Dilemmas of Choice Facing Research Universities." *Daedalus* 122, no. 4 (22 September 1993): 1ff.

Collins, Denis and Steven L. Wartick. "Business and Society/Business Ethics Courses: Twenty Years at the Crossroads." *Business and Society* 34, no. 1 (April 1995): 51ff.

Comstock, Gary. "Ethics and Scientific Research." *SRA Journal* 26, no. 2 (22 September 1994): 33ff.

Cordova, Teresa. "Power and Knowledge: Colonialism in the Academy." *Taboo: A Journal of Culture and Education* (spring 1996).

Desimore, Laura M. "Racial Discourse in a Community: Language and the Social Construction of Race." *Journal of Negro Education* 62, no. 4 (fall 1993).

D'Souza, Dinesh. "We the Slaveowners; In Jefferson's America, Were Some Men Not Created Equal?" *Heritage Foundation, Policy Review* no. 74 (fall 1995): 30ff.

Du Bois, W. E. B. *The Souls of Black Folk.* New York: Bantam Books, 1989.

———. *The Autobiography of W. E. B. Du Bois.* New York: International Publishers, 1991.

———. ed. *Black Reconstruction in America, 1860–1880.* David Levering Lewis, ed. New York: Macmillan, 1991.

Fein, Bruce. "By Every Other Name Racism Smells as Foul." *New Jersey Law Journal* (2 May 1991): 14ff.

Foner, Eric. "Reconstructing Reconstruction." *Newsday,* 16 February 1992.

Forrest, Anne. "Women and Industrial Relations Theory: No Room in the Discourse." *Industrial Relations* 48, no. 3 (22 June 1993): 409ff.

Garza, Melita Marie. "Culture Wars; Across the Nation, Universities Find Themselves on the Front Line of the Ethnic Studies Debate." *Chicago Tribune,* 18 July 1995.

Genovese, Eugene D. "Voices Must Unite for Victory in the Cultural War." *Chicago Tribune,* 22 December 1993.

Gewirtz, Paul. "On 'I Know It When I See It.'" *Yale Law Journal* 105, no. 4 (January 1996): 1023–47.

Giddens, Anthony. "In Defense of Sociology." *New Statesman & Society* 8, no. 347 (7 April 1995): 18ff.

Goetz, Thomas. "Oh, the Humanities!" *The Village Voice,* 18 April 1995.

Goodman, Neville W. "Paradigm, Parameter, Paralysis of Mind; Use of Language and Statistics in Biomedical Research; Includes List of Poorly Chosen Parameters." *British Medical Journal* 307, no. 6919 (18 December 1993): 1627ff.

Gough, Barry. "Goodbye Columbus? Canada's Chains of History; Christopher Columbus Quincentenary Uncelebrated in Canada." *History Today* 43 (March 1993): 8ff.

Gramsci, Antonio. *Selections from Political Writings 1910–1920.* New York: International Publishers, 1977.

———. *Selections from Political Writings 1921–1926.* New York: International Publishers, 1978.

Gray, Katti. "Black Group Rallying for Curriculum." *Newsday,* 22 July 1990.

Guzda, Henry P. "Workplace Industrial Relations and the Global Challenge." *Monthly Labor Review* 118, no. 7 (July 1995): 80ff.

Hamburg, Jill E. "Who Speaks for the Sephardim? Israeli Elections." *Nation* 254, no. 25 (29 June 1992): 891ff.

Handlin, Oscar. *Truth in History.* Cambridge: Harvard University Press, 1979.

Harding, Sandra. *The Science Question in Feminism.* Ithaca, N.Y.: Cornell University Press, 1986.

Himmelfarb, Gertrude. "The Group: Bourgeois Britain and Its Marxist Historians." *New Republic* 194 (10 February 1986): 28ff.

———. "What To Do About Education: The Universities." *Commentary* 98, no. 4 (October 1994): 21ff.

Hondagneu-Sotelo, Pierrette. *Gendered Transitions: Mexican Experiences of Immigration.* Berkeley: University of California Press, 1994.

Howkins, Alun. "A Past for the People: History Workshop Journal." *New Statesman & Society* 8, no. 337 (27 January 1995): 36ff.

Huggins, Nathan I. "The Deforming Mirror of Truth: Slavery and the Master Narrative of American History." *Radical History Review* 49 (winter 1991): 25–47.

Hunt, Shelby D. "Positivism and Paradigm Dominance in Consumer Research: Toward a Critical Pluralism and Rapprochement." *Journal of Consumer Research* 18, no. 1 (June 1991): 32ff.

Illich, Ivan. *Deschooling Society*. New York: Harper & Row, 1971.

Innerst, Carol. "Putting Africa on the Map: 'Racist' History Assailed." *The Washington Times*, 13 November 1990.

Jimenez, Manuel. "Scholar Challenges Latino Stereotypes." *Nuestro Tiempo* (Los Angeles) 18 March 1993.

Jones, Marc T. "Missing the Forest for the Trees: A Critique of the Social Responsibility Concept and Discourse." Special Issue: New Perspectives on Business and Society. *Business and Society* 35, no. 1 (March 1996): 7ff.

Katz, Fred E. *Ordinary People and Extraordinary Evil: A Report on the Beguilings of Evil*. Ithica, New York: State University of New York Press,1993.

Kealy, Gregory S. "Herbert G. Gutman, 1928–1985, and the Writing of Working-Class History." *Monthly Review* 38 (May 1986): 22ff.

Kuhn, Thomas S. *The Structure of Scientific Revolutions*. 2d ed., enl. Chicago: The University of Chicago Press, 1970.

Lewy, Guenter. "Academic Ethics and the Radical Left." *Policy Review* no. 19 (winter 1982): 29ff.

Lively, Donald E, and Stephen Plass. "Equal Protection: The Jurisprudence of Denial and Evasion." 40 American Universal Law Review 1307, Summer 1991.

MacNeil, Robert. In Washington: Judy Woodruff; Guests: Sen. Joseph Biden, [D] Delaware; William Bennett, National Drug Policy Director; Patricia Williams, Law Professor; John Bunzel, Former University President; Roderick Park, University Administrator; Ronald Takaki, Ethnic Studies Professor; Correspondent: Charlayne Hungter-Gault, "Hooked: Divisions Over Diversity." The MacNeil/Lehrer NewsHour, 10 May 1990, Transcript #3729.

Maloney, Linda M. "Who Killed Jesus? Exposing the Roots of Anti-Semitism in the Gospel Story of the Death of Jesus." *America* 173, no. 6 (9 September 1995): 24ff.

Marquez, Myriam. "Insensitive Words but Fair Actions? Lay That on the Jurors, Judge." *Orlando Sentinel* (Fla.) 12 December 1994.

Marriott, Michel. "Educators See Need for Diversity on Campus, but Debate How to Achieve It." *New York Times,* 19 December 1990.

Martin, Ralph Drury. "Cracking Crimes Through Language; In Fascinating Detail, Roger W. Shuy Chronicles How the Scientist Can Bring Understanding to Something We All Think We Know So Well—Everyday Conversation." *Legal Times,* 11 July 1994.

Mills, David. "Half-Truths and History: The Debate Over Jews and Slavery." *Washington Post,* 17 October 1993.

Mitchell, Don. *The Lie of the Land: Migrant Workers and the California Landscape.* Minneapolis: University of Minnesota Press, 1996.

Morgan, Glenda, and E. J. Levy. "Debunker of 'Feminist Fictions' Is Soft on Truth Herself." *Minneapolis Star Tribune,* 3 September 1994.

Morrow, Carlotta. "This Afrocentrism is Reverse Racism." *San Diego Union-Tribune,* 12 November 1995.

Muwakkil, Salim. "The Ugly Revival of Genetic Determinism." *The San Francisco Examiner,* 6 December 1994.

Nichols, Rodney W. "Federal Science Policy and Universities: Consequences of Success; The Impact of Federal Sponsorship on American University Research." *Daedalus* 122, no. 4 (22 September 1993): 197ff.

Nicholson, David. "Whose American Dilemma?" *The Washington Post,* 1 October 1995.

Novick, Peter. *That Noble Dream: The "Objectivity Question" and the American Historical Profession.* Cambridge, U.K.: Cambridge University Press, 1988.

Olisher, Dean. "World War II History Exhibit Causes Controversy." All Things Considered (NPR), 28 March 1995, Transcript # 1800–3. Guests: Simon Shama, historian, Columbia University; Michael Heymann, Smithsonian Institute; Peter Novick, University of Chicago; John Coatsworth, historian, Harvard University.

Omi, Michael, and Howard Winant. *Racial Formation in the United States: From the 1960's to the 1990's.* 2d ed. New York: Routledge, 1994.

Owens, Madeleine. "Blameless Nation Has Bob Dole Forgotten Slavery? Vietnam? The Indians? Macarthyism? Watergate?" *Columbian,* 10 September 1995.

Page, Clarence. "Bush, Quayle, Media All Ignore 'R' Word." *St. Louis Post-Dispatch,* 31 May 1992.

Parr, Joy. "Gender History and Historical Practice." *Canadian Historical Review* 76, no. 3 (September 1995): 354–ff.

Pemberton, J. Michael. "The Importance of Theory and Research to Records and Information Management." *Records Management Quarterly* 26, no. 2 (April 1992): 46ff.

Pfeffer, Jeffrey. "Barriers to the Advance of Organizational Science: Paradigm Development as a Dependent Variable." *Academy of Management Review* 18, no. 4 (October 1993): 599ff.

Pierard, Richard V. "Denying the Holocaust: The Growing Assault on Truth and Memory." *Christianity Today* 38, no. 4 (4 April 1994): 97ff.

Pinkerton, James P. "General Schwarzkopf's New Paradigm: Domestic Lessons of Desert Storm." *Policy Review* no. 57 (summer 1991): 22ff.

Pinsker, Sanford. "Lost on Campus: Civility, Rational Debate." *Christian Science Monitor,* 30 November 1995.

Pisik, Betsy. "The Semantics of Hate: Are Racist Code Words Masquerading as Political Straight Talk?" *Washington Times,* 14 November 1991.

Popper, Karl R. *The Logic of Scientific Discovery.* New York: Harper & Row, 1968.

Purvin, George. "A Little Ethnic Cheerleading Would Do History No Harm." *Washington Times,* 1 August 1990.

Raspberry, William. "Culture, Schooling and Eurocentrism." *Chicago Tribune,* 7 September 1990.

Rasch, Sara B. "Rethinking Labor History: Essays on Discourse and Class Analysis. *Labor Studies Journal* 20, no. 2 (22 June 1995): 58ff.

Ravitch, Diane, and Arthur Schlesinger Jr. "Should Teach History, Not Ethnic Cheerleading." *Newsday,* 29 June 1990.

Regents of the University of California v. Bakke, 438 US 265; 98 S. Ct. 2733; 1978 U.S. Lexis 5; 57 L. Ed. 2d 750; 17 Fair Empl. Prac. Cas. (BNA) 1000; 17 Empl. Prac., 28 June 1978.

Reilly, Joseph. "Under the White Gaze: Jim Crow, the Nobel, and the Assault on Toni Morrison; Nobel Prize for Literature." *Monthly Review* 45, no. 11 (April 1994): 41ff.

Robinson, Paul H. "Moral Credibility and Crime: Why People Obey Law." *Current* no. 373 (June 1995): 10ff.

Rocco, Raymond. "The Theoretical Construction of the 'Other' in Postmodernist Thought: Latinos in the New Urban Political Economy." *Cultural Studies* 4, no. 3 (October 1990): 321–30.

Rosaldo, Renato. *Culture and Truth: The Remaking of Social Analysis.* Boston: Beacon Press, 1993.

Sanchez, Rosaura. "Ethnicity, Ideology and Academia." *Cultural Studies* 4, no. 3 (October 1990): 294–302.

Schlesinger Jr., Arthur M. *The Disuniting of America: Reflections on a Multicultural Society.* New York: W. W. Norton, 1992.

Searle, John R. "Rationality and Realism, What Is at Stake? Ongoing 'Debate' Over the Objectives of Higher Education Curriculum, Academic Requirements and Enhancement of Western Culture." *Daedalus* 122, no. 4 (22 September 1993): 55ff.

———. *The Construction of Social Reality.* New York: Free Press, 1995.

Senior, Peter A., and Raj Bjopal. "Ethnicity as a variable in Epistiological Research." *British Medical Journal* 309, no. 6950 (30 July 1994): 327ff.

Shivakumar, Dhananjai. "The Pure Theory as Ideal Type: Defending Kelsen on the Basis of Weberian Methodology." *Yale Law Journal* 105, no. 5 (March 1996): 1383–1414.

Shore, Marlene. "'Remember the Future': The *Canadian Historical Review* and the Discipline of History, 1920–95." *Canadian Historical Review* 76, no. 3 (September 1995): 410ff.

Shuy, Roger W. *Language Crimes.* Oxford: Blackwell Publishers, 1993.

Singer, Alan. "Reflections on Multiculturalism." *Phi Delta Kappa* 76, no. 4 (December 1994): 284ff.

Sivanandan, A. "The New Racism." *The New Statesman & Society* 1, no. 22 (4 November 1988): 8–9.

Stanfield, Rochelle L. "The New Faces of Hate." *National Journal* 26, no. 25 (18 June 1994): 1460ff.

Tannen, Deborah. *Gender and Discourse.* Cambridge, U.K.: Oxford, 1994.

Thompson, E. P. (Edward Palmer). *Folklore, Anthropology and Social History.* Brighton, U.K.: Noyce, 1979.

———. *The Making of the English Working Class,* New Ed. London: Penguin, 1991.

Tobar, Hector. "Rigoberta Menchu's Mayan Vision; Revered for the Symbolic Power of Her Nobel Prize but Attacked for Her Continuing Life in Exile, the Guatemalan Leader Focuses on Bringing a 'New Dawn' to the World's Indigenous Peoples." *Los Angeles Times Magazine,* 23 January 1994: 16ff.

Turner, Sarah E., and William G. Bowen. "The Flight from the Arts and Sciences: Trends in Degrees Conferred." *Science* 250, no. 4980 (26 October 1990): 517ff.

Valenzuela, Abel Jr. "California's Melting Pot Boils Over: The Origins of a Cruel Proposition." *Dollars & Sense* no. 198 (March 1995): 28–41.

Van Dijk, Teun. *Communicating Racism: Ethnic Prejudice in Thought and Talk.* Newbury Park, Calif.: Sage, 1986.

———. *Elite Discourse and Racism.* Newbury Park, Calif.: Sage, 1993.

Vélez-Ibañez, Carlos. *Border Visions: Mexican Cultures of the Southwest United States.* Tucson: University of Arizona Press, 1996.

Weber, Eugen. "History Is What Historians Do." *New York Times,* 22 July 1984.

Weil, Eric. "Philosophical and Political Thought in Europe Today; Assessment of the Impact of Change in Traditional Social Beliefs and Cultural Ideology; Notes from the Past." *Daedalus* 123, no. 3 (22 June 1994): 185ff.

Weil, Martin, and Lisa Leff. "Naval Academy Relieves Head Of Department; Chairman Was Asked To Raise Grades." *The Washington Post,* 25 February 1990.

Wiener, Jon. "When Historians Judge Their Own; British Historian Norman Davies Denied Tenured Professorship at Stanford University." *Nation* 245, no. 17 (21 November 1987): 584ff.

Williams, William Appleman. *The Tragedy of American Diplomacy.* New York: Delta, 1962.

———. *The Contours of American History.* New York: W. W. Norton, 1988.

Willmott, Hugh. "What Has Been Happening in Organization Theory and Does It Matter?" *Personnel Review* 24, no. 8 (1995): 33–54.

Zavella, Patricia, and Paula Cruz Takash. "Gender and Power: Reconstructing Latino Ethnography." In *Urban Anthropology and Studies of Cultural Systems and World Economic Development,* 231–36. Brockport, N.Y.: Institute for the Study of Man, 1985.

CHAPTER 2

CHICANO LITERARY HISTORY: ORIGIN AND DEVELOPMENT

Luis Leal

IN 1971 TOMÁS RIVERA PUBLISHED his ground-breaking novel "*. . . y no se lo tragó la tierra/ . . . and the Earth Did Not Part,*" which immediately became a metaphor for the life of migrant workers and, by extension, for all Chicanos. The novel is structured around a series of encounters between migrant workers and the social, economic, and natural forces with which they have to contend and which they overcome. Rivera's young hero reminisces about a lost year, and is "at a loss for words" to explain what happened during that year. This sense of being lost and speechless can be considered to be the central metaphor in Rivera's novel, whose theme is the search for identity. It can also be interpreted as reflecting the author's sense of being lost in a world without a history of the literature written by his own people. In 1975 he wrote in his essay "Chicano Literature: Fiesta of the Living":

> At twelve, I looked for books by my people, by my immediate people, and found very few. Very few accounts in fact existed. When I met Bartolo, our town's itinerant poet, and when on a visit to the Mexican side of the border, I also heard of him—for he would wander on both sides of the border to sell his poetry—I was engulfed with *alegría*. It was an exaltation brought on by the sudden sensation that my own life had relationships, that my own family had relationships, that the people I lived with had connections beyond those at the conscious level. It was Bartolo's poetry . . . that gave me this awareness (439–40).

Are we to believe, as some do, that because no one had written about it, Chicano literature did not exist? Between 1836 and 1848, American critics and literary historians neglected Chicano literature published in Texas and the Southwest. Not a single article was dedicated to Chicano literary criticism, let alone literary history, before the 1950s. No wonder Rivera had difficulty in finding books written by his own people. The literature was there, but it remained for the Chicano literary historians themselves to write about it.

A number of non-Chicano critics have characterized Chicanos as a people without a past, without a voice, an illiterate people unable to record their social history, let alone their cultural endeavor. As early as 1844, Thomas Jefferson Farnham, a New England attorney visiting California, spoke of these people as being "incapable of reading or writing, and knowing nothing of science or literature" (Weber 1974, 18). In 1919 Robert Ernest Cowan, author of the book *A Bibliography of the Spanish Press in California 1833–1845*, affirmed in his introduction: "The Spanish Californian had no particular education, nor was he a writer—that is, of other than his official documents" (3). Yet, he contradicts himself, since he includes in his bibliography books in Spanish from before 1845 that are not official documents. In 1949 the much-lauded writer Carey McWilliams, in *North from Mexico*—a very useful book, considered to be the first to document the history of the Chicano people—stated the following in regard to the intellectual production of the Chicano: "In the past, Mexicans have been a more or less anonymous, voiceless, expressionless minority" (1968, 302).

The problem that arises is the following: Why is it that American literary historians have not dealt with literature written in the United States by Chicanos and other Latinos? The answer to this question comes from one of the most famous American literary historians, Robert Spiller, editor of the important *Literary History of the United States*, a required reference work for students of American history. He states, no doubt thinking about Cowan's observations and adding some of the characteristics with which the stereotype of the Californians and the Mexicans had been formulated:

> The Spanish civilization of the Pacific Coast was too thin in population, too indolent, to make a concerted stand against the Anglo-Saxon. Within a short time it underwent absorption into the cultural complex of the New West . . . lending the mass some of the richness of its pigment. Spanish language newspapers, sermons in Spanish and a few quaint remains of liturgical drama, and the

> inflow of a modest quota of books from Mexico City and Spain, were persistent enclaves in the midst of a speedy English-speaking conquest (1973, 659).

The preceding brief reference to Mexican-American literature in Spiller's book is expanded somewhat in his chapter "The Mingling of Tongues," where German-American, French (of Louisiana), Spanish-American, Italian-American, Scandinavian, and Jewish-American literatures are surveyed. In the less than a page dedicated to Spanish-American literature, Spiller first explains that "the literature that survives today among the descendants of early Colonists is an oral literature of plays, songs, ballads, and folk tales brought from Spain" (1973, 687). After mentioning the titles of a few works—among which he includes *Los Comanches,* which is definitely not of Spanish but of New Mexican origin (see Espinosa 1907), as are some of the other works that are mentioned—he states, "Of other writing there was little. The theocratic rule of the Mission period was hostile to profane knowledge. Scientific books were sometimes publicly burned, and not until 1833 was a printing press brought to California. Then it published almost exclusively official documents. The first volume printed in Texas, in 1829, was in English by an American immigrant" (1973, 687). The present century is dismissed in Spiller's *History* in three lines: "In the twentieth century," he says, "Spanish-American culture, both early and contemporary, furnished material to such American-born novelists as Gertrude Atherton, Willa Cather, Harvey Fergusson, and John Steinbeck" (1973, 687–88). This is not the place to mention all of the inaccuracies and errors that have been accumulated in such a short (mis)evaluation of Latino literature; undoubtedly there are many.

As late as 1969, the Chicano scholars Ernesto Galarza, Herman Gallegos, and Julián Samora were bemoaning "the almost total lack of historical and literary treatment of the Mexican American in the United States" (Galarza, Gallegos, and Samora 1969, 56). Suffice it to say there were documents that confirm the existence of a rich Chicano literary tradition, both oral and written, beginning as early as the 1850s, not to mention the periods before the conquest of Texas and the Southwest in 1836 and 1848. What has happened is that those materials have been neglected by historians. It was necessary to wait for Chicano scholars themselves to document their cultural heritage. They have gone back into the past, as Genaro Padilla has done in his recent book, *My History, Not Yours*, in which he analyzes numerous autobiographies by early Chicanos and Chicanas, documenting their lives and their works.

The first Chicanos to research oral literature by people of Mexican descent having lived in the United States were the folklorists Aurelio M. Espinosa, Arthur L. Campa, and Juan B. Rael. These early critics, however, had dedicated themselves only to the study of oral literary tradition, neglecting written literary works. Espinosa began by studying the folklore of New Mexico and then went on to include that of other regions in the Southwest, especially California. His study of *Los Comanches*, a play dating from 1780, appeared in 1907. He is also remembered for the study of a nineteenth-century play, *Los Tejanos* (1943), an important source of information on the history of the conflicts between Texas and New Mexico between 1836 and 1848. In the introduction to his book *Folktales of Mexico*, Américo Paredes states that Espinosa's study, "New-Mexican Spanish Folk-lore," which appeared in the *Journal of American Folklore* in 1910–11, represents "the first truly scholarly work on Mexican folk-lore," as well as being "the first real collection of Mexican folk narrative" (Paredes 1970, lxxiii).

Espinosa published his most important works during the first two decades of this century, which he dominated as a scholar. During the 1920s, however, there were other scholars who followed Espinosa's example. Among them, in Texas, Jovita González was active publishing in the *Annals* of the Texas Folklore Society. Dr. Paredes tells us that she was "one of the first Mexican Americans to write in English about her own culture" (1972, 8).

The work of Espinosa was continued by his own son, José Manuel, by Arthur Campa, and by Juan B. Rael. José Manuel's collection of 114 Mexican folktales from the southwestern United States, which appeared in 1937, has been surpassed in quantity only by Juan B. Rael's *Cuentos españoles de Colorado y Nuevo México...Spanish Tales from Colorado and New Mexico* (1940). Campa, on the other hand, can be considered a pioneer in bibliographical studies. His article, "A Bibliography of Spanish Folk-lore in New Mexico," published in 1930, was important because it opened a new field in Chicano historiography, since this was the first bibliography published in any field of Chicano studies.

Mexican-American historians began to diversify in the 1950s. Scholars interested in other fields besides folklore and bibliography began to appear, especially in the political sciences, anthropology, sociology, literature, and the arts. To this group belongs Américo Paredes, whose book *With His Pistol in His Hand*, published in 1958, has served as a model for the type of history that takes into consideration a human approach. It was during the late 1950s that the first Chicano literary history appeared. It is a brief survey in Spanish published in 1959 by José Timoteo López, Edgardo Núñez, and Roberto Lara Vialpando, giving an account of the literature written by the contemporary writers of a region in New Mexico. At first it was said that Chicano literature was born that year, which coincides with the publication of *Pocho* by José Antonio Villarreal, considered by some critics as the first Chicano novel. This historical literary event led some critics to theorize that Chicano literature did not exist before 1959. And to confirm such a view, they claimed that the word *Chicano*, although it existed, was not applied specifically to designate those who were then called Mexican Americans, or *pochos*, as they are called in Villarreal's novel. It was even said that Chicanos and Mexican residents (Mexican nationals with permanent visas) living in the United States were incapable of writing literary works.

Since Chicano letters were excluded from histories of American literature, it was necessary for Chicanos themselves to write their own histories. Thus it was necessary to train literary historians at universities. It was there that they produced the first comprehensive histories of Chicano literature, in the form of doctoral dissertations.

Since the early 1970s the space occupied by the history of Chicano literature has been expanding rapidly. Literary historians are now beginning to find the lost steps left by past writers. It was in 1971—an important year in the development of Chicano literary historiography—that the first doctoral dissertations dealing with the history of Chicano literature were accepted at leading universities. That year, Alba Irene Moesser wrote about "La literatura mejicoamericana del suroeste de los Estados Unidos," and Philip D. Ortego presented for his doctorate a well-researched "Background of Mexican-American Literature," in which for the first time an extraordinary amount of information on Chicano literature in the nineteenth century was collected. Both critics, however, place the birth of Chicano literature in 1848. In 1971 Herminio C. Ríos wrote in his introduction to the first edition of Rivera's novel: "1848 is the beginning point of Mexican-American literature. Literature written prior to this date by the Spanish speaking inhabitants of the Southwest must properly belong to the Mexican period, and thus to Mexican literature" (1971, xiv). Nevertheless, he immediately adds:

> The year 1848, however, is simply a capricious chronological device that does not take into consideration human experiences, human sentiments, and human loyalties. It reveals nothing of the myths, legends, archetypal experiences, and the rich oral tradition whose birth and development precede this date. It remains silent about the literary currents that came and went, but left their mark upon the writers that were present among the Mexican-American population. Also, this date does not tell us at what point in history artistic sentiment revealed itself as being no longer totally Mexican, but rather as consciously reflecting a Mexican-American reality. Perhaps this particular point of a Mexican-American consciousness reflected in literature will neither quickly nor easily be resolved, but certainly it will inspire considerable discussion as the Mexican-American literary tradition is reconstructed and interpreted by literary historians, and enriched by such gifted writers as Tomás Rivera (1971, xiv).

The literature written before 1848 by Mexicans in the Southwest was given an appropriate name by Ray Padilla, a critic associated with the group at the University of California, Berkeley, that in 1967 began to publish the pioneering periodical *El Grito*. In the number published during the winter of 1971–72 he wrote: "[A]ll works prior to 1848 can be treated as pre-Chicano *Aztlanense* materials" (19). Therefore, the problem to be solved was: How could we justify including the works of authors who wrote before 1848 in a history of Chicano literature? Calling them pre-Chicano *Aztlanense* without explaining why did not seem to me to be a sufficient reason to include them.

In 1973 at Indiana University, Luis Dávila and Nicolás Kanellos were preparing to publish the *Revista Chicano-Riqueña* and they asked me to write an article for the first number. It was then that I began to think about establishing a chronology of Chicano literature. Inspired by Ríos's words, I began to do research about pre-Chicano writers, not only during the Mexican period, but also since the first explorers and settlers came to the Southwest during the sixteenth century. I titled my study "Mexican-American Literature: A Historical Perspective," and it appeared in the first number of the *Revista* in the spring of 1973.

During my second year at the University of California at Santa Barbara, that is, in 1977—the late Joseph Sommers, of the University of California at San Diego, asked me for permission to reproduce my article. Since the materials available in the library at UCSB were more abundant than those at the University of Illinois, where I had formerly taught, I decided to enlarge the study, which appeared in the book *Modern Chicano Writers,* published in 1979. The first part of this book, titled "A Conceptual Framework," includes four other studies, by Américo Paredes, Joseph Sommers, Rosaura Sánchez, and Juan Gómez Quiñonez. Paredes studies "The Folk Base of Chicano Literature"; Sommers examines several "Critical Approaches to Chicano Literature"; Sánchez deals with "Spanish Codes in the Southwest"; and Gómez Quiñones contributes an article titled "Towards a Concept of Culture." In the introduction, Sommers states: "While many of the critical studies we present focus on modern works, we have tried to show that a perspective indispensable to full critical understanding is the historic process of cultural continuity and change" (2).

In my 1973 study I did not make an attempt to delve deeply into the nature of Chicano literature, but I did include some of the topics suggested by Ríos, such as literary currents, the fact that artistic sentiment was no longer totally Mexican but consciously reflecting a Mexican-American reality, and the presence of a rich oral tradition, the only aspect of that literature that had been previously studied by early Chicano historians, as we have seen. Conscious of the fact that these critics had dedicated themselves only to the study of the oral literary tradition, and had neglected earlier written literary works, I decided to see if the inclusion of these writers in a history of Chicano literature was justified.

I found that in the literature produced by the Mexican people living in the *provincias internas* (Spanish Borderlands) we can find the roots of Chicano literature, as well as the nature of the culture of the people who wrote it. Most of this literature, to be sure, was neglected by literary historians, and was never published. Fortunately, sufficient manuscripts remain in public libraries. In my 1973 article I wrote:

> We can consider Chicano literature to include that literature written by Mexicans and their descendants living or having lived in what is now the United States. We will also consider those works, especially those before 1821, written by the inhabitants of this

> region having a Spanish background, as forming part of an early stage of Mexican-American literature. We aren't overlooking the fact that before 1848 Mexican-Americans legally did not exist as a group; however, they have a long uninterrupted literary tradition. The year 1848 is a political point in time, and it is important in the literary field since English then became the official language of the Mexican territory that became part of the United States, and for this reason it affected the development of the literature of the region, but did not interrupt it. By accepting this definition of Chicano, we can say, then, that Mexican-American literature had its origin when the Southwest was settled by the inhabitants of Mexico during Colonial times and continues uninterrupted to the present (Leal 1973, 35).

In a subsequent article, not published until 1985 but written earlier, I argued that the literature of the Mexican people living in the northern provinces—that is, north of the border set in 1848 by the Treaty of Guadalupe Hidalgo—is somewhat different from that of central Mexico. In this literature we already find a new sensibility, due mainly to the presence of different environmental factors, such as a new landscape and a different climate, as well as the nature of the cultures of the native people, unlike those of central Mexico. No less important is the fact that during this colonial period the settlers who came from central Mexico established the bases upon which Chicano culture was to develop. The institutions and the cultural elements brought to the Southwest United States from Mexico are the ones that shaped Chicano culture, and therefore its literature.

This new sensibility can be observed in most *cronistas* (chroniclers). In the *Relación de los Naufragios* (1542) of Alvar Núñez Cabeza de Vaca—an account of his trip across the continent from 1528 to 1536—we find the first description of the landscape of Texas, New Mexico, and Arizona, as well as an account of the life and customs among the native inhabitants; he speaks of the great prairies and rivers, the native villages, the bison, the prickly pear, the *tlacuache* (opossum) and other flora and fauna. His description of the buffalo, the first to appear in literature, is of interest, since this animal would later become an obligatory motif in "Western" and Southwest folklore as well.

In his *relación* (account) about the *Descubrimiento de las siete ciudades* (1539), Fray Marcos de Niza fosters the myths of Cíbola and the seven cities, which he claimed to have found in New Mexico, and at the same time provides us with the first description of the homes of the New Mexico natives, whose structures we consider today as appearing somewhat magical, for, after four centuries some of them still exist, although made of adobe. Years later Antonio de Espejo, in *El Viaje que hizo Antonio de Espejo* (1586), spoke of rich mines in Arizona. This awakened the interest of Juan de Oñate, who in 1598 led an expedition into New Mexico. He was accompanied by Gaspar Pérez de Villagrá, the author of the first epic poem, *Historia de la Nueva México* (1610), considered as the first state history of the United States, since the general history of Virginia by John Smith was not published until fourteen years later. He begins his long poem by recounting the pilgrimage of the Aztecs, who left Aztlán in search of Tenochtitlán, the promised land. Villagrá is also the first writer to describe the *vaquero,* a character that much later, as a result of the influence of Mexican culture, became one of the most popular prototypes of the North American "West," but with the name of *cowboy* (the English translation of *vaquero*).

It is interesting to point out, since it reveals the mestizo origin of border culture, that Villagrá gave the name of *vaquero* to the Indians who helped with the cattle roundup. On the plains, Oñate and his group found, as Villagrá tells us, "gran número de vaqueros que a pie matan aquestas mismas vacas que decimos, y dellas se sustentan y mantienen" (a great number of cowboys who on foot kill those same cows of which we speak, and from them feed and sustain themselves, canto XVII: 93v). He also describes, in anecdotal discourse, the activity known as *aventada,* which much later was encompassed by the popular word *rodeo.* It is in Villagrá's poem that we find also the origin of the name of the now famous river that divides Mexico from the United States. He observes: "del caudaloso río que del norte desciende manso, tanto se embravece que también Río Bravo le llamamos" (of the mighty river which from the north flows quietly, so much does it rage, that we called it Wild River, canto XI: 56v).

It has been said of this epic poem that it is more history than poetry, and it carefully documents Oñate's *entrada* (expedition) into New Mexico. Other *cronistas,* among them Fray Alonso de Benavides, and Isidro Félix de Espinoza have left important documents necessary to reconstruct the early history of the Mexican people in the Southwest. These and other early writers left us a history of the founding of the social institutions upon which Chicano culture was to develop. These institutions and the cultural elements brought to the Southwest from Mexico helped to shape Chicano culture, and therefore its literature.

This literary tradition was strengthened after 1821, when Mexico received its independence from Spain. During this short period (1821–48), the printing presses were introduced, important in the production of books and the development of periodical literature. In California in 1835, Governor José Figueroa published his *Manifiesto a la nación mexicana,* and in Texas Juan N. Seguín published his *Personal Memoirs* covering the years 1834–42.

All these political and cultural changes, however, did not affect the writing of popular literature, whose uninterrupted existence from colonial days to the present attests to its enduring nature.

After reading these early works, I reached the conclusion that the history of Chicano literature should also include everything written before 1848 by inhabitants of the region (both published and in manuscript form), as it rightfully forms part of the Chicano cultural inheritance. As far as we know, no people has rejected its literary inheritance. The history of American literature does not begin in 1776; it includes all works in existence since the arrival of the Pilgrims in the seventeenth century. The literary history of Mexico does not begin in 1821; nor do we say that Sor Juana's poetry belongs to the history of Spanish literature. The same can be said of other countries, such as India and the African nations.

After 1836 in Texas and 1848 in the Southwest, there is no question about the history of Chicano literature. Most literary historians have accepted those years as marking the beginning of Chicano literature, and not 1959, as previously stated. This early period has been better documented than other periods by Chicano literary historians, among them Philip Ortego and Ray Paredes.

The theory that Chicano literature had its beginning during the sixteenth century was influential in the establishment in 1990 at the University of Houston, with a generous grant from several foundations, of the ambitious project called "Recovering the U.S. Hispanic Literary Heritage." The indices of the literary contents of nineteenth-century Spanish-language newspapers are now complete. Recently, novels in English by Maria Amparo Ruiz de Burton, published in San Francisco in 1872 and 1885, have been reedited. In general, the broad scope of the project includes recovery not only of the Chicano literary heritage, but of all the conventional literary genres of Latinos. When completed, we will be able to say that we are no longer lost, no longer a people without a literature, without a literary history, as Rivera wrote only two decades ago.

References

Campa, Arthur L. 1930. "A Bibliography of Spanish Folk-lore in New Mexico." *University of New Mexico Bulletin* 2, no.3 (September). Report. in *Hispanic Folklore Studies of Arthur L. Campa*. New York: Arno, 1976.

Castañeda, Carlos E. 1936–58. *Our Catholic Heritage in Texas*, 1519–1936. 7 vols. Austin, Tex: Von Boeckmann-Jones. Report. New York: Arno Press, 1976.

Cowan, Robert Ernest. 1919. *A Bibliography of the Spanish Press in California 1833–1845*. San Francisco, Calif.: Robert Ernest Cowan.

Espejo, Antonio de. 1586. *El Viaje que hizo Antonio de Espejo*. . . . Madrid.

Espinosa, Aurelio M. 1907. "Los Comanches: A Spanish Heroic Play of the Year Seventeen Hundred and Eighty." *University of New Mexico Bulletin* 1, no.1 (December): 5–46.

———. 1910. "New-Mexican Spanish Folk-lore." *Journal of American Folklore* Parts I and II 23: 395–418; Part III 24: 397–444.

———, and J. Manuel Espinosa. 1943. "The Texans: A New Mexican Spanish Folk Play of the Middle Nineteenth Century." *New Mexico Quarterly Review* 13: 299–308.

Espinosa, José Manuel. 1937. *Spanish Folk-tales from New Mexico*. New York: American Folklore Society.

Figueroa, General José. 1835. *Manifiesto a la nación mexicana*. . . . Monterrey, Calif.: imprenta del C. Agustín V. Zamorano.

Galarza, Ernesto, Herman Gallegos, and Julián Samora. 1969. *Mexican-Americans in the Southwest*. Photographs by George Ballis. Santa Barbara, Calif.: McNally & Loftin.

Gonzales, Rodolfo "Corky." 1967. *I Am Joaquín*. Delano, Calif.: Farm Workers Press.

Leal, Luis. 1973. "Mexican-American Literature: A Historical Perspective." *Revista Chicano-Riqueña* 1, no.1 (spring): 32–44. An enlarged version is included in Sommers 1979, 18–30.

———. 1985. "Periodización de la literatura chicana." In *Aztlán y México: Perfiles literarios e históricos*. Binghampton, N.Y.: Bilingual Press/Editorial Bilingue, 44–50.

López, José Timoteo, Edgardo Núez, and Roberto Lara Vialpando. 1959. *Breve reseña de la literatura hispana de Nuevo México y Colorado*. Juárez, Chihuahua: Imprenta Comercial.

McWilliams, Carey. 1949. *North from Mexico*. Reprint, New York: Greenwood Press, 1968.

Moesser, Alba Irene. 1971. "La literatura mejicoamericana del suroeste de los Estados Unidos." Ph.D. diss., University of Southern California.

Niza, Fray Marcos de. 1865. *Descubrimiento de las siete ciudades por el P. Fr. Marcos de Niza*. Madrid: Imp. de Manuel B. de Quirós.

Núñez Cabeza de Vaca, Alvar. 1542. *Cabeza de Vaca's Adventures in the Unknown Interior of America*. Reprint, newly trans. and ed. by Cyclone Covey, New York: Collier, 1961.

Ortego, Philip D. 1971. "Background of Mexican American Literature." Ph.D. diss., University of New Mexico.

Padilla, Genaro. 1993. *My History, Not Yours: The Formation of Mexican American Autobiography*. Madison: University of Wisconsin Press.

Padilla, Ray. 1971–72. "Apuntes para la documentación de cultura chicana." *El Grito* 5, no.2 (winter): 3–36.

Paredes, Américo. 1958. *With His Pistol in His Hand: A Border Ballad and Its Hero*. Austin: University of Texas Press.

———. 1970. *Folktales of Mexico*. Ed. and translated by Américo Paredes. Foreword by Richard M. Dorson. Chicago, Ill.: University of Chicago Press.

———. 1972. *Mexican-American Authors*. Américo Paredes and Raymund Paredes, eds. Boston: Houghton Mifflin.

———. 1977. *Humanidad. Essays in Honor of George I. Sánchez*. Américo Paredes, ed. Los Angeles: UCLA Chicano Studies Center.

Pérez de Villagrá, Gaspar. 1610. *Historia de la Nueva México*. Alcalá: Luis Martínez Grande. Reprint, 2 vols., edited by Luis González Obregón. México: Museo Nacional de México, 1900.

———. 1992. *Historia de la Nueva México, 1610*. A Critical and Annotated Spanish-English Edition. Translated and Edited by Miguel Encinias, Alfred Rodriguez, and Jack P. Sanchez. Albuquerque, N.M.: University of New Mexico Press.

———. 1933. *History of New Mexico*. Translated by Gilberto Espinosa. Los Angeles: Quivira Society. Prose translation of Villagra's poem.

Rael, Juan B. 1940. *Cuentos españoles de Colorado y Nuevo México/Spanish Tales from Colorado and New Mexico. Spanish Originals with English Summaries*. Stanford, Calif.: Stanford University Press. (2nd ed. 1957).

Ríos, Herminio C. 1971. Introduction to "...y no se lo trago la tierra," by Tomás Rivera. Berkeley, Calif.: Quinto Sol. (In Spanish and English).

Rivera, Tomás. 1971a. ." . . y no se lo tragó la tierra /. . . and the earth did not part." Berkeley, Calif.: Quinto Sol.

———. 1976. "Chicano Literature: Fiesta of the Living." *Books Abroad* 49 (summer): 439–52.

———. 1971b. "Into the Labyrinth: The Chicano in Literature." In *New Voices in Literature*. Edited by Edward Simmen. Edinburg, Tex.: Pan American University.

Ruiz de Burton, Maria Amparo. 1992. *The Squatter and the Don*. Edited and introduction by Rosaura Sánchez and Beatriz Pita. Houston, Tex.: Arte Público Press.

———. *Who Would Have Thought?* 1995. Edited by Rosaura Sánchez and Beatriz Pita. Houston, Tex.: Arte Público Press.

Sánchez, George I. 1936. *Mexico: A Revolution by Education*. New York: Viking Press.

Sánchez, Rosaura. 1983. *Chicano Discourse. A Socio-historic Perspective*. Rowley, Mass.: Newsbury House.

———. 1940. *Forgotten People*. Albuquerque: University of New Mexico Press.

Seguín, Juan N. 1858. *Personal Memoirs of Juan N. Seguín from the Year 1834 to the Retreat of General Woll from the City of San Antonio, 1842*. Printed at the Ledger Book and Job Office. Report in David J. Weber, ed., *Northern Mexico on the Eve of the United States Invasion*. New York: Arno, 1976.

Sommers, Joseph, and Tomás Ybarra-Frausto, eds. 1979. *Modern Chicano Writers*. Englewood Cliffs, N.J.: Prentice-Hall.

Spiller, Robert E., et al., eds. 1973. *Literary History of the United States*. 3d rev. ed. in 1 vol. New York: Macmillan.

Weber, David J. 1974. "Stereotyping of Mexico's Far Northern Frontier." In *An Awakened Minority: The Mexican-American.*, edited by Manuel P. Servín, 15–26. Beverly Hills: Glencoe Press.

CHAPTER 3

ASYMMETRY

Ramón Eduardo Ruiz

I

AT THE U.S.-MEXICAN border, two nations colossally unequal in wealth and military might face off in a modern version of David and Goliath. Nowhere else in the world does the asymmetry loom greater, as the huge gap in per capita income between the two neighbors verifies. The border is an "open wound," writes Gloria Anzaldúa, the Chicana poet, "where the Third World grates against the first and bleeds"; or, in the words of a Mexican, where people fleeing from ubiquitous poverty, the ceaseless search for jobs, and political thuggery are drawn northward by the mirage of the First World.

Distinct historical heritages and cultures clash at the border, one Catholic and Spanish, a society resting on Roman law, and the other, by language and values, Protestant and, despite its surging minority population, English at heart. South of the Rio Grande lies Latin America, the *Ariel* of Enrique Rodó, the Uruguayan essayist and to the north, his *Caliban,* Anglo-America. With Canadians, Americans share one of the world's two longest international borders and with Mexico they share the other, but the differences between the two neighbors of European origin shrink when compared to those that separate mestizo Mexico from Rodó's colossus. For nearly two centuries, the overwhelming presence of the United States has been a sword of Damocles for Mexico; little occurs north of the border that does not intrude upon the life of Mexicans.

Economics dictates this asymmetrical relationship. But for the distorted Mexican capitalism that confronts the dynamic financial and industrial capitalism of the United States, the trade and commerce that joins them together would not exist. Disparity stimulates economic exchange, giving rise to border cities that handle dissimilar exports and imports. The United States provides the finished product and the financial capital, while burgeoning populations in Mexican border enclaves serve as markets and as reserve pools of cheap labor for factories and farms on the other side. The transnational economy is hardly equal, given Mexican reliance on the United States, due largely to the absence of wealth-creating alternatives.

Unequal development spurs the border economy, which includes the movement of people and capital, the exchange of goods, commercial relations that fluctuate according to the value of the peso, and the pools of cheap Mexican labor waiting to cross the border. At best, Mexican border municipalities have only one-fifth the per capita income of their American counterparts, though twice that of their sisters to the south. In 1992, the wage rate for Ford production workers in the United States was $16.50 an hour, but the Ford plant in Hermosillo paid less than one sixteenth of that.

A story published by *The Los Angeles Times* illustrates well one of the consequences of this asymmetrical reality. In Sunland Park, New Mexico, just a skip and a jump away from El Paso, Mexican "bandits" were, in the time-honored tradition of the Wild West, plundering the cargoes of Southern Pacific trains. After robbing them, the bandits would scurry back to Mexico, in some spots just steps away. The *Colonia Anapra,* from which they emerged, is a squatter's camp of cardboard and wooden shanties, mostly discarded junk from the other side, where forty thousand unemployed and hungry Mexicans live without running water, electricity, sewers, or police. "Its residents," reported the *Times,* "store drinking water in fifty-five-gallon drums encrusted with chemical residue and cook corn tortillas over burning tires." Many of the children had "rotting teeth and gum disease," probably from drinking the polluted water. When the Border Patrol closed down the gates to jobs in El Paso, the Mexicans turned to robbing American trains in order to survive. Only Los Angeles and Chicago suffer more "train robberies." The bandits, poor Mexicans fleeing from Mexico's latest economic crisis, improvise a livelihood by robbing their wealthy neighbors.

Every Mexican city from Tijuana to Matamoros lies next-door to the United States, a condition that distorts border society. As Graham Greene once wrote, "the border means more than a custom house, a passport office . . . Over there everything is going to be different." For years, officials in Mexico City have spoken of the need to integrate the border with the rest of the nation, more so now, in these days of a global economy spearheaded by American transnational giants. They dream of reducing the satellite status of border cities without losing the economic benefits of proximity.

Nationalists worry that border Mexicans, in their supposed fondness for imitating Americans, will lose their Mexican souls. That subject, which bears careful scrutiny, is ever in the minds of writers and artists who dwell on the border, men and women caught between the powerful currents from across the border and those emanating from Mexico City, where its *Chilango* residents (resident of Mexico city) believe that only they speak for Mexican culture. Research indicates that while Americans are almost always "inflexibly ethnocentric," and give scant hoot for Mexican culture and language, Mexicans sometimes look to the United States for a source of fresh values and ideas. This goes beyond economic advantages and technological benefits derived.

The examples are obvious. Border Spanish, for example, has incorporated countless English words into its vocabulary, giving them a peculiar spelling and pronunciation. Students of language refer to its results as "Spanglish." Border residents know these words by heart: *lonche* for lunch, *troca* for truck, *breca* for automobile brake, and *quequi* for cake, plus a myriad of others. In all Mexican border communities, English-language classes are compulsory—in Ciudad Juárez, for instance, beginning in the seventh grade. Adults studying English more often than not belong to the upper tiers of society and once enrolled in American schools in El Paso. San Diego, near Tijuana, boasts of well-off Mexican residents, especially after the collapse of the peso sent them fleeing northward. An expatriate colony dubbed "Taco Towers" by unkindly neighbors inhabits a part of the Coronado shoreline across the bay; its inhabitants live in San Diego for social prestige and convenience, and out of fear of kidnappings at home. Many children of the border *burguesia* (bourgeoisie) are born on the American side; their parents covet United States citizenship for them. In his novel *El gran pretender,* Luis Humberto Crosthwaite, one of the best known border writers, has Johnny, an affluent "junior" living in San Diego with his parents and going to school at Southwestern College. Sundays he spends in Tijuana, visiting his friends and driving his father's Ford LTD.

Crossing the border is anything but an equitable experience. It all depends on where you come from. Citizens of the United States enter freely any Mexican town, so long as they stay within twelve miles of the border; on the Baja California peninsula, they travel to Ensenada, sixty miles south of Tijuana. But Mexican nationals, who endure long waits by auto at the border, must possess a permanent U.S. residence permit, visa, or other valid documentation obtained in advance. As early as 1903, United States' immigration officials at El Paso, depending on their whims on any given day, fumigated persons arriving from Mexico. My mother, a proud member of a respected family of Parral, never tired of telling how she feared having her hair fumigated for lice upon entering El Paso. Alicia Castellanos, a Mexican author, says these inequities come about because of the power of the almighty dollar.

II

The Mexico-U.S. border has thirty-one ports of entry. How far north and south the border region stretches is a subject of heated debate. Miguel León Portilla, a distinguished Mexican historian, claims it extends out at least sixty miles in both directions. By his calculation, the border exceeds in square miles the territory of such nations as Spain and France. For Jorge Bustamante, a distinguished sociologist, how you define it rests on what you are looking for. The "operational extension north and south of the region," he believes, varies according to the yardstick being used. The spatial definition is not the same if the focus is economic, as opposed to ecological concerns. The social and economic expanse of a binational zone is not determined by a geographic boundary but by the interaction of the people who live on both sides of it. It makes more sense, argues another Mexican, to define the region as the sum total of the forty-nine U.S. border counties and the thirty-nine municipalities on the other side. Others say that given the changing character of the region due to the growing economic and cultural importance of the American Southwest (which, undoubtedly, has repercussions on the Mexican side), a more flexible definition of the region is necessary.

Geographic proximity, as the experts recognize, does not by itself shape the character of a border region; clearly economic factors, as well as improvement in communication (the information highway) and transportation determine the nature of the relationship. Thus, as the American Southwest changes, so does the geographic and economic scope of the border region. Two examples of this interaction, which has altered drastically the nature of Mexican border society since the beginning of the century, stand out: one is the growing need in the American Southwest for cheap Mexican labor, and the other is the never-ending American demand for tourist facilities and commercial services south of the border. Both expand as well as dramatically alter the scope and character of Mexican society. No matter what the impact of these transformations, for Mexicans any definition of their home territory starts with the recognition that its location next door to the United States largely determines its historical, economic, and cultural outlines. That fact of life dates from the War of 1847 and the Gadsden Purchase of 1853, which by the boundary survey of 1849–55 gave form to the present demarcation line between Mexico and the United States. Relations between the two countries were initially fleeting; then, with the coming of the railroad, neighboring cities sprang up. The best examples are Ciudad Juárez and El Paso, the two Laredos, both Nogales, and Brownsville and Matamoros. Until then, it was impossible to distinguish on the Texas-Mexican frontier one cowboy from another in this sparsely populated, semibarren region. The railroads, and changes made possible by them in the early twentieth century, transformed this marginalized territory and its population, changes that came to fruition in the Sun belt with World War II and its aftermath. Until then, the boundary between the two countries retarded development; as scholars point out, regions on the edge of borders tend to develop at a slower pace as compared to similar interior areas.

For those who live on either side, the border is both a surreal and a material reality. From one end of the border to the other, to cite the *Brownsville Herald,* two battles go on. "In one, U.S. businessmen are practically begging for more Mexican customers to cross the border; in the other, politicians are demanding that we put up an assortment of fences, walls and human blockades to keep Mexicans out." Reality tends to side with the businessmen: the border is increasingly porous.

This duality is logical: an international border must be, on the one hand, an obstacle that separates two people but, on the other, porous, in order to allow a relative free exchange of goods, people and capital. The emergence of cities, to cite one more opinion, "is a barometer that measures the degree of transformation" of the region's integration. As both sides become more populated and their economies diversify the transborder swells in size and complexity. As Carey McWilliams wrote, "from El Paso to Brownsville, the Rio Grande does not separate people; it draws them together." In El Paso, a Mexican American recalled, "during the 1930s and 1940s, I can't remember the family not going to Ciudad Juárez every Sunday. I don't remember eating out in a restaurant in El Paso. Ciudad Juárez was our life."

Each year in Cochise County, Arizona, officials of the towns on the border get together with their counterparts from Sonora for a day of sports and pleasure. They have christened it a "A Celebration of Nation to Nation," a day when officials proclaim mutual goodwill, putting aside daily problems of drugs, pollution, and smuggling. The *abrazo,* or embrace, is the sign of the day, usually symbolized by a game of volleyball with conventional rules. Yet there is something amiss: the net is not a cloth mesh stretched between two poles; the seven-foot chain-link fence separating Mexico from the United States serves in its place. How do you celebrate the end of a game, however, asks Tom Miller, who tells this story, with a handshake when there is a wire fence in the way? You don't; you extend fingers through the fence, rubbing them against the fingers of your opponents.

As any Texan can tell you, the term *U.S.-Mexico border* is a misnomer; its weight, in actuality, falls on Texas. When population and cities are considered, you have to conclude that it is a Texas-Mexican border, with a few miles of New Mexico, Arizona, and California added on as an afterthought. New Mexico, moreover, has no international ports of any importance. About 9 million people live alongside the border, with perhaps 5.5 million of them on the Mexican side. One could add people in cities outside the perimeter of the geographic border who play an important role in border life, such as Los Angeles, San Antonio, and Tucson, all on the American side, and Monterrey, Hermosillo, and Chihuahua, that are Mexican.

Geographically the region is hardly homogeneous. On the Mexican side, this vast territory is defined more by its administrative and legal characteristics than by its geographic, historical, social, and economic homogeneity. The lush landscapes of the Lower Rio Grande Valley, as well as parts of the Imperial Valley of California, stand in sharp contrast to the miles upon miles of desert expanse that separates them. The urban depots run from big cities, such as El Paso, to the rustic towns of Douglas (Arizona), Roma (Texas), and Palomas (Chihuahua), a town that has hardly changed since Pancho Villa rode through it on his way to attack Columbus, New Mexico, its neighbor.

III

Since their independence at the beginning of the last century, most Latin American nations, including Mexico, tend to measure themselves by the progress and order of the United States. Even today, Mexicans evaluate their state of development by American standards, as Octavio Paz did in his famous *Labyrinth of Solitude,* retracing the steps taken by Rodó as well as the Cuban José Martí in *Nuestra América*. By this standard of measurement, the Mexican border fares poorly. But, as in life, things are more complex than they seem.

On either side of the boundary line, income levels drop as one travels south and rise as one goes north, as they do from east to west. The high family incomes on the Pacific Coast fall by as much as one-half on the Gulf of Mexico; counties on the Lower Rio Grande in Texas enjoy less than one half the income of San Diego. On the Mexican side, Tijuana boasts the highest per capita incomes and Matamoros the lowest; Ciudad Juárez straddles the middle. On the average, living standards are higher in the Mexican north than in the south; some two-thirds of Reynosa's population lives above the federally designated minimum income. Yet, we must not forget that the cost of living is also higher in the northern areas, though access to cheaper goods across the border offsets this somewhat.

In the United States, there is one automobile for every 1.9 persons; in Mexico the ratio is one car for every 16.3 persons. In Baja California Norte, where Tijuana and Mexicali lie, there is one car for every 3.8 inhabitants, many with California license plates whose owners, according to an irate letter writer to the Tijuana newspaper *Zeta,* do not pay their share of taxes. Television sets are commonplace on both sides of the international boundary. In 1991, some 97 percent of U.S. border residents had a TV set, compared to 87 percent of their Mexican neighbors.

A binational paradox exists: on the Mexican side average income rises as you near the border; on the U.S. side it falls off. If affluent Tijuana—that is, affluent by Mexican standards—were a Mexican state, its per capita income would rank fourth in the nation, after the Distrito Federal District, and the states of Tabasco (petroleum) and

Nuevo León (heavy industry). The six northern states of Mexico top the literacy rankings. But while per capita income in El Paso is low by U.S. standards, that of Ciudad Juárez is much, much lower, a symbol of the asymmetrical relationship that exists between the countries. The gross product of San Diego is twenty-five times greater than that of Tijuana, its neighbor. San Diego would have tasted rapid economic growth even if Baja California had not, but the same cannot be said of Tijuana if Southern California were unpopulated. Yet the development of such cities as El Paso and Ciudad Juárez, as well as the two Laredos, are the result of a symbiotic relationship. Between Tijuana and Mexicali there are two highways: route 8 on the U.S. side is a divided, multilane freeway; the public highway on the Mexican side is a winding and narrow road that drivers avoid taking, while the much-better private toll road is outlandishly expensive.

Mexican border cities, to underline once more, feel every fluctuation of the American economy, particularly those in Baja California, given the overwhelming presence of Los Angeles and San Diego. In the 1930s, they suffered most from the effects of the Great Depression, reeling from the massive decline in American tourists, with the subsequent rise in unemployment of restaurant cooks, bartenders, waiters, street vendors, and even prostitutes. Simultaneously, thousands of jobless Mexicans, driven out of the American Southwest, congregated along the border, adding to the woes of city fathers. However, the ability to earn dollars through tourism, entertainment, or auto repair, to name a few of the channels, fuels the well-being of Mexican border cities. Exceptions exist, nonetheless, one being Matamoros, probably the most "Mexican" of the border cities, where tourism and the Prohibition era of the 1920s had less impact on its development. Today, the assembly plants of Matamoros are one of the largest producers of auto parts in all of North America, with products including wiring assemblies for car factories in the United States, Canada, and Mexico.

IV

When we speak of a Mexican border, we speak of cities. Not until one reaches the Lower Rio Grande Valley do farmers inhabit the expanses between cities; the one exception is Mexicali. West of Nuevo Laredo, virtually empty, arid lands greet the occasional visitor. This is a unique development; in few of the international borders do cities loom so large. Today, 80 percent of border residents reside in localities of more than 100,000 people. These are no longer border towns that conjure up images of dusty streets, girlie joints, and cantinas. As Rick Cahill says in *Border Towns of the Southwest,* the cities gleam with neon lights, here and there a high-rise building dots the horizon, and automobiles rumble down a few tree-lined avenues.

Urbanization started early in the nineteenth century, first in the northeast, due mostly to an export agriculture and the steel industry of Monterrey. The arrival of the railroad and migration northward from central Mexico further stimulated urban growth, as did tourism and the service industries, offshoots of the "Golden Years" of the Volsted Act in the United States, which banned the manufacture and sale of booze. As sin palaces blossomed, so did Tijuana and Ciudad Juárez. The Great Depression slowed urbanization but World War II and the Korean conflict spurred it once more. Until the coming of the *maquiladora* (foreign-owned assembly plants), the service and tourist industries were the backbone of Mexican border urbanization. Spectacular urbanization walks hand in hand with the arrival of the *maquiladoras*.

Over time, the character of urbanization has changed. Some of the cities, formerly tourist havens, underwent transformations with the onset of the *maquiladoras*. As the fate of Avenida Revolución and downtown Ciudad Juárez testify, old core areas, where tradition holds forth, were relegated to the periphery by suburbs replete with their own shopping malls. Both retain their tourist attractions—restaurants, nightclubs, and curio shops—but the heart of the local economy no longer beats there.

During the last three decades, the border has emerged as one of the most urbanized regions in Mexico. In 1950, its population totaled less than 1 million, but today it is millions more. In the last sixty years, the population has multiplied more than fourteen times, with growth centered in the largest cities, each with over 100,000 inhabitants. In rank order, the six largest are Ciudad Juárez, Tijuana, Mexicali, Matamoros, Reynosa, and Nuevo Laredo; only Nuevo Laredo shows signs of population stagnation. The others are among the fastest growing in the Western Hemisphere. Ciudad Juárez, Mexicali, and Tijuana house half of the total border population. If current projections hold up, by the year 2000 Tijuana alone will have more than 2 million inhabitants; its population growth rate is beyond the national average of 3.5 percent a year. Tijuana, unlike other the border cities, never went through an agricultural or mining phase; it was urban from the start. In 1996, northern Mexico, with the border municipalities leading the way, was the most urbanized area of the Republic. Cities are the heartland of the border, and this trend is increasing. In 1940, for example, 71 percent of border residents were rural; today the percentages are virtually the reverse. Of Baja California Norte's inhabitants, 90 percent are urbanites. This process parallels world developments; from 60 to 70 percent of the earth's population now lives in cities.

Migrants play a huge role in the population of the border enclaves. In Tijuana, for instance, more than half of the population is of recent origin. Its inhabitants have a saying: "We are all immigrants. Our only difference is that some of us arrived earlier and some of us later." Mostly poor, the migrants settle largely on the outskirts of cities, in shacks or *jacales,* as they are known. Urbanization encircles the cities with slums, beltways of poverty and misery, in the pattern of the Third World.

Middle-class people, a symbol of the changes occurring, increasingly inhabit border cities. Until recently, these cities were largely administrative centers, customs depots, and tourist meccas. More and more, with the coming of the *maquiladoras,* they are becoming industrial bastions. Their tertiary activities, while still important, no longer set the tone. According to official government statistics, which largely equate middle class with urban residency, 37.9 percent of Mexicans fit this category. By this definition, the urbanized border has a high percentage of middle-class residents, surpassing the figure for the Republic as a whole. Topping the list of middle-class cities, according to Bustamante, stands Tijuana, based, as he explains, on distribution of income, years of schooling, and standards of health. No other city in the Republic, he maintains, is more middle class, a pragmatic society that worships capitalist values and is highly individualistic.

Be that as it may, the old survives alongside the new. On the Coahuila frontier, an area that borders Texas, agricultural settlements still play a role. Guerrero, Hidalgo, and Jiménez are largely agricultural towns; the absence of cities on the U.S. side permits them to develop on their own. Agriculture also survives in the hinterlands of Ciudad Juárez and Nuevo Laredo, and it employs more people than industry does in Matamoros and Reynosa. Eagle Pass and Del Rio, both Texas cities, live off Piedras Negras and Ciudad Acuña, their Mexican cousins.

V

On the Mexican side of the border, municipal subservience is much in order. At the top of the political hierarchy sits the federal government in Mexico City; next comes state authority; at the tail end of this system lies municipal authority. Except for Baja California Norte and Chihuahua, where the Partido de Accion Nacional (PAN) briefly wrested political control from the Partido de la Revolución Institucional (PRI), local political officials, the *presidente municipal* (mayor) included, require the blessings of the Priista hierarchy; their election, until recently, was a foregone conclusion. Political manipulation and chicanery even include the PRI financing campaigns of opposition party candidates in order to give elections a veneer of democracy. "When I ran for the job of *presidente municipal* of Tecate" (a town not far from Tijuana), Crispín Valle Casteñeda recalled, "though I was the candidate of the PAN, the campaign cost me not a penny."

For all intents and purposes, local budgets are made and unmade in Mexico City. Some 80 percent of municipal revenues come from federal and state coffers. Conversely, federal authorities collect nearly 80 percent of national income but return just over 20 percent of it to the states and municipalities. Rural municipalities often do not even have the funds to hire a clerk. Of the nearly 3 million public employees in Mexico, only 150,000 serve municipal governments. The power of *ayuntamientos* (city councils) to levy taxes is virtually nonexistent. Federal intervention dictates even the nature and location of public services such as water systems and street lighting, and municipal services also must await state decisions. Despite the reforms of 1983, which theoretically granted more local autonomy, the centralization of power in the hands of the federal executive remains steadfast, like the Rock of Gibralter.

This structural underdevelopment stems from the long-standing intervention of federal authorities in the economic affairs of states and municipalities. Undemocratic and bureaucratic interference by federal officials reaches extremes in the border provinces. In the rest of the Republic, only far-off Yucatan endures similar travails. Decentralization, the catchword of current political reform, seeks to expand municipal control of public monies for use on local projects. The platform of the PAN, which has won voter support along the border, highlights local autonomy. Municipal independence also means freedom from the intervention of state governors, though not all of them dictate in identical ways. Municipalities in the State of Sonora, for example, are freer to act on their own, followed by those of Coahuila, Baja California Norte, then Chihuahua and Tamaulipas.

From Ciudad Juárez to Matamoros, one bone of contention that mirrors the differences between municipal and federal priorities, is the collection of tolls on the international bridges. The City of El Paso receives 20 percent of its budget from these tolls, which it uses to pay police and repair streets, among other services. At the opposite end of the bridges, Ciudad Juárez keeps none. Federal officials collect the revenue. In the spring of 1995, with a municipal budget on the brink of bankruptcy, the Panista presidente municipal of Ciudad Juárez decided to challenge this inequity. To the surprise and anger of Mexico City, he installed municipal toll booths at one of the bridges, thus preventing federal officials from collecting the revenues. For this audacious usurpation of federal prerogatives the presidente spent days in jail, but in elections later that year the PAN retained control of Ciudad Juárez.

VI

Diverse factors explain the development of these border cities; the coming of the railroad is one of them. Between 1882 and 1892, the iron horse joined Ciudad Juárez, Nogales, Matamoros, Nuevo Lardo, and Piedras Negras to Mexico City and the United States. Another line linked Reynosa to Monterrey by way of Nuevo Laredo, and then to Mexico City. All connected these Mexican border enclaves with counterparts across the border, and, interestingly, by opening up jobs, halted, at least temporarily, the flight of Mexican workers to the United States. As in the case of El Paso, these railroads also converted American cities into important commercial depots by joining them with Mexico City. Nevertheless, the railroad networks of the two countries were quite different; while El Paso had intercontinental links to both the West and East Coasts of the United States, the railroad from Ciudad Juárez ran only to the south, which made it economically subservient to El Paso. The trains that ran out of Ciudad Juárez encouraged the export of minerals and raw materials from Mexico but, conversely, opened the Republic to a flood of U.S. exports. The railroad failed to join together the Mexican north. Mexican passengers had to travel on trains equipped with wooden benches and brave hostile customs and immigration agents at the border, while Americans rode on upholstered seats and took pleasure in clean coaches.

The railroad ushered in an era of transformation in the life of the border towns. There were jobs for their clerks, telegraph operators, and track workers, and through the expansion of commercial activity, in warehouses, construction, and the service industries. Because of the railroads, all built by American capital, the population of the border enclave's multiplied. Ciudad Juárez and Nuevo Laredo blossomed into the major Mexican ports of entry. The railroad helped Reynosa weather the hard times brought about by the end of the "zona libre," a green light to importation of American goods.

Agriculture, too, had a hand in this drama. Despite the paucity of arable land (only l million hectares out of a total of 13.1 million), in the hinterlands of cities such as Mexicali, San Luis Río Colorado (Sonora), Matamoros, Reynosa, Ciudad Juárez, and Miguel Alemán (a dusty but thriving metropolis across from Roma, Texas), agriculture became one of the pillars of the economy. Early in the century, cotton drove agricultural enterprise; in the Mexicali Valley, Americans invested millions of dollars on irrigation projects and planted cotton. With the advent of World War II, Mexicans in northern Tamaulipas (Lower Rio Grande) and Mexicali, free of the American presence, did the same. Water from the newly constructed Boulder Dam on the Colorado River, and later from the binational Amistad and Falcon Dams on the Rio Grande, helped spur this green revolution. Conversely, in the Valley of Juárez, the lack of adequate supplies of water blunted the cotton boom. Nearly all of the cotton, a wartime necessity, was sold in the United States, with American companies controlling its ginning, sale, and financing. When the war ended, a plague labeled *pudrición texana* by Mexican planters killed off crops, and scientists developed synthetic fibers, the bottom fell out of the cotton market; by 1970 cotton sales represented only a third of the value of all agricultural production.

Large quantities of Mexican produce still find their way to markets in the United States. Mexicali, once an oasis for cotton, now produces vegetables for California, principally onions, broccoli, celery, and asparagus. Much of the production is done by Americans, who rent the land from *ejidatarios* (farmers on communal plots) and employ cheap Mexican labor. A handful of Mexicans, financed by American dollars, participate in this activity, labeled *agromaquila* or assembly-line farming, where a few, mostly foreigners, come away with the profits, which they gain by exploiting land that is not theirs and water subsidized by Mexican taxpayers. In 1990, the *agromaquilas* used up as much water as that consumed in two years by the cities of Mexicali and Tijuana. Local residents claim that because of its historic reliance on agriculture, Mexicali is unique, home to "self-made" men.

From Matamoros to Ciudad Alemán, corn, alfafa, sorghum, wheat, and cotton are farmed while fruits and vegetables are shipped by truck to Hidalgo, Texas. From Sonora and Sinaloa, vegetables destined for households in the Southwest enter the United States. During the winter months, up to three thousand trucks daily pass through Nogales; the highest monthly volume of shipments occurs in March, the peak of the tomato harvest. The people of Ciudad Juárez buy virtually all the vegetables they consume from American farmers: potatoes, cabbage, lettuce, tomatoes, onions, cauliflower, carrots, and spinach. City merchants, say critics, are the culprits. By buying and reselling leftover crops from nearby farms in Texas and New Mexico, they make impossible their cultivation in the Valley of Juárez.

The fruits and vegetables, and some cotton, derive from modern, largely privately owned farms. In Sonora and Sinaloa, some of the big growers are Americans who finance their crops through U.S. banks and supermarket chains. Their seeds, fertilizers, and pesticides come from there. In the north, *ejidos* take a backseat to private property. It is not uncommon for *ejidatarios* in Tamaulipas, most of whom cultivate fewer than ten hectares, to rent out their lands and walk over the border to work on American farms. Only large, private farms can cultivate sorghum, the chief crop of the region, at a profit. A similar pattern characterizes farming in Mexicali, where 80 percent of the *ejidos* are rented out. In these regions, agriculture, by providing jobs and attracting hundreds of thousands of migrants from the interior of Mexico, encouraged the growth of cities. Yet today agriculture engages only a quarter of the population of the border states. At Las Palomas, a Chihuahua border hamlet, at Agua Prieta in Sonora, and particularly at Piedras Negras and Ciudad Acuña, both in Coahuila, ranching, too, is a key to the economy. At the turn of the century, mining helped lay the foundations of Nogales, Agua Prieta, Ciudad Juárez, and Piedras Negras.

VII

On opposite sides of the border, twin cities face each other, their destinies inextricably linked. As neighbors, they depend on one another, rather than integrating into the social and economic fabric of their respective nations. One American, a man by the name of L. M. Holt, was the founder of two of these cities. Known as "Limpy" because of a game leg, he baptized both Mexicali and Calexico, combining in both the names of Mexico and California.

The key twins are El Paso and Ciudad Juárez, the two Laredos, and Brownsville and Matamoros. Some wrongly add Tijuana and San Diego, forgetting that San Diegans never think of themselves as a border town. Of these cities, only San Diego is bigger than its Mexican sister. Since the 1950s, economic growth has been impressive on the Mexican side, due largely to proximity to the United States rather than to internal dynamics. The response to demands and circumstances from across the border explain Mexican demographics.

Tijuana, the youngest of border cities, symbolizes this axiom. The machinery of American tourism originally drove its tertiary economy; the saloons, restaurants, and curio shops on Avenida Revolución stood at the end of the highway from San Diego. Since the late 1960s, the *maquiladoras*, also sporting an American label, are more and more, Tijuana's bread and butter. Although dating from the colonial times, Ciudad Juárez, too, has a tourist past, as do other Mexican border enclaves. Tijuana's past, present and, most probably, future are linked closely to the ups and downs of the California economy, more so than to that of the Mexican Republic. The health of Nuevo Laredo took a turn for the better with the arrival of railroad connections to the United States that, by the 1930s, transformed it into the most profitable Mexican port of entry.

The tertiary economy suffered a setback with the advent of the Great Depression and the repeal of Prohibition in 1933. The number of border crossings plummeted, while a peso devaluation and the demise of gambling in 1936 led to rising unemployment. To correct this disastrous turn of events, officials in Mexico City declared Baja California Norte a *zona libre,* or free zone, and two years later included the border towns of Sonora. Opening up the border to the importation of American goods restored life to the economy and, as a consequence, the area's population nearly doubled.

The story of these Mexican cities cannot be told without reference to the stationing of American soldiers along the border, beginning with El Paso's Fort Bliss in 1848 and the naval base at San Diego during World War I. Later, World War II brought millions of visiting soldiers, sailors, and marines from military bases, and ushered in years of phenomenal prosperity that, in the matter of urban growth, endures until the present. Mexicans from other regions of the Republic came as braceros, as a part of a lend-lease program of cheap labor for the war effort in the United States. With the war economy in high gear and money to spend, war workers from San Diego (a major aircraft production center), and El Paso (a military bastion), as well as other border cities, looked to Mexico for scarce silk stockings, chewing gum, hairpins, and gasoline, while local merchants accepted U.S. ration coupons for the purchase of shoes and meat.

As the stories of Ciudad Juárez and Tijuana testify, WWII and its aftermath spurred the economies of Mexican border communities. The tourist trade exploded in El Paso when the number of soldiers at Fort Bliss and Biggs Field multiplied manyfold. Similar experiences were shared by Tijuana, invaded by legions of sailors and marines and, to a lesser extent, by Nuevo Laredo, Reynosa, and Matamoros, also neighbors of U.S. army camps. The Ciudad Juárez of adobe buildings began to crumble, replaced by marmol (stone) mansions, a Casino Juárez that catered to rich Mexicans, plush movie houses such as Cine Plaza and Cine Victoria, and, for the first time, suburbs. The military bases and wartime industries of El Paso provided jobs for *juarenses*. For Tijuana, the bonanza years meant massive invasions of poor people from the south, who moved into "spontaneously settled *colonias populares*." The well-off occupied the downtown *colonias* of Chapultepec, Bolaños Cacho, and Hipódromo. After 1965, especially with the advent of PRONAF, a federal program to beautify border communities, the *Zona del Río* became the new business district, the renovation of Avenida Revolución followed, and the suburb of Playas de Tijuana appeared. With this growth and the changes it wrought, the old inhabitants of Tijuana found themselves a minority. As one of them confessed in *Puente México,* "I am saddened because I cannot find an old friend from those early days. The city I knew then no longer exists."

The war and what followed in its wake more closely integrated the communities that straddle the border. The classic examples are Ciudad

Juárez and El Paso. Residents of the two cities speak of a binational metropolitan area that, by 1990, had nearly two million inhabitants. The three international bridges, the first dating from 1882, weekly ferry one million El Paso-bound Mexicans, as well as nearly 300,000 vehicles. In 1994, more than 750,000 trucks passed through Laredo. At times traffic backs up for hours.

There are antecedents for this development. As early as 1926, Ciudad Juárez residents, with their purchases of fruits, vegetables, clothing, and other necessities, were spending fifteen million dollars in El Paso. From 1882 to 1935, when a Mexican concern replaced it, El Paso's Electric Company furnished the electricity used by the people of Ciudad Juárez, while another American enterprise provided the telephone service there. In 1892, a trolley began to run between the two cities, first pulled by mules and later fueled by electricity. At the time of its demise in 1973, the trolley carried thirteen thousand passengers daily. During the days of the Mexican Revolution of 1910, Ciudad Juárez banks deposited their funds across the border for safekeeping, while the rich and prominent saw fit to move north.

A population explosion is one more phenomenon of this era. The growth can be attributed to migrants from the south, especially after the appearance of the *maquiladora* industry in 1965; lower mortality rates; and fecundity, the survival of the newborn. According to the census of 1990, more than half of *tijuanenses* were born in another state. One other factor bears mentioning: the appeal of living next door to a wealthy neighbor who may, under favorable circumstances, provide dollar-paying jobs for Mexicans who commute to work in United States. The population grew by as much as 3.36 percent a year until 1975, then tapered off to about 2.10 percent yearly. What this meant was that between 1930 and 1980, while the population of the entire Republic grew annually by 4.2 percent, from 16.6 million to nearly 70 million, that of the border increased 10.5 percent, from 276,000 to 3.7 million inhabitants. Today, the United States-Mexico border is the most heavily populated international region in the entire world.

Ciudad Juárez and Tijuana, with nearly half of Mexican border residents, lead the urban population explosion. In 1940, Tijuana had a population of a little more than sixteen thousand people; today it is home to nearly one million. Whether Ciudad Juárez is bigger than Tijuana is a subject of passionate debate. Whatever the truth, the population of the Ciudad Juárez-El Paso metropolitan area has quadrupled since 1950. Ciudad Juárez, however, is twice as large as El Paso, and is projected to have up to 1.2 million people by the year 2000.

The two cities represent one of the fastest-growing urban regions in both Mexico and the United States. By 1980, Tijuana had grown to over ten times its size in 1950; until the 1970s, annual growth rates reached an incredible 12 percent, putting Tijuana alongside of the fastest-growing cities in the Western Hemisphere. Of the fifteen largest cities in Mexico, three are on the border; only Mexico City, Guadalajara, and Monterrey have more inhabitants than Tijuana and Ciudad Juárez. Even Reynosa, which fronts on one of the poorest areas of the United States, had 750,000 inhabitants by 1995. None of the American border cities, despite their impressive population explosions, kept pace. The population of these cities is young; according to a recent census, more than half of the residents of Ciudad Juárez, a mirror of the demographic picture all along the border, are eighteen years old or younger.

Demographers predict that ten million people will inhabit the two sides of the border by the turn of the century. For Mexico and the United States, this poses policy implications of the first order. As a binational region, it is a source of revenue for both Mexicans and Americans—at the local, state, and federal level. Decisions on the environment, crime, drug enforcement, migrants, and trade, just to mention the heavyweights, are international matters. Even national issues may be matters of foreign policy. As Lawrence A. Herzog, the author of a fine book on the subject, writes, the border "is one of the few places in the world where urban and environmental planning are elevated to the level of foreign policy."

VIII

This distorted propinquity, to bring this point to the fore once again, plays out in the urban enclaves that lie between the Pacific Ocean and the Gulf of Mexico. Its roots, as the pageant of the 1920s, for the most part an American melodrama featuring American actors performing on a Mexican stage, bears out, are not always deep. The historical legacy of these border towns ranges from the seventeenth century to the twentieth. The oldest, Ciudad Juárez, known originally as El Paso del Norte, dates from 1659, while San Ysidro, which faces Tijuana, did not exist until the 1920s. Both Laredos, as well as Reynosa and Matamoros, go back to the years of the eighteenth century, Piedras

Negras to the middle of 1849, and the others to the turn of the last century. With the exception of Brownsville, their U.S. equivalents began life at the same time. From the start, therefore, they were sister towns.

Ciudad Juárez—*la mejor frontera de México* (the best border of Mexico), boast its eulogists—was born as a Spanish mission, as was Ojinaga, on the edge of the Big Bend country of West Texas. The Misión de Nuestra Señora de Guadalupe, what is now Ciudad Juárez, served as a strategic gateway to the Spanish towns of New Mexico. The mission, the brainchild of a Franciscan monk, Fray García de San Francisco y Zúñiga, is a symbol of mission architecture, with thick adobe walls and hand-carved beams. Paso del Norte became Ciudad Juárez in 1888, named after the patriot president who took refuge there during the French occupation of Mexico in the 1860s. Even as late as the 1920s, Ciudad Juárez was, to quote one account, "a poor and dirty little town, full of saloons and whores." El Paso, by the same account, was only slightly better off. Ciudad Juárez always had one advantage: it remained the principal gateway, even more so after the coming of the railroad, for the exchange of goods between Mexico and the United States.

The old downtown core of the city still shelters bars, hotels, *discotecas,* and curio shops, as well as the *plazuela de los mojados,* where the jobless congregate. On the east side, which is expanding rapidly, are modern shopping malls, luxury hotels and the homes of the rich—garish mansions sitting behind walls of one kind or another and landscaped in the American style. On the west side, out of sight of tourists, the contrast could not be greater: the landscape is dotted with *jacales,* or huts of adobe.

The Spaniards came across the site of Ojinaga in 158l; they baptized it Presidio, now the name of its American sister. Ojinaga was not settled until 1759, when it became a stopping point on the trade route between San Antonio, Texas, and Chihuahua City. The building of the Southern Pacific railroad to El Paso and Los Angeles cost Ojinaga its geographic importance. Today, historic buildings cluster around a quaint central plaza; the tidy homes of the well-to-do stand on a paved side street, far from the *colonias* of dusty streets and eroding adobe homes. Ojinaga, wrote Tom Miller, is one of the last remnants of the Mexican West, where flour tortillas and cowboy hats are the vogue. Far removed from the big city, it is a "pueblito in Mexico's interior rather than a town facing its northern neighbor."

Far to the east, Palomas, the other border town in Chihuahua, once the headquarters of a huge American cattle ranch, as well as the site of a gambling casino patronized by Americans during Prohibition days, is a place on the map that reminds one of the way border towns looked decades ago. For three months each year the streets of Palomas, a shabby place of no more than eight square blocks, are filled with cowboys herding cattle waiting to be shipped by truck to U.S. buyers. Columbus, New Mexico, a barbwire fence away, is even smaller than Palomas. To the east, in the state of Coahuila, lies Ciudad Acuña. Named after a poet who wrote garbled verse, Ciudad Acuña is a neighbor of Del Rio, Texas, and was not linked by highway to Mexico City until the 1950s. Piedras Negras, lying east of Ciudad Acuña, is six times larger than its sister city Eagle Pass. It bears the name of coal deposits in its vicinity; in 1900 it was the third largest Mexican border town.

Nuevo Laredo, which lies further east, holds a special place in the hearts of Mexican nationalists. When founded by José de Escandón in 1755, the city was located on the north bank of the Rio Grande. After the War of 1847, when the international boundary was shifted to the Rio Grande, its Mexican inhabitants moved their town to the opposite shore rather than live under Yankee rule. Its patriotic settlers baptized it Nuevo Laredo; the "old" Laredo, now part of Texas, stayed put. Since Nuevo Laredo's early growth revolved around its Texas cousin, ties between families in the cities still survive. Nuevo Laredo became a major international port of entry with the coming of the railroad in the 1880s. This was reinforced by the completion of the Pan-American highway to Mexico City in the 1950s. By 1910, Nuevo Laredo was the second largest Mexican border town. The historic business districts of the two Laredos face each other; Mexicans shop on the American side by walking across the bridge. Since the 1940s, Nuevo Laredo's growth has been to the south, alongside the railroad tracks to Mexico City and Monterrey, and to the west, where a third rail line joins Nuevo Laredo to Piedras Negras. In the late 1930s a town of "dark and unsurfaced streets," to quote Graham Greene, today it has 350,000 inhabitants who tolerate its hot summers and cold winters. For years after the War of 1847, gangs of armed Americans invaded Tamaulipas, wanting to establish a Republic of the Sierra Madre and, in the pattern of Texas, annex it to the United States. Later, the American Civil War had a powerful impact on Tamaulipas, in particular Matamoros. Monterrey, the hub city of nearby Nuevo León, reaped a financial harvest. Trying to avoid the Union blockade, southern planters shipped their cotton through the ports of northeast Mexico, much of it through Matamoros. The war brought prosperity to these Mexican towns; until then their inhabitants, favored by climate, rainfall, and soil, had raised cotton and cattle, adding to their incomes by smuggling goods into Mexico.

The city of Matamoros, the biggest in Tamaulipas, honors a hero of the Mexican struggle for independence. Its Spanish father, Captain Alfonso de León, was seeking a maritime port to give the region, eventually filled with small cattle ranches, access to the sea. It is the oldest town in the Lower Rio Grande. Old colonial buildings dot its downtown. In 1928, a highway joined Matamoros to Ciudad Victoria, the capital of Tamaulipas, and, with the cotton boom of the 1950s, the city expanded rapidly after the establishment of cotton gins, cotton-seed oil plants, and warehouses. After the boom collapsed, Matamoros turned to commerce and tourism. Its latest phase, characterized by explosive population growth, corresponds to the arrival of the *maquiladora* industry at the end of the 1970s.

Reynosa, unlike Matamoros, has only a glimmer of a historical past. One does not see architectural reminders; colonial cathedrals do not sit on the edges of the city's central plaza. Only a tiny fraction of its residents have ties to families who lived there before the 1930s. Founded in 1749, Reynosa became a border city with the signing of the Treaty of Guadalupe Hidalgo in 1848. Unlike Matamoros, which added population rapidly, Reynosa remained a small town until recently; in 1930 it had fewer than five thousand inhabitants. However, federal irrigation projects for large-scale farming—basically cotton—and the coming of the PEMEX oil refinery in 1955 changed that. The region from Reynosa to Nuevo Laredo is rich in deposits of natural gas. Initially the gas went to Texas, but with the rise of industry in northern Mexico PEMEX now ships more and more of it to the cities of Monterey, Monclova, Torreón, Saltillo, and Chihuahua. PEMEX, which pays good wages and employs large numbers of men, is one of the pillars of the local economy. Thus, until the arrival of the *maquiladora* industry in the late 1970s, particularly Zenith, the economy of Reynosa, unlike that of the rest of the Mexican border communities, had an internal dynamic of its own. Its geographic location did not dictate its economics.

An international bridge, inaugurated in 1926, joins Reynosa and tiny Hidalgo, Texas, but McAllen, the more important American city, lies just eight miles beyond. Each day, thousands of Mexicans wend their way to work over the bridge; hundreds of women, traveling on American company buses, shop in Hidalgo or McAllen; and heavy trucks loaded with merchandise rumble back and forth. On weekends, countless Mexican Americans cross the bridge to shop, see dentists and physicians, or visit relatives. The distance between Reynosa and McAllen helps keep at bay the American cultural influence, so pervasive in many other Mexican border communities; Reynosa, they say, is another border city adhering closely to Mexican culture, partly because of its physical isolation from a big American metropolis; partly because it lies not far from Monterrey, one of largest and richest cities in the Mexican Republic; and partly due to the presence of PEMEX. The availability of cheap, used autos bought across the border partly explains its chaotic, sprawling nature, a pattern not atypical of other Mexican border cities. With the aid of the automobile, Reynosas's residents overran *ejido* lands, overcame the absence of bridges across its numerous canals, and circumvented the installations of PEMEX.

Nuevo Progreso, Tamaulipas, the youngest city on the border, was born less than half a century ago, when a businessman in Progreso, Texas, who wanted to import Mexican vegetables built a bridge across the Rio Grande. By then, Mexican farmers had planted corn, broccoli, tomatoes, and corn on former brushland. Soon Nuevo Progreso had streets full of curio shops and restaurants catering to American tourists. Some were "far younger" than the "Old Mexico" these tourists came to see.

Tijuana, Baja California Norte, lies miles away. Called the "most visited city in the world," its history is intimately bound up with that of San Diego, the California metropolis just eighteen miles beyond. Until 1957, no paved road connected Tijuana with the capital of the Republic, despite unwelcome and repeated attempts by Americans to acquire the peninsula from Mexico. For all the overlap of historic events, a huge gulf separates Tijuana, a Third World City, from San Diego, a wealthy haven. To quote the editorial lament of the *San Diego Union and Tribune,* "the sad truth is . . . that, throughout modern history, our two cities have maintained a distinct distance from each other—a divide that is far greater than that separating most other cities along . . . the border."

The economic boom of southern California fueled the transformation of Tijuana from a *ranchería* (village) to an urban settlement. A

Mexican by the name of Ricardo Orozco, formerly an employee of a Hartford, Connecticut, real estate agency that developed the town of Ensenada, laid out the city plan for Tijuana; he placed its downtown adjacent to the boundary line. The tourist industry dictated its location and the land-use plan. The bars, cabarets, and restaurants, all owned by Americans, were on Avenida Revolución, and the residential *colonias* to the west, around the Parque Teniente Guerrero. As San Diego expanded as a naval base, so did Tijuana. Tourism fed on the reform movement in California between 1900 and 1929. Gambling, the mainstay of the local economy, began in 1908 and horse racing in 1915, both American enterprises. When the United States began closing the international gates at 9 p.m., a hotel industry sprang up in Tijuana. For Mexicans, recalled one of them who arrived in 1927, Tijuana inspired nostalgia *por mi tierra;* "the sight of the town saddened me . . . everywhere houses of wood, unlike the adobe, brick, and stone of my hometown."

Tijuana is changing. You still see Mixtec women selling trinkets on the streets; striped donkeys still stand on Avenida Revolucion; and the fetid smell of poverty hangs heavy on its outskirts. But now there are also modern department stores, majestic hotels, elegant boutiques, and condominiums for lawyers and physicians, banks and freeways. *La Avenida de los Heroes,* a wide boulevard lined with trees and green lawns, is the heart of the new *zona del río,* where high-rises darken the sky. It includes a twenty-five million dollar shopping mall and a new cultural center. To build it, "Bobby" de la Madrid, a callous governor with a heart of stone, drove out five thousand poor families living in a slum—an eyesore on Tijuana in his opinion—and spent millions of federal dollars to channel the floodplain of the river. On the east side lies La Mesa, a dusty suburb of shops and apartment complexes where American tourists, in their shorts and polo shirts, seldom venture. On the Mesa de Otay are the buildings of the *maquiladoras*; the campus of the Universidad Autónoma de Baja California lies nearby.

Middle-class Mexicans—*maquiladora* managers, government bureaucrats, businessmen, and professionals—can be seen everywhere in Tijuana. It is not uncommon to find their wives, yuppies in dress and values, in restaurants with cellular phones to their ears. Anthropologists, economists, and demographers staff the Colegio de la Frontera Norte, a government think tank on the highway to Ensenada. *Tijuanenses* enjoyed bonanza years until the late 1980s, when the bottom fell out of the neighboring California economy. Border crossings, always an index of local conditions, then dropped dramatically, hurting commercial and service activities associated with tourism. Lower levels of public and private investment limited the construction industry, halting expansion and laying off masons, carpenters, and other tradesmen. Evidence suggests that per capita income may have decreased between 1970 and 1990, undermining living standards as economic expansion lagged behind the population growth rate. According to one study, the golden years may be a memory; "are we seeing," its authors ask, "the first signs of a bleak future economic performance by Tijuana?"

Mexicali, the only border city with a state capital, lies east of the coastal range, in one of the world's hottest and driest climates. Its citizens often drive to Tijuana to escape the heat; the better-off buy homes along the coastal highway to Ensenada, largely an American paradise. Every year the poor die from the summer's heat and the winter's biting cold. Tourists seldom visit Mexicali; it is a government town, replete with office buildings for bureaucrats. Once a tiny village of Cocopah Indians, Mexicali today, despite its inhospitable climate, has nearly one million inhabitants.

Like Tijuana, Mexicali owes its original existence to American enterprise, an offshoot of the Colorado River Land Company, which, due to the largess of Mexican federal authorities, enjoyed a monopoly on the land. Early Mexicali, a dirt street with a few wooden houses on opposite sides, was, for all intents and purposes, a cotton plantation. As late as 1930, its population was one-third Chinese, a legacy of the days when thousands of them were brought over by their American patrons to till the fields. Principally from Canton province, these laborers lived in the barrio *Chinesca* that stood on the international border. Another American company, the Jabonera del Pacífico, served as the sole bank, sold the machinery and equipment, and, as owner of the only cotton baler, monopolized its sale. The Compañia Mexicana de Terrenos y Aguas de Baja California, also American, held the rights to the water of the Colorado River. Less than 2 percent of the planters controlled 95 percent of the land. Few Mexicans lived in Mexicali, though they toiled planting and harvesting cotton. Even in 1929, recalled a visitor, Mexicali was a small town filled with cabarets and whorehouses, patronized by Americans from the Imperial Valley.

Calexico, its U.S. neighbor, is the tail on the dog. Dating from 1902, when it was a U.S. customs house, it remains a small town. Mostly populated by persons of Mexican descent, its stores, which cater to low-income Mexican shoppers, line the main street that runs parallel to the international border. It is a poor town, where workers earn some of the lowest wages in California. Of the families in Mexicali, many have relatives in Calexico; visits across the border are commonplace. American tourists rarely visit Tecate, the third of the Baja California border communities, which lies thirty-three miles east of Tijuana and sits at 1,600 feet above the sea. For many years it was principally known for its Tecate brewery, established in 1930, and its pottery, tile, and red brick industry.

Between Mexicali and Ciudad Juárez lie the Sonora border towns on the edge of Arizona: Nogales, San Luis Río Colorado, Naco, Sásabe, and Agua Prieta. Of the five, Nogales, which straddles a deep canyon, is the most important and Sásabe the least. Naco, according to one observer, has "not stirred in one hundred years." At the turn of the century, it was a depot for copper trains from the Cananea mines of William C. Greene; now its corrals only seasonally hold cattle from Sonora ranches headed for Arizona feedlots. San Luis Río Colorado, a colorless town, and more and more a shelter for *maquiladoras*, acts as a service center for the cotton and sorghum hinterland. Agua Prieta, which dates from 1897, faces Douglas, Arizona. Before the closing of the smelter in Douglas, the copper mines of Cananea and Nacozari used it to process their ore. Cowboys herd thousands of Mexican cattle through Agua Prieta on their way north to market. An international accord links together the power, water, and sewer systems of the two towns; fire departments respond to each other's calls. Agua Prieta is three times as big as Douglas. Even less significant than Naco is Sásabe, which stands on cactus-covered hills; lacking a PEMEX station, its residents buy their gasoline in the United States.

Only a chain-link fence separates Nogales, Sonora, from Nogales, Arizona; eliminate it and the two would be one city. In 1990, Mexico's Nogales, with over one hundred thousand inhabitants, was more than six times as large as its U.S. neighbor. Without a decent bookstore or a library of note, or even first-class restaurants, Nogales is a homely entrepôt clinging to two hillsides that abut a rail line and the highway.

IX

Scores of American pundits wax eloquently about binational economies, but surely they must be disciples of G. B. Shaw, who, in *Pygmalion*, asked, "Independence? That's middle-class blasphemy. We are all dependent on one another, every soul of us on earth." The reply is yes—and no; not everyone is equally dependent, and certainly not on the U.S.-Mexico border, where an asymmetrical relationship dictates the nature of life.

CHAPTER 4

CHICANO HISTORY: PARADIGM SHIFTS AND SHIFTING BOUNDARIES

Ramón A. Gutiérrez

"TOWARDS A NEW CHICANA/O HISTORY," the title of this conference, excellently summarizes the theoretical tensions and philosophical divides that have developed in the field of Chicano history over the last forty years. What is Chicano History? Who and what are its proper frames of reference? Forty years ago, the answers to these questions were simple and clear. Chicanos were men. As Mexican-American civil rights activism metamorphosed into the militant nationalism of the Chicano Movement between 1955 and 1970, Chicanos were defined as immigrant working men of Mexican peasant origin. They were heroic, indefatigable men, struggling against an exploitative capitalist labor regime; nevermind that more than half of all Mexican emigrants to the United States since 1945 had been women. This demographic reality rarely precipitated scholarly reflection. "Man" was the universal subject of historical inquiry, and as the persons who populated the professorate, men unhesitantly dictated what was worthy of study as Chicano.

"Towards a New Chicana/o History" evidences a major transformation. How did Chicano evolve into Chicana/o? What does the slash in the word Chicana/o signify? Exactly how did it slip in? The movement from the "Old" Chicano history to the "New Chicana/o history," which this symposium hopes to summarize, perhaps to synthesize, and maybe even to heal, is indicative of larger professional debates about the nature of historical writing and its relationship to the past. Thus, Chicano history is but one of the many fields grappling with the feminist critique of universal "Man." At this moment, when belief in the Enlightenment project of universal human emancipation has waned, and positivism and empiricism are under attack, historians have begun to question their methods and their own most cherished myths.

Struggles between the "old" and the "new," be it in Chicano history or any other field, can, in part, be explained demographically as a generational shift in the professorate. Scholars who began their careers in the late 1940s and early 1950s have reached retirement age, and are trying to perpetuate their concerns into the next millennium. Some are resisting change with the poison power of their pens. But to view these struggles only demographically would be to deny the fundamental epistemological shifts that are also afoot. The old economic and political certitudes of the 1950s have crumbled. Capitalism has been denationalized and has taken a more global and more mobile form. Just about everywhere, communism has been eclipsed. And from our own postmodern condition and perspectives, many proclaim the exhaustion of Enlightenment tenets and modernity's failure.

The starting point for many of these debates is an assessment of modernity. From the perspective of the postmodern critic, which herein I evoke, modernity was that extraordinary intellectual effort on the part of Enlightenment thinkers to develop objective science and a universal morality and law. The idea was to use the accumulation of knowledge, generated by many individuals working freely and creatively, for the pursuit of human emancipation and the enrichment of daily life. The scientific domination of nature promised freedom from scarcity, want, and the arbitrariness of natural calamities. Rational forms of social organization and thought would liberate one from irrationality, myth, religion, and superstition.

History as a university discipline and profession was born out of this modernist impulse. Historians sought universal truth, laws of human progress, and ways to liberate citizens and subjects. In the late-nineteenth century, objectivity and the quest for truth became the collective myths of the historical profession. By reading sources in a detached and dispassionate manner, it was believed, one could reveal the truth of the past. That knowledge, gained in an "objective" manner, enhanced its scientific value. If scientific rules were imposed on documentary bodies of evidence, the past would be reflected in written history.

At least three major political and ideological interpretations of the past have dominated modernist historical writing over the last hundred years. All three are found in Chicano histories. There was a bourgeois version of the past, a proletarian analogue, and a history that eschewed theory and metanarrative and claimed to be written for its own sake. [1] Bourgeois narratives of history were anchored in the logic and development of liberal market capitalism. Shackled by the past, the entrepreneurial individual constantly progressed toward the absolute freedoms of the market economy. The proletarian version of history shared with the bourgeois tale a common starting point in the capitalist economy, but relied on class and class conflict as its moving force. Karl Marx summarized this version of the past well when he wrote in *The Manifesto of the Communist Party*, "The history of all hitherto existing society is the history of class struggle."[2]

Characteristic of bourgeois and proletarian constructions of the past was a linear and progressive historical trajectory. Whether a burgeoning capitalist grabbing for markets or a worker yearning for better wages, these narratives of history took one from a dark and bleak past to a bright and bountiful future. Events cumulatively and progressively unfolded in evolutionary sequence. From savagery to barbarism, to feudalism, to capitalism, to socialism, and ultimately to communism, Karl Marx predicted, was the inevitable path of history.

The writing of history for its own sake peacefully coexisted alongside bourgeois and proletarian interpretations of the past. Sometimes called historicist, sometimes antiquarianism, this was plain, "common sense" history, local and particularistic. Eschewing larger metanarrative claims, it did not pretend to be discovering laws of history, trajectories of the past, or larger schema for understanding human progress. Characteristic of encyclopedias, almanacs, handbooks, and guides to particular themes, these histories were written by local elites for the mastery of local needs, and thus implicitly shared a bourgeois outlook and goal.

Chicano history, rooted in an older tradition of writing on Mexican immigrants in the United States and of their assimilation over time, was deeply enmeshed in these modernist models. Those who began writing Chicano history in the 1960s were, after all, largely trained in American universities, where modernist frameworks still reigned hegemonic. Though in the wake of the Feminist and Civil Rights Movements the meanings of truth and objectivity were being hotly debated in the late 1960s and early 1970s, alternative frameworks had yet to be satisfyingly articulated.

For the bourgeois version of Chicano history one need not look beyond two still popular college textbooks: Matt S. Meier and Feliciano

Rivera's *The Chicanos: A History of Mexican Americans*, and James Diego Vigil's *From Indians to Chicanos: The Dynamics of Mexican American Culture*. "Mexican American history begins with the early study of man [*sic*] in the Western Hemisphere," wrote Meier and Rivera.[3] And so began chapter 1 of their epic, a story that went "back as much as 50,000 years," starting with Asian migration across the Bering Straits, and culminating in 1960s Chicano protest. According to Meier and Rivera:

> The history of the Mexican American can be conveniently divided into five broad periods: the Indo-Hispanic period, the Mexican period, a period of cultural conflict during the last half of the nineteenth century, a period of resurgence in the first four decades of the twentieth century, and a period of regeneration from World War II to the present.[4]

The principle motor for this history of "resurgence" and "regeneration" was the economy. "[I]nvestment of capital in mines, railroads, cattle, and agriculture . . . " ultimately attracted ethnic Mexicans north into the United States and, once there, relegated this population "*la raza* to a minority position of second-class citizenship in what had been its own land."[5] For Meier and Rivera, the word "improvement" critically described the Mexican-American past. The labor demands of the American economy shattered the "traditional provinciality" of ethnic Mexicans and made them aware "of new possibilities for improving their social status."[6]

In *From Indians to Chicanos: The Dynamics of Mexican American Culture*, James Diego Vigil took readers on a similar odyssey from the Ice Age to the 1960s, offering what he called "a dynamic history."[7] Painfully using a life cycle model of human development as his template, Vigil argued that Chicano history could be divided into four major historical periods, each of which corresponded to an evolutionary stage in the human life cycle. The first period, the pre-Columbian, dated from 30,000 B.C. to 1519, and was appropriately the period of Chicano "embryonic life and infancy." Chicanos progressed to "childhood" during the Spanish colonial period, from 1521 to 1821. Mexican independence and nationalism between 1821 and 1846 catapulted Chicanos toward "adolescence." In the Anglo period, from 1846 to the 1960s, Chicanos reached "early adulthood." And as a result of the social struggles in the 1960s, "Chicanos have reached a new plateau, adulthood, in which they can learn from previous stages and gain further maturity . . . . The metaphor of history as an individual pattern of growth and development becomes awkward at this point: the declining strength of old age, followed by death, does not seem to be in the future of the Chicano people."[8]

Vigil compounded the history of Chicano maturation with an intersecting matrix, which he called the Six C's: class, culture, color, contact, conflict, and change. Vigil explained:

> The categories of class, culture, and color provide a vehicle to highlight the continuous social order and the way in which several major social features intertwine to make a social history.... A contact-conflict-change explanatory sequence clarifies the transformations that a fully functional social system undergoes and pinpoints specific aspects of the upheaval.[9]

All contact-conflict-change situations that Chicanos had historically faced pivoted around "the class factor," Vigil opined. Racial and cultural issues simply "obscured the real problem source—economic competition."[10] But the economic engine that Vigil, as well as Meier and Rivera, constructed in their histories was rather weak. It was a variant of the old "push-pull" immigration model, in this case the economic power of capitalism to "pull" population into Mexico's north, and from there into the United States.

Interpretive histories of the ethnic Mexican in the United States have been few and far between. More weighty, both in page counts and sheer number, are the historical dictionaries, documentary collections, and biographical handbooks. Matt Meier and Feliciano Rivera edited *The Dictionary of Mexican American History* in 1981, and since then there has been a proliferation of biographical aids on the history of Chicanos, Mexican Americans, Hispanic Americans, and Latinos.[11]

Many of the men who first wrote self-consciously as Chicanos were themselves of ethnic Mexican working-class origin. The proletariat model of the past best resonated with their own life experiences and aspirations, and quite naturally came to dominate Chicano histories. Following the great modernist paradigm almost verbatim, Chicano historians told the story of foreign rural peasants being transformed into immigrants and American workers in the cities of the United States, and in its "factories in the fields," as Carey McWilliams called them.[12]

While Meier and Rivera, and Vigil, clearly gave workers a role in their tracts, it was a peripheral one. The economy and capitalist development moved history forward. Worker resentment, resistance, and revolt were quite secondary.

Mario García's *Desert Immigrants: The Mexicans of El Paso, 1880–1920* stands out as an exemplar of the proletarian version of Chicano history.[13] Advancing a conservative interpretation by advocating assimilation rather than revolution, the story García told was of Mexican peasants gradually assimilating American lifeways and culture as marginalized workers in the United States. As García wrote:

> Mexican immigrants . . . shared a common tie with the larger wave of Eastern and Southern European immigrants as well as with black workers who migrated from the rural South to the urban North. . . . Mexican immigrants, like black migrants to the North, may have experienced less economic and social advances owing to persistent racial and cultural discrimination, yet they were significant additions to an expanded multiracial American working class by World War I.[14]

The Mexican "saga" in the United States was "the immigrant story commencing in the late nineteenth century, which is inextricably linked with the growth of American industrial capitalism," wrote García.[15] By embracing the immigrant analogy, he and other historians of the Mexican experience in the United States were simply echoing the regnant social science paradigm of the day.[16] Theorists of ethnicity then believed that, like white European immigrants, Mexicans would eventually be assimilated fully into American life as beneficiaries of full equality and justice.[17]

Juxtaposed with this conservative proletarian history that imagined progress for Chicanos through assimilation and Americanization was a much more radical variant anchored in class struggle and faith in a socialist future. Historian Juan Gómez-Quiñones and the cadre of doctoral students he trained at UCLA have been most identified with this interpretation. Much of Juan Gómez-Quiñones's own writing was on the history of Mexican workers on both sides of the United States-Mexico border, particularly their heroic attempts to unionize. These histories studied worker radicalism, labor unionization and strikes, the relationship between Mexican workers and state authorities, political organizations on both sides of the border, and the culture of Mexican workers and Chicanos.[18]

Gómez-Quiñones's students, and scholars influenced by his work, wrote histories on the origins of labor activism in fraternal organizations and mutual aid societies.[19] Francisco Balderrama studied the role of the Mexican consulates in protecting workers in the United States.[20] The relationship between Mexican workers and the Communist Party of the United States gained Luis Arroyo's attention.[21] Class and class formation in the United States were one of the central threads that unified this work. The dynamics of racism were deemed of less import. Race was but an ideological ploy the ruling class used to divide workers, these scholars maintained. It was false consciousness best ignored. If workers were ever to seize state power, it would be only by organizing along strict class lines, or so claimed Socialist and Communist organizers of ethnic Mexican workers in the United States between the 1920s and the 1960s, as did their historians.

Even further to the political left, eschewing class struggle, assimilation, and civil rights activism, was a radical Chicano nationalism that militated for self-determination and human emancipation. *The Chicano's Struggle Toward Liberation* was thus the subtitle of Rodolfo Acuña's 1972 book, *Occupied America*.[22] Allying himself with movements of oppressed peoples in the Third World, and invoking the lessons of Paulo Freire's *Pedagogy of the Oppressed*[23] and Franz Fanon's works on French colonialism in Algeria, Acuña proposed that Chicanos were an internal colony of the United States and would be liberated only through a national revolution:

> [T]he conquest of the Southwest created a colonial situation in the traditional sense—with the Mexican land and population being controlled by an imperialistic United States. Further, I contend that this colonization—with variations—is still with us today. Thus, I refer to the colony, initially, in the traditional definition of the term, and later (taking into account the variations) as an internal colony. . . . The parallels between the Chicanos' experience in the United States and the colonization of other Third World peoples are too similar to dismiss.[24]

Internal colonialism as an analytical model for understanding the status of Chicanos in the United States was first imported into Chicano history through the writings of Berkeley sociologist Robert Blauner and Tomás Almaguer, who was then his student.[25] The theory of internal colonialism initially emerged in the social sciences in the 1950s as an attempt to explain the "development of underdevelopment" in Africa, Asia, and Latin America.[26] Employed by Latin American Marxists as an explanation for the backwardness of areas in which Indians lived, internal colonialism eventually was developed as a theory of ethnic relations between indigenous groups and the larger mestizo (mixed blood) class societies in Mexico, Guatemala, and Peru. The theory proposed that structural constraints, very similar to those through which the metropolis systematically underdeveloped the periphery (colonies), were reproduced internally in a nation-state in relations between the dominant center and Indian communities. Thus the discrimination Indians suffered had not only a cultural manifestation, but a structural foundation as well.[27]

Nationalist protest movements in the United States were deeply influenced by this colonial paradigm. Harold Cruse, as early as 1962, characterized race relations in the United States as "domestic colonialism."[28] Three years later, in 1965, Kenneth Clark in his book *Dark Ghetto* advanced the proposition that the political, economic, and social structure of Harlem was essentially that of a colony, a model Stokely Carmichael and Charles Hamilton employed explicitly as internal colonialism in their 1967 book, *Black Power*.[29] It was Robert Blauner who best articulated the theory in relationship to American minorities, however, maintaining that while the United States was never a colonizer in the nineteenth-century European sense, it had nonetheless developed economically through the conquest and seizure of indigenous lands, the enslavement of Africans, and the usurpation of Mexican territory through war. "Western colonialism," wrote Blauner, "brought into existence the present-day patterns of racial stratification; in the United States, as elsewhere, it was a colonial experience that generated the lineup of ethnic and racial divisions."[30]

Blauner admitted that race relations and social change in the United States could not be explained entirely through internal colonialism because the country was a combination of colonial, racial, and capitalist class realities. Internal colonialism was a modern capitalist practice of oppression and exploitation of racial and ethnic minorities within the borders of the state characterized by relationships of domination, oppression, and exploitation. Such relationships were apparent as: (1) forced entry: "The colonized group enters the dominant society through a forced, involuntary, process"; (2) cultural impact: "The colonizing power carries out a policy which constrains, transforms, or destroys indigenous values, orientations, and ways of life"; (3) external administration: "Colonization involves a relationship by which members of the colonized group tend to be administered by representatives of the dominant power. There is an experience of being managed and manipulated by outsiders in terms of ethnic status"; and (4) racism: "a principle of social domination by which a group seen as inferior or different in terms of alleged biological characteristics is exploited, controlled, and oppressed socially and psychically by a superordinate group."[31]

White racial privilege was at the heart of the colonial relationship, manifested as an "unfair advantage, a preferential situation or systematic 'headstart' in the pursuit of social values, whether it be money, power, position, learning, or whatever." White people had historically advanced at the expense of blacks, Chicanos, and other Third World peoples, particularly in the structure of dual labor markets and occupational hierarchies. Given these material facts, racism was not a form of false consciousness; it resulted in concrete benefits for whites.[32]

Chicanos quickly saw themselves as an internally colonized population within the United States that was socially, culturally, and economically subordinated, and regionally segregated by white Anglo-Saxon America. Sociologist Tomás Almaguer gave these ideas their fullest scholarly elaboration as applied to Chicanos. Others soon followed Blauner and Almaguer's lead: Rodolfo Acuña and me in history; Joan W. Moore in sociology; and Mario Barrera, Carlos Muñoz; and Charles Ornelas in political science.[33]

When internal colonialism was taken from the global to the local level of analysis, the barrio, or ghetto, became its focus, as apparent in the titles of important historical works by Albert Camarillo (*Chicanos in a Changing Society: From Mexican Pueblos to American Barrios in Santa Barbara and Southern California, 1848–1930*), Richard Griswold del Castillo (*The Los Angeles Barrio, 1850*–1890), and Ricardo Romo (*East Los Angeles: A History of a Barrio*).[34] In all of these works Chicano history began in 1848, at the end of the U.S.-Mexico War with the legal and political incorporation of ethnic Mexicans into the United States. If anything defined the ethics of the Chicano moral community of memory and history in the barrio, it was the belief in collectivism and an explicit rejection of individualism. *Chicanismo* meant identifying with *la raza* (the race or people), and collectively promoting the interests of *carnales* (or brothers) with whom they shared a common language, culture, religion, and Aztec heritage.

The Feminist Critique

A Chicana feminist critique of the personal politics of Chicano history and its historians was first articulated in political practice. Only later, as women gradually began to earn advanced academic degrees, was it voiced in scholarship. Couched first as an assault on male chauvinism, by 1969 radical Chicanas were beginning to see themselves as triply oppressed, by race, class, and sex.[35] Within the Chicano student movement women were being denied leadership roles and were being asked to perform only the most traditional stereotypic roles—cleaning up, making coffee, executing the orders men gave, and servicing their needs. If women did manage to assume leadership positions, as some of them did, they were ridiculed as unfeminine, sexually perverse, promiscuous, and all too often, taunted as lesbians.[36]

The sexism rampant in the Chicano Movement prompted Irene Rodarte to ask rhetorically of movement men, "Machismo or Revolution?"; a question Guadalupe Valdés Fallis reformulated as "Tradition or Liberation?"[37] Others, such as Anna Nieto-Gómez, Velia García [then Hancock], and Mirta Vidal, spoke out about the sexism in the movement, militated for the liberation of women, and drew attention to the ways that racial and sexual oppression operated in the mythic Chicano nation of Aztlán.[38]

Chicano men initially deemed the feminist critique an assault on their Mexican cultural past, on their power, and by implication, on their virility. If Chicanos were going to triumph in their anti-capitalist, anti-colonial revolt, divisiveness could not be tolerated.[39] Chicana feminists who were influenced by ideas foreign to their community—namely bourgeois feminist ideology—were, according to the men, "malinchistas," traitors to the race. Be "Chicana Primero," the men exhorted, asking the women to take foremost pride in their cultural heritage and to reject women's liberation.[40] Adelaida R. del Castillo, among others, retorted that women were not seeking to dominate the movement. They only sought full equality: "True freedom for our people can come about only if prefaced by the equality of individuals within La Raza."[41]

Just as Chicano scholars who were interested in interpreting the history of the Southwest as a history of racial conflict between Anglos and Mexicans explicitly chose 1848 as the beginning of Chicano history, Chicana historians began re-visioning a past ordered by a very different sense of time. For women, it was not the U.S.-Mexican War that was most important. It was instead the first major act of conquest in the Americas, Spain's defeat of the Aztec empire. Judith Sweeney, in her 1977 historiographic essay on Chicanas, was the first person to propose a new chronology for Chicana history. That history, she stated, began in 1519 and could "be divided into three major periods: the colonial period (1519–1821); the nineteenth century (1821–1910); and the contemporary period (1910–76)."[42] Others writing on the history of Chicanas quickly followed Sweeney's lead.[43]

A chronology for Chicana history that began in 1519 rather than 1848 was not an arbitrary and mindless act. Rather, it placed at the very center of the political debate about the future and the past the issues of gender and power. By choosing 1519, women focused attention on one of Mexico's most famous women, Doña Marina. Doña Marina was a Mayan woman of noble ancestry who befriended Hernán Cortés in 1517. Cortés availed himself of Doña Marina's considerable knowledge of the local political geography and of her knowledge of various indigenous languages. Acting as his mistress, translator, and confidant, Marina helped Cortés to forge local antipathies toward the Aztecs into a fighting force that Cortés successfully unleashed on Tenochtitlan. In Mexican history, Doña Marina, also known as La Malinche, had often been seen as a villain, as the supreme betrayer of her race.[44] On this point many Chicanos were in accord. Malinche was a traitor, stated Luis Valdez in his 1971 play, *The Conquest of Mexico*, because "not only did she turn her back on her own people, she joined the white men and became assimilated . . ."[45]

Adelaida R. del Castillo, Cordelia Candelaria, and others were quick to respond, rehabilitating Malinche in historical writing as the primordial source of the two concepts that women were eager to place at the core of the Chicana Movement—*mexicanidad* (Mexicanness, or a unity of Mexican culture on both sides of the border) and *mestizaje* (race mixture or a belief in cultural hybridity). "Malinche is the beginning of the *mestizo* nation," wrote del Castillo, "she is the mother of its birth, she initiates it with the birth of her *mestizo* children."[46] Whatever the facts—in the case of Malinche there are dreadfully few—the crafting of a her/story and feminist chronology shifted the debate. Racism and sexism were now of equal importance. The male ethos of *carnalismo,* or brotherhood, and *Chicanismo,* so central as organizing themes in Chicano histories, were now complicated by *mexicanidad* and *mestizaje.*[47] *Mexicanidad* subverted *Chicanismo* because it asserted that Mexicans on both sides of the border shared a common culture and past, and had never been isolated and insulated as an internal colony in the United States. Thus, implicitly an ethno-class struggle for liberation was being proposed, not one of national unity. By emphasizing *mestizaje,* women drew attention to their role in the reproduction of the nation, not a pure-bred nation, but one based on extensive racial mixing and hybridity.

If the aim of Chicano history had been to decolonize the mind, making ethnic Mexicans in the United States more than the arms with which they toiled in the factories and fields, Chicanas were intent on decolonizing the body. Male concerns over job discrimination, access to political power, entry into educational institutions, and community autonomy and self-determination were augmented by female demands for birth control and against forced sterilization, for welfare rights, for prison rights for *pintas* (female prisoners) for protection against male violence, and most importantly, for sexual pleasure both within marriage and outside of it.[48]

Despite the rhetoric that "La Nueva Chicana" (the "New Woman") had to shatter cultural stereotypes to define herself, those definitions were initially contained within the still hegemonic proletariat model of the past.[49] The condition of Mexican-American working women was but a shorter, less important chapter of the working-class struggles men had waged.[50] Nevertheless, feminism forced a change in historical interpretation, heightening the centrality that the intersection of race, gender, and class assumed. Histories of Mexican emigration to the United States are a good case in point. As was noted, although more than half of all of the Mexican immigrants entering the United States since 1945 had been women, this fact was frequently ignored. The works of Vicki L. Ruiz and Susan Tiano, Margarita B. Melville, Gilbert Cardenas and Estevan T. Flores, and Rita J. Simon and Caroline B. Brettell, offered important correctives to this oversight.[51]

Even more exciting, however, were the studies by Chicanas that linked race, class, and gender domination at the workplace with gender domination within the home. Patricia Zavella's splendid work, *Women's*

Work and Chicano Families, studied women cannery workers in the Santa Clara Valley of northern California, showed how mechanization had contributed to female labor segregation and how the labor market reinforced traditional family roles within the household.[52] Vicki L. Ruiz covered very similar terrain in her masterful *Cannery Women, Cannery Lives* a study of Mexican women's unionization attempts in the California food processing industry.[53]

In addition to these very traditional topics, what was perhaps most revolutionary was that Chicanas began to write and to express a complex inner emotional life. Reflecting in 1970 on the participation of Chicanas in the liberation movement, Enriqueta Longauex y Vásquez stated that while the role of the Chicana previously "has been a very strong one—[it has been] . . . a silent one."[54] That silence has been shattered, and as the veil that shrouded the subordination of women has been ripped apart, exposing sexism and homophobia as ills just as debilitating and intensely experienced as racism and class oppression, modernism itself has been rethought.

The Postmodern Turn

There were many reasons why the certitudes and beliefs of modernism started to crumble, why intellectuals groped for other interpretive frameworks and critiques. Two world wars, death squads, the Holocaust, the obliteration of Hiroshima and Nagasaki, and the constant threat of nuclear annihilation prompted some to wonder about modernity's promises. Around the globe, everywhere that nationalist and socialist revolutions had been won in the name of liberation had become systems of human oppression. Capitalism, too, had been radically transformed, given global and mobile form, deterritorialized, and also denationalized. Simultaneously, deindustrialization was taking place, displacing workers and eclipsing the labor movement's importance. As these changes transpired, modernist versions of the past, both bourgeois and proletariat, seemed less plausible trajectories toward a liberatory future. The moment to theorize something beyond modernism was at hand. Postmodernism was born.

Postmodernism is a term that means different things in different disciplines. A postmodern culture is one in which a formerly unified subject is split into its constituent parts, in which a single homogeneous style is superseded by a number of heterogeneous fashions.

Postmodernism usually refers to a particular constellation of styles and tones in cultural practice, most notably pastiche; blankness; a mixing of forms, level, and styles; and a relish for repetition, revealing the constructed nature of work.[55] In philosophy and history, postmodernism has been associated with an aversion to any project that proposes universal human emancipation through reason, science, and technology. While eschewing such metanarratives as Marxism and Freudianism, it has acknowledged "the multiple forms of otherness as they emerge from differences in subjectivity, gender and sexuality, race and class, temporal (configurations of sensibility) and spatial geographic locations and dislocations."[56]

Mexican-American, Chicana, and Chicano intellectuals embraced postmodernism as an analytic mode in the late 1980s to explode the fictions of Chicano history, showing that there never really was one "Chicano" culture or community with a capital "C." Instead, they viewed Chicanos and Chicanas as an eclectic composition of peoples and traditions. Tomás Almaguer's essay, "Ideological Distortions in Recent Chicano Historiography," began the demystification of Chicano history, exposing the false epistemological closures and the simplistic ideas that he, as well as other Chicano intellectuals, had claimed as their credo in the 1960s. Almaguer argued that, motivated primarily by the desire to challenge the dominant assimilationist model of the 1950s, Chicanos had embraced a colonial analysis that depicted the history of Chicanos as that of a colonized minority waging a neo-colonial struggle against racism and imperialism.[57]

However strongly these sentiments were felt in the 1960s, the analysis was wrong, Almaguer argued. Historically, ethnic Mexicans in the United States had straddled several classes and had never been viewed monolithically, either by themselves or by outsiders. In the racial hierarchies that had evolved in the U.S. Southwest, ethnic Mexicans occupied an intermediate position between Anglos and Indians. In short, much of what had been written was an ideological distortion of the past, fashioned to fit the political tenor of the day. Almaguer developed all of these themes more systematically in his *Racial Fault Lines: The Historical Origins of White Supremacy in California*.[58]

The call for the elaboration of an analytic schema that better reflected the complexity of the ethnic Mexican population in the United States had various exponents. In her 1987 book *Borderlands/La Frontera: The New Mestiza*, Gloria Anzaldúa explored language in order to illustrate the complexities of ethnic Mexican culture on both sides of the U.S.-Mexico border. Anzaldúa identified six forms of Spanish, and two of English she spoke and described how and when each was used:

> My "home" tongues are the languages I speak with my sister and brothers, with my friends. They are [Pachuco (called caló), Tex-Mex, Chicano Spanish, North Mexican Spanish dialect, and Standard Mexican Spanish, with Chicano Spanish] being the closest to my heart. From school, the media and job situations, I've picked up standard and working-class English. From Mamagrande Locha and from reading Spanish and Mexican literature, I've picked up Standard Spanish and Standard Mexican Spanish. From los recién llegados, Mexican immigrants and braceros, I learned Northern Mexican dialect. . . .[59]

Anzaldúa's point was that the relationship between language and identity was not as neat and easy as Chicano nationalists had once imagined.

David Gutiérrez similarly shattered the unity in a former theme, immigration, in his book *Walls and Mirrors: Mexican Americans, Mexican Immigrants, and the Politics of Ethnicity*.[60] While in many ways this book can be categorized as a traditional history of an immigrant group—what some might call the "old" Chicano history—what was particularly innovative about this book was the ethnic complexity that it recorded. History here was not the backward projection of 1960s Chicano identity, but the struggle among workers from various regional cultures in Mexico, stratified by generation, gender, class, and occupation, competing with, and only occasionally allying with, older resident populations in the United States Southwest of Mexican and Hispanic origin. Identity and culture were contested among the members of these groups, and were also in opposition to the constraints and limits placed by states and dominant ethnicities.

If the "old" Chicano history depended on certitude, on objectivity, on disinterestedness, and on "facts" gathered in a systematic and unbiased fashion to reveal the truth, "new" Chicana and Chicano historical writings have been presented as "readings," "positionings," "perspectives," and "constructions" of the past. Far from certitude or even a search for truth, historical writing has been presented as a narrative prose discourse that is invented, constructed, and positioned in relationship to power. The unmarked universal "Man" of modernism who was disembodied and spoke from no particular place, in postmodern narratives was embodied in females and males, in bodies that are marked as brown, black, white, Asian, Latino, and hybrid, and that operate in erotic economies of multiple possibilities: heterosexual, homosexual, bisexual, transgendered.

The conjunction of such complex subject positions has led to the development of intersectionality as a powerful theme in historical writings on Chicanas and Chicanos. When a person occupies two or three overlapping statuses, does that intersection create a particular and different type of reality? Gloria Hull, Patricia Bell Scott, and Barbara Smith first asked this question about intersectionality in a now famous anthology entitled *All the Women Are White, All the Blacks Are Men, but Some of Us Are Brave.*[61] Here Hull and her collaborators highlighted the ways in which the hegemonic category "woman" really only meant white, middle-class women. Black women were being excluded in feminist theory and practice. Black only meant men in black nationalist thought. Black women were thus eager to understand how the status of black and women intersected in distinct ways. Ultimately these women theorized "women of color" as a distinct subject position and identity. Critical race theorist Kimberlé Crenshaw gave intersectionality its most rigorous legal examination, noting how U.S. Courts allowed black women to litigate only as women for gender discrimination, only as blacks for racial discrimination, but not as black women when these two statuses compounded discrimination in unique ways.[62]

Writing as a Chicana, Jewish, lesbian, *tejana* of working-class origin, Gloria Anzaldúa uses the concept of intersectionality to explore the realities of the U.S.-Mexico border zone. The international border creates a clear dichotomous separation, but the complicated cultures that underlie this divide produce numerous ways of living and loving, not just two. For Anzaldúa, cultures creatively blend in the border zone into something new that is not quite Mexican, not quite part of the United States. In this borderland, she writes, "you are neither hispana india negra española ni gabacha, eres mestiza, mulata, half-breed caught in the crossfire between camps while carrying all five races on your back."[63]

Writing on the history of the Spanish conquest and the domination of New Mexico's Pueblo Indians during the seventeenth and eighteenth centuries, Ramón A. Gutiérrez further elaborated on the intersection and conjunction of statuses. Gutiérrez wrote:

> The conquest of America was not a monologue, but a dialogue between cultures, each of which had many voices that often spoke in unison, but just as often were diverse and divisive. . . . As such, the historical process that unfolds here is a story of contestation, of mediation and negotiation between cultures and between social groups. This is not a history of Spanish men or of Indian men, or of their battles, triumphs, and defeats. It is a history of the complex web of interactions between men and women, young and old, rich and poor, slave and free, Spaniard and Indian, all of whom fundamentally depended on the other for their own self-definition.[64]

The works of Hull, Crenshaw, Anzaldúa, and Gutiérrez were exemplary of a move away from sharp oppositional binaries in social theory and practice. Oppositions have increasingly been theorized as generative tensions at polar ends that mutually require each other and that are constantly in process and flux. The recent literature on racial ideology, most notably on the social construction of whiteness, is a good example of this. Novelist Toni Morrison correctly analyzed the polar opposites and the fluidity of the racial order in the United States when she observed that each new generation of racialized immigrants had moved upward and been whitened by "buying into the notion of American blacks as the real aliens."[65] In his important article, "The Possessive Investment in Whiteness," George Lipsitz examined the central but uninterrogated role of whiteness, which emerged in the United States as a legal identity and cultural practices created out of "slavery and segregation, by immigration restriction and Indian policy, by conquest and colonialism." Lipsitz showed how the U.S. government had invested in particular forms of whiteness through family and welfare policy, through mortgage loan policies, through tax policy, and through the very wage structure of urban places.[66] Karen Brodkin Sacks similarly studied the impact of real estate practices on Jews and African-Americans in "How Did Jews Become White Folks?" showing how the latter had been disadvantaged by restrictive covenants.[67]

Following these leads, as well as the pathbreaking work of David Roediger, historian Neil Foley has recently completed *The White Scourge: Mexicans Blacks, and Poor Whites in the Cotton Culture of Central Texas*.[68] Herein Foley studies land, labor, and race relations in south-central Texas to understand the complex social heterogeneity and hybridity that were there created when cotton culture from the U.S.

South and cattle culture from Mexico's north were fused. By interrogating the great unmarked category of race—whiteness—as it applied to Mexicans he has splendidly shown the dynamism of racial ideology, the fluidity of racial categories, the complex web of socio-racial positions created through the overlap of race, class, and gender statuses, and the meanings of blackness at the denigrating bottom of the labor regime.

Postmodern scholarship on identity makes us aware of the radical restructuring of the ways in which capital operates, the ways in which workers migrate around the globe, and of the complex communication technologies that simultaneously link persons across wide spaces. In such a context, ethnic identities, despite appearances, are never fixed and timeless. They do not move unidirectionally as governed by those laws that theoretically should regulate modes of production, psychic economies, and the assimilation of immigrants in host societies. Rather, ethnic identities are produced locally, in the here and now, as creative and contestatory responses to complicated global structural and cultural processes. As local productions, ethnicities are always organized around the generational, gender, occupational, and residential experiences of a group, and thus are quite complex. As I have tried to show through an exposition of the logic of their arguments, Marxists, nationalists, and feminists have all been critical of such postmodern understandings of identities because they claim that historical actors are left without an explicit theory of agency. Michael Peter Smith's retort is that: "The focus upon the process of cultural production of politically and socially salient differences in race, class, ethnicity, gender, and sexual preference are intended to show, as art theorist Victor Burgin points out, that the meaning of such differences is 'something mutable, something historical, and therefore something we can do *something* about.'"[69]

Notes

1. Keith Jenkins, *On 'What is History?': From Carr and Elton to Rorty and White* (New York: Routledge, 1995), 1–14.
2. Karl Marx, "The Manifesto of the Communist Party," in Karl Marx and Friedrich Engels, *Basic Writings on Politics and Philosophy* (Garden City, N.Y.: Anchor, 1959), 7.
3. Matt S. Meier and Feliciano Rivera, *The Chicanos: A History of Mexican Americans* (New York: Hill and Wang, 1972), 3.
4. Ibid., xiv.

5. Ibid., *The Chicanos,* xv.
6. Ibid., *The Chicanos,* 189–90. (For other examples of Chicano improvement, see pp. 166–67, 185, 200.)
7. James Diego Vigil, *From Indians to Chicanos: The Dynamics of Mexican American Culture* (St. Louis: C.V. Mosby Co., 1980; reissued in 1984).
8. Ibid., 2–4, 223.
9. Ibid., 4–6.
10. Ibid., 5, 128.
11. Matt Meier and Feliciano Rivera, comps. *Dictionary of Mexican American History* (Westport, Conn.: Greenwood Press, 1981); Albert Camarillo, *Mexican Americans in Urban Society* (Berkeley Calif.: Floricanto Press, 1986); Angela E. Zavala, ed., *Anuario Hispano-Hispanic Yearbook* (McLean, Va.: T.I.Y.M. Publishing Company, 1991); Nicolás Kanellos and Claudio Esteva-Fabregat, eds., *Handbook of Hispanic Cultures in the United States* (Houston: Arte Público Press, 1993).
12. Carey McWilliams, *Factories in the Field* (Santa Barbara, Calif.: Peregrine, 1971).
13. Mario T. García, *Desert Immigrants: The Mexicans of El Paso, 1880–1920* (New Haven, Conn.: Yale University Press, 1981).
14. Ibid., 233.
15. Ibid., 1.
16. Manuel Gamio, *Mexican Immigration to the United States: A Study of Human Migration and Adjustment* (Chicago: University of Chicago Press, 1930); John Martinez, *Mexican Emigration to the U.S., 1910–1930* (San Francisco: R&E Research Associates, 1972); Mark Reisler, *By the Sweat of Their Brow: Mexican Immigrant Labor in the United States* (Westport, Conn.: Greenwood Press, 1976).
17. Michael Omi and Howard Winant, *Racial Formation in the United States: From the 1960's to the 1990's* (New York: Routledge, 1994), 9–23.
18. Juan Gómez-Quiñones, "The First Steps: Chicano Labor Conflict and Organizing 1900–1920," *Aztlán* 3, no. 1 (1972): 13–50; "Piedras contra la luna, México en Aztlán y Aztlán en México: Chicano-Mexican Relations in the Mexican Consulates, 1900–1920," in *Contemporary Mexico: Papers of the IV International Congress of Mexican History* (Mexico City: El Colegio de México, 1975), 53–72; "On Culture," *Revista Chicano-Riqueña* 5, no. 2 (1977): 35–53; *Development of the Mexican Working Class North of the Rio Bravo: Work and Culture among Laborers and Artisans, 1600–1900* (Los Angeles: Chicano Studies Research Center Publications, UCLA, 1982); *Chicano Politics: Reality and Promise, 1940–1990* (Albuquerque: University of New Mexico Press, 1990).
19. K. L. Briegel, *The Alianza Hispano Americana, 1894–1965: A Mexican Fraternal Insurance Society* (Ph. D. diss. University of Southern California, 1974); J. A. Hernández, *Mutual Aid for Survival: The Case of the Mexican Americans*

(Malabar, Fla.: Krieger, 1983); Carlos Vélez-Ibañez, *Bonds of Mutual Trust: The Cultural Systems of Rotating Credit Associations Among Urban Mexicans and Chicanos* (New Brunswick, N.J.: Rutgers University Press, 1983).

20. Francisco E. Balderrama, *In Defense of La Raza: The Los Angeles Mexican Consulate and the Mexican Community, 1929–1936* (Tucson: University of Arizona Press, 1982).
21. Luis Arroyo, "Notes on Past, Present and Future Directions of Chicano Labor Studies," *Aztlán* 6, no. 2 (1975): 137–50.
22. Rodolfo Acuña, *Occupied America: The Chicano's Struggle Toward Liberation* (San Francisco: Canfield Press, 1972).
23. Paulo Freire, *Pedagogy of the Oppressed* (New York: Seabury Press, 1970)
24. Acuña, *Occupied America*, 3.
25. Robert Blauner, "Internal Colonialism and Ghetto Revolt," *Social Problems* 16, no. 4 (spring 1969): 393–408; Robert Blauner, *Racial Oppression in America* (New York: Harper and Row, 1972); Tomás Almaguer, "Toward the Study of Chicano Colonialism," *Aztlán* 2, no. 1 (1971): 7–21; "Historical Notes on Chicano Oppression: The Dialectics of Racial and Class Domination in North America," *Aztlán*, 5, nos. 1, 2 (1974): 27–56; "Class, Race, and Chicano Oppression," *Socialist Revolution* 25 (1975): 71–99.
26. Andre Gunder Frank, *Capitalism and Underdevelopment in Latin America* (New York: Monthly Review Press, 1967).
27. Pablo González-Casanova, "Internal Colonialism and National Development," in *Latin American Radicalism*, I. L. Horowitz, ed. (New York: Anchor Press, 1969), 118–37. Rodolfo Stavenhagen, "Classes, Colonialism, and Acculturation," *Studies in Comparative International Development* 1, no. 6 (1965): 53–77; Julio Cotler, "The Mechanics of Internal Domination and Social Change in Peru," *Studies in Comparative International Development* 3, no. 12 (1967–68): 229–46.
28. Harold Cruse, *Rebellion or Revolution* (New York: Morrow, 1962).
29. Kenneth Clark, *Dark Ghetto* (New York: Harper and Row, 1965); Stokely Carmichael and Charles Hamilton, *Black Power* (New York: Random House, 1967).
30. Blauner, *Racial Oppression in America,* 12.
31. Ibid., 84.
32. Ibid., 22.
33. Ramón A. Gutiérrez, *Mexican Migration to the United States, 1880–1930: The Chicano and Internal Colonialism* (Ph.D. diss., University of Wisconsin, 1976); Joan W. Moore, "Colonialism: The Case of the Mexican Americans," *Social Problems* 17, no. 4 (spring 1970): 463–72; Mario Barrera, Carlos Muñoz, and Charles Ornelas, "The Barrio as Internal Colony," *Urban Affairs Annual Reviews* 6 (1972): 465–98; Mario Barrera, *Race and Class in the Southwest: A Theory of Racial Inequality* (Notre Dame, Ind.: Notre Dame University Press, 1979).

34. Albert Camarillo, *Chicanos in a Changing Society: From Mexican Pueblos to American Barrios in Santa Barbara and Southern California, 1848–1930* (Cambridge, Mass.: Harvard University Press, 1979); Richard Griswold del Castillo, *The Los Angeles Barrio, 1850–1890* (Berkeley: University of California Press, 1979); Ricardo Romo, *East Los Angeles: A History of a Barrio* (Austin: University of Texas Press 1983).
35. Adelaida R. Del Castillo, "Mexican Women in Organization," in *Mexican Women in the United States: Struggles Past and Present,* Magdalena Mora and Adelaida R. Del Castillo, eds. (Los Angeles: Chicano Studies Research Center Publications, 1980), 7–16.
36. The critique of machismo was powerfully articulated in poetry. See Marcela Christine Lucero-Trujillo, "Machismo Is Part of Our Culture," in *The Third Woman* 3 (1988): 401–2; and Lorna Dee Cervantes, "You Cramp My Style, Baby," as reprinted in Yvonne Yarbro-Berjarano, "The Female Subject in Chicano Theatre: Sexuality, 'Race,' and Class," *Theatre Journal* 38, no. 4 (December 1986): 402. On Chicanas being taunted as lesbians, see Una Chicana, "Abajo con los Machos," *La Raza* 1, no. 5 (1971): 3–4.
37. Irene Rodarte, "Machismo vs. Revolution," in *La mujer en pie de lucha,* Dorinda Moreno, ed. (Mexico City: Espina del Norte Publications, 1973); Guadalupe Valdes Fallis, "The Liberated Chicana: A Struggle Against Tradition," *Women: A Journal of Liberation* 3, no. 4 (1974): 20–21.
38. Anna Nieto-Gómez, "Sexism in the Movimiento," *La Gente* 6, no. 4 (March 1976): 10; Velia Hancock, "La Chicana: Chicana Movement and Women's Lib," *Chicano Studies Newsletter* (February-March 1971): 1; Mirta Vidal, *Chicanas Speak Out* (New York: Pathfinder Press, 1971).
39. Bernice Zamora, "Notes from a Chicana COED," *Caracol* 3 (1977): 19, as quoted in M. Sanchez, *Contemporary Chicana Poetry* (Berkeley: University of California Press, 1985), 231–32.
40. Enriqueta Longauex y Vásquez, "Soy Chicana Primero," *El Cuaderno* 1, no. 1 (1972): 17–22; Enriqueta Longauex y Vásquez, "The Mexican-American Woman," in *Sisterhood is Powerful,* Robin Morgan ed. (New York: Random House, 1970), 379–84.
41. Adelaida R. del Castillo, "Mexican Women" 16; Theresa Aragón de Valdez, "Organizing as a Political Tool for the Chicana," *Frontiers: A Journal of Women Studies* 5, no. 2 (1980): 11.
42. Judith Sweeney, "Chicana History: A Review of the Literature," in *Essays on la Mujer,* Rosaura Sánchez, ed. (Los Angeles: Chicano Studies Research Center Publications, 1977), 99–123, quotation on p. 100.
43. Alfredo Mirandé and Evangelina Enríquez wrote in 1979 that the "roots of the Chicana . . . in the United States date back to the conquest of Mexico in 1519." See *La Chicana: The Mexican-American Woman* (Chicago: University of Chicago Press, 1979), 2.

44. T. R. Fehrenhach, *Fire and Blood: A History of Mexico* (New York: Collier, 1973), 131. See also Octavio Paz, *The Labyrinth of Solitude: Life and Thought in Mexico* (New York: Grove, 1961).
45. Luis Valdez, "La Conquista de Méjico," in *Actos y el Teatro Campesino* (San Juan Bautista, Calif.: Menyah Productions, 1971), 131.
46. Adelaida R. del Castillo, "Malintzin TenEpal: A Preliminary Look into a New Perspective," in *Essays on la Mujer,* Rosaura Sánchez, ed. (Los Angeles: Chicano Studies Research Center Publications, 1977), 124–49, quotation on p. 126; Cordelia Candelaria, "La Malinche, Feminist Prototype," *Frontiers: A Journal of Women Studies* 5, no. 2 (1980): 1–6.
47. Norma Alarcón, "Chicana's Feminist Literature: A Re-Vision through Malintzín/or Malinche: Putting Flesh Back on the Object," in *This Bridge Called My Back: Writings by Radical Women of Color,* Cherríe Moraga and Gloria Anzaldúa, eds. (New York: Kitchen Table, Women of Color Press, 1983), 182–90; Rachel Phillips, "Marina/Malinche: Masks and Shadows," in *Women in Hispanic Literature: Icons and Fallen Idols,* Beth Miller, ed. (Berkeley: University of California Press, 1983), 97–114; Shirlene Soto, "Tres modelos culturales: La Virgen Guadalupe, La Malinche y la Llorona," *fem* 10, no. 48 (October–November 1986): 13–16.
48. On birth control see: Sylvia Delgado, "Young Chicana Speaks Up on Problems Faced by Young Girls," *Regeneración* 1, no. 10 (1974): 5–7; Kathy Flores, "Chicano Attitudes Toward Birth Control," *Imagenes de la Chicana* (vol. 1): 19–21; Melanie Orendian, "Sexual Taboo y la Cultura?" *Imagenes de la Chicana* (vol. 1): 30. Theresa Aragón de Valdez chronicles a 1971 San Antonio case in which Mexican-American women were used as guinea pigs for a birth control experiment without being informed in "Organizing as a Political Tool for the Chicana," *Frontiers: A Journal of Women Studies* 5, no. 2 (1980): 9. On forced sterilization see: Carlos G. Velez-I, "Se me Acabó la Canción: An Ethnography of Non-Consenting Sterilizations among Mexican Women in Los Angeles," in *Mexican Women in the United States,* Magdalena Mora and Adeliada del Castillo, eds., (Los Angeles, UCLA, Chicano Studies Research Center Publications 1980), 71–94. On welfare rights see: Clemencia Martínez, "Welfare Families Face Forced Labor," *La Raza* 1, no. 7 (January 1972): 41; Mary Tullos and Dolores Hernández, "Talmadge Amendment: Welfare Continues to Exploit the Poor," *La Raza* 1, no. 7 (January 1972): 10–11; Anna Nieto-Gómez, "Madres Por la Justicia," *Encuentro Femenil* 1, no. 1 (spring 1973): 12–19; Alicia Escalante, "A Letter from the Chicana Welfare Rights Organization," *Encuentro Femenil* 1, no. 2 (1974): 15–19. On prison rights see: Renne Mares, "La Pinta: The Myth of Rehabilitation," *Encuentro Femenil* 1, no. 2 (1974): 27–29; Josie Madrid, Chata Mercado, Priscilla Pardo, and Anita Ramirez, "Chicanas in Prison," *Regeneración* 2, no. 4 (1973): 53–54.
49. Viola Correa, "La Nueva Chicana," in *La Mujer en Pie de Lucha,* Dorinda Moreno ed. (Mexico City: Espina del Norte Publications, 1973); Maxine

Baca Zinn, "Gender and Ethnic Identity among Chicanos," *Frontiers: A Journal of Women Studies* 5, no. 2 (1980): 18–24.

50. Ruth Allen, *The Labor of Women in the Production of Cotton* (New York, 1933, reprinted 1975); Ruth Allen, "Mexican Peon Women in Texas," *Sociology and Social Research* 16 (November–December 1931): 131–42; Mary Loretta Sullivan and Bertha Blair, "Women in Texas Industries: Hours, Working Conditions, and Home Work," *Bulletin of the Women's Bureau* 126 (1936); Selden C. Menefee and Orin C. Cassmore, *The Pecan Shellers of San Antonio: The Problem of Underpaid and Unemployed Mexican Labor* (Washington, D.C.: U.S. Government Printing Office, 1940); Melissa Hield, "Union-Minded: Women in the Texas ILGWU, 1933–1950," *Frontiers* 4, no. 2 (Summer 1979): 59–70; George N. Green, "ILGWU in Texas, 1930–1970," *Journal of Mexican-American History* 1, no. 2 (1971): 144–69; Mario F. Vásquez, "The Election Day Immigration Raid at Lillie Diamond Originals and the Response of the ILGWU," and Douglas Monroy, "La Costura en Los Angeles, 1933–1939: The ILGWU and the Politics of Domination," both in *Mexican Women in the United States,* Magdalena Mora and Adelaida Del Castillo, eds. 145–48, 171–78; Jane Dysart, "Mexican Women in San Antonio, 1830–60: The Assimilation Process," *Western Historical Quarterly* 7 (October 1976): 365–75; Ester Gallegos y Chávez, "The Northern New Mexican Woman: A Changing Silhouette," in *The Chicanos: As We See Ourselves,* Arnuldo D. Trejo, ed. (Tucson: University of Arizona Press, 1979), 67–80.
51. Vicki L. Ruiz and Susan Tiano, eds., *Women on the U.S.-Mexico Border: Responses to Change* (Boston: Allen and Unwin, 1987); Margarita B. Melville, "Mexican Women Adapt to Migration," in *Mexican Immigrant Workers in the United States,* Antonio Ríos-Bustamante, ed. (Los Angeles: Chicano Studies Research Center Publications, 1981), 119–26; Gilbert Cárdenas and Estevan T. Flores, *The Migration and Settlement of Undocumented Women* (Austin: Sociology Department, University of Texas, 1986); Rita J. Simon and Caroline B. Brettell, eds., *International Migration: The Female Experience* (Totowa, N.J.: Rowman and Allanheld, 1986).
52. Patricia Zavella, *Women's Work and Chicano Families: Cannery Workers of the Santa Clara Valley* (Ithaca N.Y.: Cornell University Press, 1987).
53. Vicki L. Ruiz, *Cannery Women, Cannery Lives: Mexican Women, Unionization, and the California Food Processing Industry, 1930–1950* (Albuquerque: University of New Mexico Press, 1987).
54. Enriqueta Longauex y Vásquez, "Mexican-American Woman," 380.
55. Todd Gitlin, "Postmodernism: Roots and Politics," in *Cultural Politics in Contemporary America,* Ian Angus, ed. (New York: Routledge, 1988), 347–85.
56. Andreas Huyssens, "Mapping the Post-Modern," *New German Critique* 33 (1984): 5–52, as quoted in David Harvey, *The Condition of Postmodernity: An*

Enquiry into the Origins of Cultural Change (Oxford, England: Basil Blackwell, 1989), 41.

57. Tomás Almaguer, "Ideological Distortions in Recent Chicano Historiography," *Aztlán* 18 (1989): 7–27.
58. Tomás Almaguer, *Racial Fault Lines: The Historical Origins of White Supremacy in California* (Berkeley: University of California Press, 1994).
59. Gloria Anzaldúa, *Borderlands/La Frontera: The New Mestiza* (San Francisco: Ante Lute Press, 1987), 55–56.
60. David Gutiérrez, *Walls and Mirrors: Mexican Americans, Mexican Immigrants, and the Politics of Ethnicity in the American Southwest, 1910–1986* (Berkeley: University of California Press, 1994).
61. Gloria Hull, Patricia Bell Scott, and Barbara Smith, eds., *All the Women Are White, All the Blacks Are Men, but Some of Us Are Brave* (Old Westbury, N.Y.: Feminist Press, 1982).
62. Kimberlé Crenshaw, "Mapping the Margins: Intersectionality, Identity Politics, and Violence Against Women of Color," in *After Identity: A Reader in Law and Culture,* Dan Danielsen and Karen Engle, eds. (New York: Routledge, 1995), 332–54; "Demarginalizing the Intersection of Race and Sex: A Black Feminist Critique of Antidiscrimination Doctrine, Feminist Theory and Antiracist Politics," *Legal Forum: Feminism in the Law: Theory, Practice and Criticism* (1989), 139–67.
63. Gloria Anzaldúa, *Borderlands/La Frontera,* 194.
64. Ramón A. Gutiérrez, *When Jesus Came, the Corn Mothers Went Away: Marriage, Sexuality and Power in New Mexico, 1519–1846* (Stanford Calif.: Stanford University Press, 1991), xvii–xviii.
65. Toni Morrison, "On the Backs of Blacks," *Time* 142 (fall 1993): 57.
66. George Lipsitz, "The Possessive Investment in Whiteness: Racialized Social Democracy and the White Problem in American Studies," *American Quarterly* 47, no. 3 (September 1995): 369–87.
67. Karen Brodkin Sacks, "How Did Jews Become White Folks?" in *Race,* Steven Gregory and Roger Sanjek, eds. (New Brunswick, N. J.: Rutgers University Press, 1994).
68. David Roediger, *The Wages of Whitenesss: Race and the Making of the American Working Class* (New York: Verso, 1991); *Towards the Abolition of Whiteness* (New York: Routledge, 1994); Neil Foley, *The White Scourge: Mexicans, Blacks, and Poor Whites in the Cotton Culture of Central Texas* (Berkeley: University of California Press, 1997).
69. Michael Peter Smith, "Postmodernism, Urban Ethnography, and the New Social Space of Ethnic Identity," *Theory and Society* 21, no. 4 (August 1992): 493–531, quote on pp. 525–26.

CHAPTER 5

REGION, NATION, AND WORLD-SYSTEM: PERSPECTIVES ON MIDWESTERN CHICANA/O HISTORY

Dennis N. Valdés

Introduction: Chicana and Chicano Paradigms and the Midwest

DURING ITS YOUTH IN the late 1960s and early 1970s, Chicano historical scholarship emphasized its distinctive past and setting. While paying cursory homage to indigenous roots among the Aztecs in Central Mexico, authors initiated serious investigation in early-nineteenth-century Texas, New Mexico, and California, immediately prior to the mass migration of English-speaking people from the United States (Acuña 1972; Meier and Rivera 1972; Vigil 1980). The choice had important political and interpretive implications. Acknowledging ancient roots and a geography comprising former Mexican territory permitted Chicano scholars to challenge historians of the United States, whose story flowed from east to west, and portrayed Mexicans, if at all, as the last of the immigrants. It emphasized incorporation of Mexicans as a result of military conquest, in contrast with Europeans, who were voluntary immigrants. Legal and political mechanisms imposed on Mexicans without consent deprived them of a land base and resulted in widespread downward mobility, while dominant political culture continued to restrict Mexicans who entered the United States in the twentieth century. The focus on conquest and the Southwest also drew attention to the creation and proximity of the U.S.-Mexican border, which further distinguished Mexicans from individuals of European, African, and Asian backgrounds. The political border was considered critical in the formation and maintenance of a unique Chicano identity and history. In effect, the distinct chronology and geography unified a group of scholars adhering to a wide range of political and theoretical perspectives.

Key features of this Chicano history did not apply to Mexicans in the Midwest, whose continuous presence dates only from the turn of the twentieth century. The early midwesterners were overwhelmingly immigrants from Mexico who lived and worked among their European predecessors and more recently arrived African Americans. With roots mostly in the interior of Mexico, they did not share a collective memory of U.S. conquest or the concomitant loss of ancestral lands. Finally, the U.S.-Mexican border had little immediate meaning, located more than one thousand miles away from most Mexicans in the Midwest. I was born in Detroit, and the borderlands I knew best during my youth straddled the United States and Canada. The political border dividing the two nations was marked by the Detroit River, easily crossed by tunnel or bridge to reach Windsor, Ontario, located immediately to the south.

Neglect in general and theoretical literature has prompted midwestern Mexicans to complain that the discipline of Chicana/o studies displays a lack of consideration similar to that Anglo-dominated academia showed toward Chicanas/os in the Southwest a generation ago. The exclusion is replicated even in recent overviews and bibliographies, where reference to the Midwest is sparse and often lacking entirely (Gutiérrez 1993; Ríos-Bustamante 1993; González and Fernández 1994; I. García 1996; Griswold del Castillo 1997).

In this chapter I will examine interpretive historical frameworks adopted by twentieth-century scholars toward midwestern Mexicans, including the literature of the Chicano generation. While placing the authors in their contemporary contexts, I will simultaneously discuss how a world-system perspective, which is not new in Chicano historical scholarship, offers theoretical opportunities to address a number of important issues in the field and incorporate broader geographical and chronological frameworks.

"Mexican Folk" in the Industrial Heartland

When Mexicans arrived in the Midwest in large numbers in the early-twentieth century, academics adopted preconceived notions about their place in society. Scholars based their views on the applicability of cultural models of assimilation, the experiences of European immigrants, and the memory of world conquests during a previous century of industrial capitalist expansion. They shared assumptions that the United States, a modern, democratic, and industrial nation, offered superior economic, social, and political incentives for capable individuals from poorer, more backward countries who sought a better life.

They did not agree, however, on the capacities of Mexicans as compared with those of Europeans, or on the propriety of encouraging assimilation. Some considered Mexicans as capable and meritorious of assimilation with their European counterparts, while others vehemently disagreed. The debate among midwestern and other mainstream academics centered on acceptance of models of Anglo conformity versus cultural pluralism. Proponents of the former supported their arguments with popular social and scientific notions including social Darwinism and Eugenics. They were influenced by the political realities of imperialism, particularly European conquests in Africa and Asia, and the U.S. conquests of Mexico and Spain during the nineteenth century, which shaped their notions of racial superiority. Yet most denied that the United States fit within the imperialist family of nations.

The conviction of inherent U.S. superiority over Mexico was shared by Europeans, conservative and radical alike, including Karl Marx. In an 1854 letter to Frederick Engels, he viewed the U.S. conquest and acquisition of Mexican territory positively, contrasting what he considered superior traits of Americans to those of inferior Mexicans:

> It is the Yankee sense of independence and individual efficiency, perhaps even greater than among the Anglo-Saxons. The Spaniards are already degenerated. But now a degenerate Spaniard, a Mexican, is an ideal. All encumbrances, braggings, loudmouthedness, and quixoticism of the Spaniards here [are] raised to cubic power (Marx 1972: 41).

Marx's views were informed by contemporary scholarship and newspaper coverage in England and the United States and influenced by the Black Legend, initially part of England's ideological battle against Spain in its centuries-long struggle for world hegemony that accompanied military battles on land and sea. Yet such expressions make understandable the reluctance of many Chicano scholars to accept the leadership or conclusions of Marx's self-appointed followers in subsequent generations.

By the 1920s, adherents of Eugenics, Social Darwinism and other bias theories occupied posts in the most prestigious academic institutions in the nation, including Ivy League schools like Harvard, Yale, and Princeton, and the Universities of Wisconsin and Michigan in the Midwest. Few had conducted investigations or claimed expertise on immigration from Mexico. Yet like contemporary "experts" at the end of the twentieth century, they considered their credentials sufficient to participate in the public debate on immigration restriction, based largely on their views regarding the capacity of Mexicans to assimilate. They supported restriction, basing their arguments on an assumption of inherent Mexican biological and cultural deficiencies (U.S. Congress 1927: 1904).

A noteworthy 1930 study of Flint, Michigan, by sociologist William Albig suggests that such opinions were in conformity with dominant popular culture in the Midwest. Consistent with other midwestern investigations, he found very negative attitudes toward Mexicans by European immigrants, with nuanced differences by age, gender, and formal schooling. He observed that, "young adults were, in general, much more critical of divergent customs than were the elders." A nineteen-year-old male student claimed that: "they're dirty as hogs. . . . I don't know how they get along. I used to work in an A&P store. They always bought good food, what they did buy, when they had money. The women are pretty dumb, they never do learn to talk." A seventeen-year-old girl asserted: "I think they're all awful. I've heard that when the Mexican men get mad at their wives they just leave them and exchange wives for a month or so. The people of the neighborhood think they're all bad about things like that, anyway.... I'm glad we're going to move." A twenty-year-old immigrant woman who had recently moved from Detroit reported: "I keep away from the whole district now as much as possible. I don't like it, and I wish we'd move. I dislike the Mexicans very much" (Albig 1930: 63–70).

Albig found that among adult men, few considered Mexicans economic competitors, in contrast with a majority of women and younger adults. He also observed that adult women of European background more openly expressed negative views than men. A woman interviewee stated, "once we were going to sell the house, and a family wanted it, but wouldn't buy it because of the Mexicans next door." Another

Flint woman asserted: "we moved because of the Mexicans and Negroes. There was [*sic*] Mexicans next door." The study suggested that as southern and eastern European immigration, predominantly male in its early phases, became more evenly balanced by gender, prejudice increased. Albig also found that individuals with the most schooling were the most prejudiced. His work implied that schooling and Americanization, touted in popular culture and among educators as the most effective means of upward mobility and a better life in the United States, contributed to heightened prejudice against Mexicans. Academic hostility toward Mexicans did not occur in isolation (Albig 1930: 63–70).

Several contemporary midwestern studies manifested racial bias theories. In a 1926 article, sociologist Ruth Camblon asserted that Chicago Mexicans were overwhelmingly descendants of Indians, which accounted for cultural traits including "mysticism," and accounted for why "the Mexican lacks physical resistance. His inherited lack of health habits or scientific health standards, combined with his migratory life make him peculiarly susceptible to disease" (Camblon 1926: 211). Mexicans' racial background also accounted for their being "honest, gentle, industrious, self-abnegating and religious. They accept their misfortunes sadly but quietly." Camblon feared that as greater numbers of Mexicans came to Chicago in response to economic incentives, "we shall be faced with these acute problems in increasing numbers." She had grasped the shifting tide of dominant opinion that was creating the "Mexican Problem" and would soon pervade academic and popular thought (Camblon 1926: 208–11).

Paternalism was also rampant in midwestern scholarship, including the work of geographer Earl Sullenger. His study of Mexicans in Omaha sought to account for Mexican migration through biology: "the intermarriage of the Spaniards and Indians has produced the migrating Mexicans." He urged greater institutional intervention to offset cultural deficiencies, including "passive" and "mentally lazy" natures that hindered self-advancement and participation in Americanization programs. He suggested that, "we should not neglect them as is usually done. We should meet them with a kindly attitude and show that we have regard for them," to help them "solve their difficulties" (Sullenger 1924: 289–93).

Scholars who viewed midwestern Mexicans within cultural pluralist perspectives tended to portray them as the last of the immigrants, and potentially good citizens capable of assimilation. Research interest was greatest at the University of Chicago, home of the "Chicago School," where works on midwestern Mexicans appeared in the social sciences, particularly in sociology, social work, and anthropology. This school was led by anthropologist Robert Redfield, best known for his investigations on Mexico, who popularized a model depicting Mexicans as representing "folk society," in contrast with modern urban industrial society. In his 1930 classic, *Tepoztlán: A Mexican Village,* he wrote: "the folk culture is a fusion of Spanish and Indian elements," comprised of preindustrial rural and small town peoples whose local cultures display "relatively small diversity of intellectual interest." A critical problem for Mexican folk culture, he suggested, was the "spread of city ways" (Redfield 1930: 1–13). As folk people, Mexicans in Chicago encountered "disorganization" and were subject to a myriad of difficulties in "reorganization" and adjustment to the big city.

Redfield and the "folk" model influenced writings by University of Chicago students and faculty in the 1920s and 1930s. Their assessments of Mexicans in Chicago generally were much more positive than those of their contemporary counterparts. Sociologist Anita Edgar Jones, in a 1928 essay, "Mexican Colonies in Chicago," concluded: "on the whole, the Mexicans have been much like the other immigrant groups in many respects, living under hard conditions when necessary and gradually finding their condition improving with their period of American life.... The picture may fairly be called an encouraging one" (Jones 1928b: 597).

Redfield also collaborated with other scholars, including economist Paul Taylor and anthropologist Manuel Gamio in their massive studies on Mexican immigrants in the United States, which included Chicago and other midwestern settings (Redfield 1929). Funded by the Social Science Research Council, the works of Taylor and Gamio generally conformed with the framework posited by Redfield. Both accepted push-pull models of immigration and discussed conditions in Mexico rather than simply focusing on the United States. They agreed generally that Mexicans, whose folk society was being disrupted in Mexico, were also being lured northward. Yet in certain ways the two authors differed. Taylor found important regional differences Mexicans faced in Chicago and Bethlehem, Pennsylvania, in comparison with those in the Southwest. He regarded Mexicans as the last of the immigrants and as equally as talented and intelligent as recent European arrivals to

Chicago, who also came from a folk culture. He suggested that environment rather than heredity primarily accounted for different outcomes among Mexicans and Europeans. One environmental factor, geography, was particularly important, as Mexicans in the urban Midwest faced a "greater stress of adjustment" than those in the Southwest. Yet he concluded that the Chicago environment generally offered more favorable opportunities for Mexican immigrants. In the urban Midwest, segregation of Mexicans in work, residences and schools was less marked, and the impact of color prejudice as a hindrance to assimilation "is less effective than in the rural West and Southwest," or even in Los Angeles (Taylor 1932: 280).

Gamio considered Mexican immigration as a temporary episode in Mexican history and did not focus as specifically as Taylor on differences between the urban Midwest and the rural Southwest. His overall assessment of immigration was positive: "although the immigrant often undergoes suffering and injustice and meets many difficulties, he undoubtedly benefits economically by the change," and by learning to work in the modern industrial setting, becomes, "much more efficient than before." Unlike Taylor, Gamio regarded permanent settlement negatively, both because Mexicans faced constant prejudice and because he believed they should return and apply their experiences in modern agriculture and industry to Mexico's economic development (Gamio 1931: 49).

The studies of Taylor and Gamio portrayed Mexican migration within an international framework, emphasizing its simultaneous impact in Mexico and the United States. Furthermore, they observed that Mexican workers were recruited to almost every state in the union, where they formed "colonies," which they referred to as *colonias*. Clearly their studies of Mexicans were not confined to the Southwest. Gamio also offered a compromise in the intensifying public debates of the 1920s and early 1930s regarding whether immigration from Mexico should be placed on a quota, as desired by conservatives, progressives, and even labor historians. The conservative position was not in keeping with the relatively free movement allowed residents from countries of the Western Hemisphere, and many liberals feared that restrictive legislation would offend Mexico and other neighbors in the Americas. Rather than create an international political embarrassment by writing new laws, Gamio suggested the creation of an administrative mechanism to assist Mexicans who wanted to return voluntarily, with the support of the Mexican government.

From a world-system perspective, the public discussion was implicitly predicated on the existence of an international world economic and political order in which the United States had become the industrial core, with Mexico and the rest of Latin America its periphery. The latter had replaced industrializing rural sectors of Europe as the source of a reserve of cheap labor for U.S. capitalists, and repatriation confirmed Mexicans' expendability.

Second Generation "Problems"

With the onset of the Great Depression, scholarship on midwestern Mexicans took a negative turn. Students from the University of Chicago emphasized disruption, which they attributed to the extremely difficult conditions attending to the urban life of Mexican folk. In his study of juvenile delinquency among Mexican youth in Chicago, Edward Bauer discussed recent history in South Chicago. Adopting from Redfield, he emphasized the "disorganizing influences of urban society" on Mexican families, compounded by fathers' job losses in the early 1930s. He suggested that economic and social disorder during the Great Depression increased family tension and induced youth to find company with gangs. Yet he concluded that reports on gang activities of Mexican boys were highly exaggerated, while girls were almost never delinquent. Bauer also found that the integration of the South Chicago Mexican colony was very low, that adolescents still identified overwhelmingly as Mexicans, and that their close friends were almost all Mexicans, factors that could account also for low levels of delinquency. Furthermore, he suggested, "they may become culturally assimilated, and at the same time remain in a semi-caste status," between that of blacks and whites. Bauer predicted that "unless Mexicans are able to move out of the colony and establish themselves in the larger community the process of assimilation will be much slower than has been the case in ethnic groups of European origin." As among observers in the 1920s, he concluded that assimilation remained more potential than actual for youth of the second generation (Bauer 1938: 1–4, 55).

Portrayals of midwestern Mexican immigrants and their children as a problem continued to pervade academic literature. The most prolific regional scholar of the second generation, sociologist Norman D. Humphrey, wrote many articles in the 1940s and 1950s based on a thesis and dissertation on Mexicans in Detroit. Trained at the University of

Michigan, he accepted many ideas popularized by the Chicago School, including a push-pull explanation of immigration, portrayal of Mexicans as "folk" culture, and their consequent difficulties adjusting to modern urban society. Humphrey emphasized cultural factors more heavily than the Chicago School, while he portrayed the "folk" overwhelmingly as "peons." He frequently offered cultural explanations for economic decisions, including why Mexicans frequently resided in basement and attic apartments, which, "being lightless and airless, approximate the adobe huts of the peasant village." Like Taylor, he predicted that Mexicans would prefer the urban Midwest to Texas, suggesting that, "while germinal elements for a Mexican caste are present in the northern states, they are not as developed, nor as overt in their expression, as they are in the south," due largely to the small Mexican population (Humphrey 1944: 332). He concluded that acculturation of Detroit Mexicans tended toward "a merging of Mexican peasant and American working class culture," which involved "the acquisition of relatively superficial layers of American culture and the shedding of equally shallow Mexican elements" (Humphrey 1946: 433, 437).

Dominant midwestern academic literature tended to view positively those features of Mexican culture that were consistent with assimilation while regarding the rest as a "problem." In seeking to account for differences between two generations of Mexicans in St. Paul, sociologist Norman Goldner suggested that "fathers" started and remained at the bottom of the occupational hierarchy. By contrast, "sons," who also started at the bottom, "have become occupationally diversified and upwardly mobile" as a result of job training and English-language skills. He also suggested the occurrence of a "leveling and democratization of the family" from its former patriarchal form, due to the experience of family labor in the fields and the "competitive-utilitarian urban system." Yet Goldner acknowledged that despite greater acculturation, schooling, and participation in electoral politics and Anglo organizations, "sons" "felt that Anglos were prejudiced about twice as often as did the 'fathers.'" As Albig had found a generation earlier, Anglo prejudice continued to hinder assimilation (Goldner 1961: 105, 107, 110).

Studies extending into the 1960s and 1970s continued to seek cultural deficiencies to account for the failure of midwestern Mexicans to assimilate. Carolyn Matthiasson, in a 1968 dissertation concerned with acculturation, asserted that "Mexican-Americans in Milwaukee tend to be very suspicious" of outsiders and social agencies (Matthiasson

1968: 7). In a 1973 study of the history of Chicago Mexicans in the 1920s, Mark Reisler, after detailing widespread prejudice and racial antipathy, concluded that "only his effort to preserve his native identity and his hope of returning to the homeland alleviated the despair of the culture of poverty" (Reisler 1973: 158).

Toward a Midwestern Chicana/o History

During the generation prior to the Chicano Movement, a handful of works of historical significance written by Mexicans in the Midwest appeared, including the unpublished but influential studies of Frank X. Paz. Born in Morelia, Michoacán, and reared in Illinois, he received a degree in engineering at the University of Illinois and was the first president of the Mexican Civic Committee in Chicago. Paz was one of the few individuals in the Midwest to adopt the term *Mexican-American* in the 1940s, which he used interchangeably with Mexican. Yet his assessment of Mexicans' Americanization was not positive. He observed that, "the status of Mexicans in Chicago is not too good if we examine it from the standpoint of the values of the American way of life" (Paz 1949: 6). He questioned the usefulness of assimilation, noting that conditions for Chicago Mexicans had not improved in the previous twenty years, even in the labor unions they had joined enthusiastically. He observed that when Mexicans complained about exclusion and lack of upward mobility, "we get the same old answers: 'well, your people are not trained,'" an excuse he considered no longer acceptable. Rhetorically, he asked, "where is the equality of opportunity? Where is the American way of life?" (Paz 1949: 8–9).

"The Mexican in Adrian," perhaps the first scholarly article in a professional historical journal written by a Mexican on Mexicans in the Midwest, appeared in 1958. Its author, Reymundo Cárdenas, addressed both identity and the Redfield paradigm. He asserted that, "many of the native born refer to themselves as Latin-Americans, Spanish, or Spanish-Americans. . . to give the impression that they are not of Indian blood." He asserted that a Mexican identity was maintained by immigrants, who scoffed at such terms. Cárdenas was more sympathetic to the notion of "folk culture," which he viewed positively and as less an impediment to improved material conditions than ill treatment by Anglo-Americans. He emphatically challenged current academic literature that addressed Mexicans as a "problem," suggesting that culture was not responsible, but rather Indian appearances, which prompted Anglo-American discrimination. Mexicans responded by resisting Anglo-American culture. Cárdenas thus concluded that ongoing immigration and discrimination helped maintain a Mexican identity in the Midwest (Cárdenas 1958: 343–49).

In the best-known historical work of the generation, *North From Mexico*, Carey McWilliams offered a socialist interpretation of the history of Mexicans in the United States. His study began with initial contact between native and European in the sixteenth century and ended in the middle of the twentieth century. In contrast to many early Chicano scholars who claimed inspiration from his text, McWilliams addressed the Midwest and stories familiar to me during my youth. He suggested that urban midwestern *colonias* could be readily distinguished from the Southwest: "the colony is strikingly similar to that of the typical 'foreign' settlement." Its boundaries were not sharply defined, as Mexicans worked and were more likely to socialize among European immigrants and their children, and racial discrimination was less visible than in the Southwest. He asserted that, "in Chicago and Detroit, Mexicans are merely another immigrant group; in the Southwest they are an indigenous people" (McWilliams 1949: 221).

McWilliams attributed the limited Mexican presence in the north at the time to economic and political factors. First, he suggested that sugar beet and southwestern agricultural employers had combined to limit Mexican workers in northern industry through legislative and administrative measurers. They did not fear that industrial employers would take workers from them, but were more concerned about a political backlash against a large Mexican presence in the north that might halt immigration, and threaten their labor supply. Second, when the federal government decided to restrict Mexican immigration at the onset of the Great Depression, he concluded, "the doors of midwestern industrial employment were closed almost as soon as they were opened," and he thought the colonias were destined to disappear (McWilliams 1949: 184–85, 221–23). Although renewed migration upset his prediction, later Chicano historians paid little attention to his interest in regional distinctions. Furthermore, only a handful of midwestern studies produced during the Chicano generation extended their chronology beyond the early 1930s, as he had done much earlier.

DENNIS N. VALDÉS

The Midwest as Chicana/o History

According to Ignacio García, the roots of Chicano historical scholarship appear in the Mexican-American generation, and can be found in the works of folklorists and a handful of historians like Carlos Castañeda. García suggested that the writers of this generation were conventional scholars who "stayed within the mainstream of their departments and their field" (I. García 1996). Although many authors were indeed conventional, others, including Castañeda, engaged in writing and political activism that set them sharply apart from their European-American peers. As a member of the League of United Latin American Citizens (LULAC), Castañeda worked with the Fair Employment Practices Commission during World War II, investigating employment discrimination against Mexican Americans while providing information for lawsuits that challenged the dominant racial order in Texas (Daniels 1991: 146–84; Perales 1948). Castañeda also contributed Mexican perspectives that countered Anglo-dominant Texas history (Castañeda 1928: 1976).

Among folklorists, Americo Paredes's scholarship was also tumbling paradigms. In addition to his better-known works on folklore, his ideas reverberated in works like a 1939 Poem, "A Sandino" (To Sandino), a tribute to early twentieth-century Nicaraguan soldier, guerrilla leader and patriot Augusto Sandino (Paredes 1980). It was an indictment of United States imperialism in Nicaragua and a challenge to contemporary hegemonic scholarship that supported views popularized by the U.S. government and military leaders, including prominent Latin American historian Charles E. Chapman of the University of California. Two years before Paredes's poem, Chapman published the influential text, *Republican Hispanic America: A History,* which depicted Sandino's actions as the "depredations of a bandit" afraid to confront the United States Marines in open battle. He further asserted that, "when roads were impassable" in the rainy seasons, Sandino would hide in the woods, while during the dry season he fled to Mexico to avoid capture. Chapman refused to acknowledge that Sandino, vastly outnumbered as he challenged the leading military power of the hemisphere, was engaged in guerrilla activities, or that he found widespread support among neighboring countries, including Mexico. He concluded that, "the intervention in Nicaragua has accomplished at least one thing, however. It has pretty well banished the fears Central

America once had of impending United States conquest . . . It merely behooves the Nicaraguans to avoid 'chronic wrongdoing'—to Europeans and Asiatics, at any rate—and their country is safe" (Chapman 1937: 270–71).

Paredes was explicit in his challenge to Chapman's view of Sandino as a bandit in the woods:

las selvas fueron tu mejor escudo,	The jungles were your best shield
alma indominable de jaguar suriano	Unconquerable soul of the southern jaguar,
todo el poder del notreamericano	All the power of the North American
ceder no quiso ni vencerte pudo.	Wanted you to yield but could not conquer you.
Empuñando el acero ya desnudo,	Clawing the now barren steel,
el mañoso sajón volvióse fuera,	the dangerous Saxon who came from far away,
quiso que la justicia enmudeciera	wanted to mute justice
y en el combate rudo	and in naked combat
tú desdeñaste el yugo, yo te canto,	you showed disdain for the yoke, I sing to you,
yo que he sufrido y he llorado tanto	I who have suffered and have cried so much
el yugo colectivo de mi raza.	For the collective yoke of my raza
Vives aún y vivirás, Sandino,	You still live and you will live, Sandino
más alla del furor del asesino	Beyond the furor of the assassin
y del fragor que ya nos amenaza.	And of the violence that still threatens us.

Ignacio García's assessment relies on cultural pluralist perspectives, which represent only one trend in contemporary scholarship, and whose current practitioners have been most interested in the middle-class "Mexican American generation." Their most prolific author, Mario García, considers the most influential activist scholar of that generation, Ernesto Galarza, a "semi-intellectual" (M. García 1989: 231). Galarza was a labor organizer and an author of books, articles, and poetry, who considered his own scholarship "action-oriented" research. His history of the bracero program, *Merchants of Labor* (1964), a harsh portrayal intent on influencing policy, was the most complete and detailed study of the era, bent on providing ammunition to influence politicians to abolish the program. Galarza's socialist writings provided an international vision and a familiarity with conditions among Mexican workers, including braceros in the Midwest. Many consider him and others who were breaking paradigms, rather than Mexican-American scholars who stayed within the mainstream, as having had the greatest influence on the subsequent generation of Chicano historians.

Another influential trend in early Chicano historical literature, internal colonialism, adopted a narrower geography and chronology, confined to the nineteenth and twentieth-century Southwest. Influenced by Robert Blauner, Albert Memmi, and other authors who had gained great popularity in the late 1960s and early 1970s, Chicano versions of internal colonialism were also influenced by McWilliams, Galarza, and by neo-Marxist authors including Oliver Cox and Frantz Fanon, who were concerned about anticolonial struggles against imperialist powers. As its proponents soon discovered, the internal colony suffered from major theoretical drawbacks, including a static approach to change over time. Historians of the Midwest found it particularly inapplicable, except in agriculture (Willson 1977). Many students of the Southwest soon discarded the internal colonial model as well, often without abandoning their early premises about chronology and geography (Almaguer 1989).

A lack of inclusiveness in the earliest consciously Chicano writings generated additional challenges. Many Chicanas, influenced by feminist authors, preferred a chronology dating from 1519, which stressed the conquest of Native American women by European men (Castañeda 1990; Menchaca 1994). In addition to its gendered reading, the date also drew attention to mestizas and mestizos, people of mixed Native American and European backgrounds, ignored by both cultural pluralist models, which emphasized Mexicans within a European immigrant viewpoint; and internal colonial models, which stressed indigenous elements. Meanwhile, postmodernists, influenced in particular by French historian Michel Foucault, added more diverse peoples and offered possibilities for addressing contemporary dilemmas stemming from historical discourse. Yet even the new writings offered few theoretical openings for Chicano geographic spaces outside the Southwest.

Midwestern Chicano historical literature frequently accepted "last of the immigrant" analogies, often with caveats, or sometimes rejected them outright without clearly suggesting alternatives. The strategy was influenced by chronology, for at least 80 percent of published historical literature on the Midwest examines the "immigrant" generation from the turn of the century to 1933.

During the highly creative 1970s, investigators focused largely on urban history in the Chicago area, highlighted by the dissertations of Ciro Sepúlveda, Francisco Arturo Rosales, and Louise Año Nuevo Kerr. Somewhat later, Zaragoza Vargas, Valerie Mendoza, and Juan García extended the geographical reach of midwestern Chicano writings. The published highlights include Vargas, *Proletarians of the North: Mexican Industrial Workers in Detroit and the Midwest, 1917–1933* (1993), focusing on immigrant workers, and Juan García's geographically broader survey based largely on writings of the Chicano generation and its predecessors, *Mexicans in the Midwest, 1900–1932* (1996).

Interpretive works adopting European immigrant analogies include Gilberto Cárdenas's tribute to Oscar Handlin's classic, *The Uprooted*, "Los Desarraigados." Cárdenas suggests that, "the predominant industrial and other manufacturing-related employment and the urban settlement of Mexican immigrants to the Midwest more closely parallel the European immigrant pattern than the earlier patterns of immigration in the Southwest." He further suggests the plausibility of a European immigrant analogy for the second generation of agricultural workers who traveled each year between Texas and northern Mexico and the Midwest: "In many respects, this seasonal labor parallels the movement of European immigrants from the Atlantic Coast to the Midwest" (Cárdenas 1976: 159–60). Meanwhile, Valerie Mendoza accepts a cultural pluralist paradigm that Mexicans sought a better life and that their desires were largely achieved, despite discrimination (Mendoza 1994). Vargas agrees that they "held expectations for a better life in the North that were shaped by the culture of consumption and new patterns of leisure activities." He also accepts the view that life was better in the Midwest than in either Mexico, where folk society was being disrupted by capitalist intrusion, or Texas, where Mexicans were compelled to accept "second-class status" (Vargas 1993: 4, 10). The authors agree that despite the hostility that Mexicans faced as newcomers, racism was less of a hindrance in the Midwest, and that they could more nearly achieve the status of Europeans.

By contrast, Arturo Rosales argues that neither European immigrant analogies nor Southwest-based models apply to the Mexican urban experience in the early-twentieth-century Midwest. European-based perspectives fail because Mexicans encountered intense patterns of discrimination and racism. Southwest-focused models are not applicable because of two factors. First, "the colonized legacy was not as acute and possibly nonexistent" in the Midwest. Second, regional origins in Mexico differed. Immigrants to the Southwest tended to come from settings closer to the border, while those who came to the Midwest originated primarily in the Mexican interior. He argued that the border people more closely approximated the "folk" culture, while those from the interior were more Hispanized and thus it was easier for them to adapt. Furthermore, he suggested, "the symbolism of the Hispanic southwest and its established Mexicano populations did not compete or mingle with the Mexican immigrant cultures in the development of the colonias" of the Midwest (Rosales 1976).

Midwestern Chicano historical scholarship addressing the twentieth century after 1933 remains limited. The most influential urban literature stems from articles by Año Nuevo Kerr, based on her dissertation. Her important article, "Mexican Chicago," challenges linear assimilationist perspectives, suggesting that assimilation appeared likely at the end of the 1930s. But it was aborted in subsequent years as a result of rising antiforeign sentiment in dominant political and popular culture as a result of World War II, the Zoot-Suit Riots, and renewed migration to Chicago, capped by "Operation Wetback" in 1954, a nationwide program aimed at mass deportation of undocumented Mexican workers (Año Nuevo Kerr 1979). In a more recent essay, Edward Escobar argues on behalf of the applicability of several features of internal colonialism in the Midwest, particularly with reference to labor, namely occupational stratification of Mexican workers, their function as a reserve labor force, and as a "buffer during times of economic distress" (Escobar 1987: 10–11).

While many former adherents of internal colonial models have abandoned them, others emphasize the importance of neocolonialism, like Américo Paredes sixty years ago, which is not incompatible with a world-system perspective (Saragoza 1987; Acuña 1988). Many scholars of the Chicano generation were influenced by the world-system analysis first popularized by Immanuel Wallerstein in an initial wave of enthusiasm in the 1970s and early 1980s, although some later abandoned it (Almaguer, 1974; *Fernand Braudel Review* 1981). World-system analysis, unlike some global models of history, considers core and periphery as symbiotic, appearing simultaneously in different contexts throughout the world. It has influenced my own writings on the Midwest.

"Perspiring Capitalists" (1981) examined international dimensions of class formation in the automobile industry. *Al Norte* and essays on agricultural workers simultaneously discussed international and regional variations in class formation and the division of labor. In the case of the twentieth-century Midwest, a core-periphery perspective suggests how hired agricultural labor became associated primarily with Mexicans, and how in a relational sense Texas has functioned as a semiperiphery between the primary source of production in the Midwest and reproduction in Mexico. World-system analysis transcends narrow political economy, as Immanuel Wallerstein has argued, offering a framework also to enhance understanding of aspects of culture and identity, suggesting that racial distinctions are a function of the axial division of labor between a core and its periphery (Wallerstein 1991).

Conclusion

From the perspectives of region, nation, and world-system, the Midwest offers challenges to Chicano historical scholarship. It demonstrates that the field cannot be examined solely within the framework of the regional history of the West or the Southwest, still a dominant approach in most current writing. Mexican communities have existed in many regions outside the Southwest for several generations, and new ones have been appearing in the Pacific Northwest, the Midwest, the Great Plains, the Southeast, and the Atlantic States. A focus on the distinctiveness of the Southwest does not enhance understanding of the links among Mexican communities in different regions of the United States and Mexico.

Consciously comparative regional perspectives on a national level counter facile generalizations, including long-popular views that conditions in one region are superior to another. In the case of the Midwest, a pervasive assumption has been that Mexicans settled there because the region offered superior opportunities to Texas and Mexico. Yet if the Midwest was so clearly superior, why did so few Mexicans remain out of the hundreds of thousands who came, and why were settled midwestern Mexicans so slow to develop a middle class? Scholars informed by international perspectives have offered promising avenues for investigation, including Robert Redfield, who addressed the dialectic between better material conditions and the disorganizing influence of the regional setting.

Features of world-system perspectives, which antedated the 1970s, offer a framework for examining many facets of Chicano history, including its place as part of Mexican history and an international framework that transcends the restricted geography of the U.S.-Mexican border. From an international framework, residents of Texas or California may justly claim to be more deeply rooted as Chicanas and Chicanos, while midwesterners are more Mexican. As Norman Humphrey, Reymundo Cárdenas, and others observed in earlier generations, midwestern Mexicans were more likely to identify themselves as Mexicana, Mexicano, or Mexican than Mexicans elsewhere, and those terms continue to be the most popular self-identifiers in the region (Davalos 1993).

International perspectives, including the world-system, offer opportunities to examine the intersection of gender, class, and race. A Chicana challenge to male-centered perspectives that opens the field symbolically in 1519 with the birth of mestizas, as well as mestizos, may not go far enough, for it cannot account for the African roots of people of Mexican background. A world-system perspective, which would not negate the importance of 1519, places it within the context of the "long" sixteenth century (1450–1650), an early phase of capitalist expansion that linked peoples of Europe, Asia, Africa, and the Americas into relationships of inequality distinguished along axes of geography, labor, and gender.

A world-system approach also permits comparisons of different types of colonial relations in historical context. The territories that became the United States and Mexico were political colonies from the time of European conquest until the late-eighteenth and early-nineteenth centuries, respectively. With political independence, less formal neocolonial features continued, as the European core was losing its dominance. The U.S. conquest of Mexico in the mid-nineteenth century marked an important shift in the direction of economic and political power between the two countries. In the late-nineteenth century, the United States, rather than England or France, gained political sway and economic domination. Capitalists from the United States first hired Mexicans to work on the railroads, in mining, and in agriculture, not in the United States but in Mexico. Soon employers including the Hearsts, the Guggenheims, and the Santa Fe railroad tapped labor sources with which they were familiar in Mexico to work in the Southwestern United States. Other employers followed the railroads into the Mexican interior to intensify their search for labor, a logical choice given the availability of transportation, dense populations, and an available labor reserve. From the early years of the twentieth century the scale of international labor migration expanded and contracted in response to local, regional, and international factors.

Henry Ford carried the relationship between the two countries a step farther in automobile manufacturing in Mexico and elsewhere around the time of World War I. He hired Mexican students to help him establish a global industrial empire by training them in Detroit, where they had slim possibilities of achieving a status equivalent to what they had in Mexico. The Ford experience further demonstrates the limited applicability of assimilationist models and enhances an understanding of why midwestern Mexicans were so slow to achieve upward social mobility. But his project lured Mexicans as industrial workers, who were an expendable labor force for employers in the core of the world economy, as evidenced during the Great Depression. During World War II, the network of migration was renewed, and it expanded rapidly but unevenly in the second half of the twentieth century. In contemporary history, nation-based models claim that Mexican labor migration has caused declining wages among U.S. workers. If applied to Mexico a similar nation-based model would predict that rapid outmigration should contribute to increasing wages in Mexico. Yet relative and absolute wages of Mexican workers in both countries have declined in recent decades. Meanwhile the increasingly racialized portrayals of Mexicans reflect demographic growth and geographic extension throughout the United States, trends paralleled elsewhere in the contemporary world.

As current investigations in the new Chicana/o history examine geography, chronology, and other issues of interest, they simultaneously challenge, modify, and adapt established methodologies and perspectives. It is important that they not be confined solely to following the latest trends and ideas. Investigators as diverse as Manuel Gamio, Paul Taylor, Reymundo Cárdenas, and Américo Paredes were writing about Mexicans in regional, national, and international contexts long before the conscious articulation of the field, and such predecessors can offer new insights and understandings in the field.

References

Abbott, Edith. 1938. *The Tenements of Chicago 1908–1935*. Chicago: University of Chicago Press.

Acuña, Rodolfo. 1972. *Occupied America: The Chicano Struggle Toward Liberation*. New York: Harper and Row.

———. 1988. *Occupied America: A History of Chicanos.* 3d. ed. New York: Harper and Row.

Albig, William. 1930. "Opinions Concerning Unskilled Mexican Immigrants." *Sociology and Social Research* 15:62–72.

Almaguer, Tomás. 1974. "Historical Notes on Chicano Oppression: The Dialectics of Racial and Class Domination in North America." *Aztlán* 5 (spring and fall): 27–56.

———. 1989. "Ideological Distortions in Recent Chicano Historiography: The Internal Colonial Model and the Chicano Historical Interpretation." *Aztlán* 18.

Anderson, Esther S. 1925. "The Beet Sugar Industry of Nebraska as a Response to Geographic Environment." *Economic Geography* 1 (October): 372–86.

Año Nuevo Kerr, Louise. 1976. "The Chicano Experience in Chicago, 1920–1970." Ph. D. diss., University of Illinois at Chicago.

———. 1979. "Mexican Chicago: Chicano Assimilation Aborted, 1939–1954." In *The Ethnic Frontier: Essays in the History of Group Survival in Chicago and the Midwest,* Melvin G. Holli and Peter d'A. Jones, eds. 293–328. Grand Rapids: William B. Eerdmans.

Badillo, David A. 1995. "The Catholic Church and the Making of Mexican-American Parish Communities in the Midwest." In *Mexican Americans and the Catholic Church 1900–1965,* Jay P. Dolan and Gilberto M. Hinojosa, eds. 239–87. Vol. 1 of the *Notre Dame History of Hispanic Catholics in the U.S.* Notre Dame, Ind.: University of Notre Dame Press.

Barrera, Mario. 1979. *Race and Class in the Southwest: A Theory of Racial Inequality*. Notre Dame, Ind.: University of Notre Dame Press.

Bauer, Edward Jackson. 1938. "Delinquency Among Mexican Boys in South Chicago." Masters thesis, University of Chicago.

Betten, Neil, and Raymond A. Mohl. 1973. "From Discrimination to Repatriation: Mexican Life in Gary, Indiana, During the Great Depression." *Pacific Historical Review* 42 (August): 370–88.

Caine, Terry Allen. 1971. "Social Life in a Mexican-American Community: Social Class or Ethnic Concept." Masters thesis, University of Minnesota.

Camblon, Ruth S. 1926. "Mexicans in Chicago." *The Family* 7 (November): 207–11.

Cárdenas, Gilberto. 1976. "Los Desarraigados: Chicanos in the Midwestern Region of the United States." *Aztlán* 7 (summer): 153–86.

Cárdenas, Reymundo. 1958. "The Mexican in Adrian." *Michigan History* 42 (fall): 343–52.

Carlson, Alvar W. 1975. "The Settling Process of Mexican-Americans in Northwestern Ohio." *Journal of Mexican-American History* 5: 24–42.

———. 1976. "Specialty Agriculture and Migrant Laborers in Northwestern Ohio," *Journal of Geography* 75 (May): 292–310.

Castañeda, Carlos. 1928. *The Mexican Side of the Texas Revolution*. Dallas: P. L. Turner.

———. 1976. *Our Catholic Heritage in Texas*. New York: Arno.

Chapman, Charles E. 1937. *Republican Hispanic America: A History*. New York: Macmillan.

Daniels, Clete. 1991. *Chicano Workers and the Politics of Fairness: The FEPC in the Southwest, 1941–1945*. Austin: University of Texas Press.

Davalos, Karen Mary. 1993. "Ethnic Identity among Mexican and Mexican American Women in Chicago, 1920–1991." Ph. D. diss., Yale University.

Delgado, Anthony. 1978. "Mexican Immigration to the Hull House and 18th Street Community Areas of Chicago, 1910–1960." Masters thesis, University of Texas at Austin.

DeVillar, María Lourdes. 1989. "From Sojourners to Settlers: The Experience of Undocumented Migrants in Chicago." Ph. D. diss., Indiana University.

Escobar, Edward J. 1987. "The Forging of a Community." In *Forging a Community: The Latino Experience in Northwest Indiana, 1919–1975*, ed. by James R. Lane and Edward J. Escobar, 3–24. Chicago: Cattails Press.

Estrada, Leobardo F. 1976. "A Demographic Comparison of the Mexican Origin Population in the Midwest and Southwest." *Aztlán* 7 (summer): 203–34.

Faught, Jim D. 1976. "Chicanos in a Medium-Sized City: Demographic and Socioeconomic Characteristics." *Aztlán* 7 (summer): 307–26.

Felter, Eunice. 1941. "The Social Adaptation of the Mexican Communities in the Chicago Area." Masters thesis, University of Chicago.

Fernand Braudel Review. 1981. Special issue focusing on Chicano History. 4: 453–636.

Flores, Edmundo. 1945. "Mexican Migratory Workers in Wisconsin: A Study of Some Aspects of the War Food Administration Program for the Use of Mexican Agricultural Workers during 1945 in the State of Wisconsin." Masters thesis, University of Wisconsin.

Galarza, Ernesto. 1964. *Merchants of Labor: The Mexican Bracero Story*. Charlotte N.C.: McNally and Loftin.

Gamio, Manuel. 1930. *Mexican Immigration to the United States: A Study of Human Migration and Adjustment*. Chicago: University of Chicago Press.

———. 1931. *The Mexican Immigrant: His Life Story*. Chicago: University of Chicago Press.

García, Ignacio. 1996. "Juncture in the Road: Chicano Studies since 'El Plan de Santa Bárbara.'" In: David Maciel and Isidro Ortiz, eds. *Chicanas/Chicanos at the Crossroads.*

García, Juan R. 1976. "History of Chicanos in Chicago Heights." *Aztlán* 7 (summer): 291–306.

———. *Mexicans in the Midwest 1900–1932.* 1996. Tucson: University of Arizona Press.

———. 1982. "Midwest Mexicanos in the 1920s: Issues, Questions, and Directions." *Social Science Journal* 19 (April): 89–99.

García, Mario T. 1989. *Mexican Americans: Leadership, Ideology and Identity, 1930–1960.* New Haven Conn.: Yale University Press.

Goldner, Norman S. 1960. "The Mexican in the Northern Urban Area: A Comparison of Two Generations." Masters thesis, University of Minnesota.

———. 1961. "The Mexican in a Northern Urban Area: A Profile of an Ethnic Community." *Proceedings of the Minnesota Academy of Sciences* 29: 102–11.

González, Gilbert G., and Raúl Fernández. 1994. "Chicano History: Transcending Cultural Models." *Pacific Historical Review* 63, no. 4 (November): 469–97.

Griswold del Castillo, Richard. 1997. "Recent Writings on Chicana/o History." Presented at NACCS National Conference, Sacramento, California, April.

Gutiérrez, David. 1993. "Significant to Whom?: Mexican Americans and the History of the American West." *Western Historical Quarterly* 24, no. 4. (November): 519–39.

Hendrickson, Kent. 1964. "The Sugar-Beet Laborer and the Federal Government: An Episode in the History of the Great Plains in the 1930s." *Great Plains Journal* 3 (spring): 44–59.

Hoffman, Abraham. 1973. "Chicano History: Problems and Potentialities." *Journal of Mexican-American History* 1 (spring 1973): 6–12.

Horowitz, Ruth. 1983. *Honor and the American Dream: Culture and Identity in a Chicano Community.* New Brunswick, N.J.: Rutgers University Press.

Huber, Peter John. 1967. "Migratory Agricultural Workers in Wisconsin." Masters thesis, University of Wisconsin.

Humphrey, Norman D. 1943. "The Mexican Peasant in Detroit." Ph.D. diss., University of Michigan.

———. 1944. "The Detroit Mexican Immigrant and Naturalization." *Social Forces* 22 (March): 332–35.

———. 1946. "The Housing and Household Practices of Detroit Mexicans." *Social Forces* 24 (May): 433–37.

Jones, Anita Edgar. 1928. "Mexican Colonies in Chicago." *Social Services Review* 2 (December): 579–97.

———. 1928. "Conditions Surrounding Mexicans in Chicago." Masters thesis, University of Chicago, 1928. Reprint, San Francisco: R&E Research Associates.

Kanellos, Nicolas. 1976. "Fifty Years of Theater in the Latino Communities of Northwest Indiana." *Aztlán* 7 (summer): 255–65.

Kiser, George C., and David Silverman. 1973. "Mexican Repatriation during the Great Depression." *Journal of Mexican American History* 3: 139–64.

Koch, Elmer Cornelius. 1927. "The Mexican Laborer in the Sugar Beet Fields of the United States." Ph. D. diss., University of Illinois.

Laird, Judith A. 1975. "Argentine, Kansas: The Evolution of a Mexican-American Community, 1905–1940." Ph. D. diss., University of Kansas.

Lambert, Louisa. 1935. "Tank Town: Mexicans in Minnesota." *Hamline Piper* (May): 24–31.

Leitman, Spencer. 1974. "Exile and Union in Indiana Harbor: Los Obreros Católicos 'San José' and *El Amigo del Hogar*, 1925–1930." *Revista Chicano Riqueña* 2: 50–57.

López y Rivas, Gilberto. 1973. *The Chicanos: Life and Struggles of the Mexican Minority in the United States*. New York: Monthly Review Press.

———. 1979. *Conquest and Resistance: The Origins of the Chicano National Minority*. Palo Alto, Calif.: R&E Research Associates.

Marx, Karl. 1972. *On the American Civil War*. Edited and translated by Saul K. Padover. New York: McGraw-Hill.

Matthiasson, Carolyn Weesner. 1972. "Acculturation of Mexican-Americans in a Midwestern City." Ph.D. diss., Cornell University.

McWilliams, Carey. 1949. *North From Mexico: The Spanish-Speaking People of the United States*. Boston: J. B. Lippincott Company.

Meier, Matt, and Feliciano Rivera. 1972. *The Chicanos: A History of Mexican Americans*. New York: Hill and Wang.

Mendoza, Valerie M. 1994. "They Came to Kansas Searching For a Better Life." *Kansas Quarterly* 25, no.2: 97–106.

Mirandé, Alfredo. 1985. *The Chicano Experience*. Notre Dame, Ind.: University of Notre Dame Press.

Oppenheimer, Robert. 1985. "Acculturation or Assimilation: Mexican Immigrants in Kansas, 1900 to World War II." *Western Historical Quarterly* 15: 429–48.

Paredes, Americo. 1980. "A Sandino." (1939). In: *Canto al Pueblo*. Houston: Arte Publico Press.

Paz, Frank X. 1949. "Status of the Mexican American in Chicago." In *Report of the Conference on the Mexican American in Chicago*, 6–12. Chicago: Community Relations Service.

Perales, Alfonso. 1948. *Are We Good Neighbors?* San Antonio, Tex.: Artes Gráficas.

Pierce, Lorraine Esterly. 1971. "St. Paul's Lower West Side." Masters thesis, University of Minnesota.

———. 1974. "Mexican Americans on St. Paul's Lower West Side." *Journal of Mexican American History* 4: 1–18.

Redfield, Robert. 1929. "The Antecedents of Mexican Immigration to the United States." *American Journal of Sociology*, 35 (November): 433–38.

———. 1930. *Tepotzlán: A Mexican Village*. Chicago: University of Chicago Press.

Reisler, Mark. 1973. "The Mexican Immigrant in the Chicago Area during the 1920s." *Journal of* the *Illinois State Historical Society* 66 (summer): 144–58.

———.1976. *By the Sweat of Their Brow: Mexican Immigrant Labor in the United States, 1900 to 1940.* Westport Conn.: Greenwood Press.

Ríos-Bustamante, Antonio. 1993. *Regions of La Raza: Changing Interpretations of Mexican Regional History and Culture*. Encinco, Calif.: Floricanto Press.

Rogers, Mary Helen. 1952. "The Role of Our Lady of Guadalupe Parish in the Adjustment of the Mexican Community to Life in the Indiana Harbor Area." Masters thesis, Loyola University of Chicago.

Rojo, Emilia Angela. 1980. "Between Two Cultures: A Phenomenological Participatory Investigation of the Enduring Struggle of the Mexican-American Community." Ph.D. diss., University of Michigan.

Rosales, Francisco Arturo. 1976. "Mexicanos in Indiana Harbor during the 1920s: Prosperity and Depression." *Revista Chicano-Riqueña* 4 (fall): 88–98.

———. 1978. "Mexican Immigration to the Urban Midwest during the 1920s." Ph.D. diss., Indiana University.

———. 1976b. "The Regional Origins of Mexicano Immigrants to Chicago during the 1920s." *Aztlán* 7 (summer): 187–201.

———. 1989. "Mexicans, Interethnic Violence, and Crime in the Chicago Area during the 1920s and 1930s: The Struggle to Achieve Ethnic Consciousness." *Perspectives in Mexican American Studies* 2: 59–97.

Rosales, Francisco Arturo, and Daniel T. Simon. 1976c. "Chicano Steel Workers and Unionism in the Midwest, 1919–1945." *Aztlán* 7 (summer): 267–75.

———. 1981. "Mexican Immigrant Experience in the Urban Midwest: East Chicago, Indiana, 1919–1945." *Indiana Magazine of History* 72 (December): 333–57.

Rutter, Larry G. 1972. "Mexican Americans in Kansas: A Survey and Social Mobility Study, 1900–1970." Masters thesis, Kansas State University.

Salas, Gumecindo, and Isabel Salas. 1972. "The Mexican Community of Detroit." In *La Causa Chicana*, 161–78. New York: Family Service Association of America.

Samora, Julián, and Richard A. Lamanna. 1967. *Mexican-Americans in a Midwest Metropolis: A Study of East Chicago*. Los Angeles: Graduate School of Business, University of California.

Santillán, Richard. 1989. "Rosita the Riveter: Midwest Mexican American Women During World War II, 1941–1945." *Perspectives in Mexican American Studies* 2:115–47.

———. 1995. "Midwestern Mexican American Women and the Struggle for Gender Equality: A Historical Overview, 1920s–1960s." *Perspectives in Mexican American Studies* 5:79–119.

Saragoza, Alex. 1987. "The Significance of Recent Chicano-Related Historical Writings: An Appraisal." *Ethnic Affairs* 1 (fall): 24–62.

Sepúlveda, Ciro. 1976. "La Colonia del Harbor: A History of Mexicanos in East Chicago, Indiana, 1919–1932." Ph. D. diss., University of Notre Dame.

———. 1976b. "Research Note: Una Colonia de Obreros: East Chicago, Indiana." *Aztlán* 7 (summer): 327–36.

———. 1976c. "The Origins of the Urban Colonias in the Midwest, 1910–1930." *Revista Chicano-Riqueña* 4 (fall): 99–109.

Simon, Daniel T. 1974. "Mexican Repatriation in East Chicago, Indiana." *Journal of Ethnic Studies* 2 (summer): 11–23.

Smith, Michael M. 1980. *The Mexicans in Oklahoma*. Norman: University of Oklahoma Press.

———. 1981. "Beyond the Borderlands: Mexican Labor in the Central Plains, 1900–1930." *Great Plains Quarterly* 1 (fall): 239–51.

———. 1989. "Mexicans in Kansas City: The First Generation, 1900–1920." *Perspectives in Mexican American Studies* 2: 29–57.

Stilgenbauer, F. A. 1927. "The Michigan Sugar Beet Industry." *Economic Geography* 3 (October): 486–506.

Sullenger, T. Earl. 1924. "The Mexican Population of Omaha." *Journal of Applied Sociology* 8 (May-June): 289–93.

———. 1935. "Ethnic Assimilation in Omaha." *Sociology and Social Research* 19 (July-August): 545–54.

Taylor, Paul S. 1931. *Mexican Labor in the United States: Bethlehem, Pennsylvania*. University of California Publications in Economics, vol. 7, num. 1. Berkeley: University of California Press.

———. 1932. *Mexican Labor in the United States: Chicago and the Calumet Region*. University of California Publications in Economics vol. 7, num. 2. Berkeley: University of California Press.

United States. Congress. House. 1927. "Our Present Immigration Policy Should Be Upheld." 69th Cong. 2d sess. *Congressional Record,* 18 January: 1904.

Valdés, Dennis Nodín. 1981. "Perspiring Capitalists: Latinos and the Henry Ford Service School, 1918–1928." *Aztlán* 12 (autumn): 227–39.

———. 1989. "The New Northern Borderlands: An Overview of Midwestern Chicano History." *Perspectives in Mexican American Studies* 2:1–28.

———. 1991. *Al Norte: Agricultural Workers in the Great Lakes Region, 1917–1970.* Austin: University of Texas Press.

Vargas, Zaragoza. 1993. *Proletarians of the North: Mexican Industrial Workers in Detroit and the Midwest, 1917–1933.* Berkeley: University of California Press.

Veness, April Renee. 1984. "'But It's Not Supposed to Feel Like Home': Ethnicity and Place on the West Side of St. Paul." Ph. D. diss., University of Minnesota.

Vigil, James Diego. 1980. *From Indians to Chicanos: A Sociocultural History.* St. Louis: C. V. Mosby.

Wallerstein, Immanuel. 1991. "Culture as the Ideological Battleground of the Modern World-System," In *Race, Nation, Class: Ambiguous Identities,* Etienne Balibar and Immanuel Wallerstein, eds., 31–55. New York: Verso.

Weber, David Stafford. 1982. "Anglo Views of the Mexican Immigrant: Popular Perceptions and Neighborhood Realities in Chicago, 1900–1940." Ph. D. diss., Ohio State University.

West, Stanley A. 1975. "The Mexican Aztec Society: A Mexican-American Voluntary Association in Diachronic Perspective." Ph. D. diss., Syracuse University.

Willson, Kay Diekman. 1977. "The Historical Development of Migrant Labor in Michigan Agriculture." Masters thesis, Michigan State University.

CHAPTER 6

STATE OF THE DISCIPLINE: CHICANO HISTORY

Louise Año Nuevo Kerr

Brief Survey of the Last Twenty Years

Prior to the 1960s, little research had been done on the history of Mexicans in the United States—or on any other aspect of the Mexican experience. Few scholars had been trained; archives were scanty, and those that existed had not been catalogued; no resources were available to support travel or other research costs; and faculty positions for professors interested in studying or teaching about Mexicans were rare. With the Chicano Movement, however, came a commitment on the part of young Chicanos to the study of Mexican Americans and the inclusion of them in curricula across the spectrum of higher education, including history.

During the 1970s, the National Council of Chicanos in Higher Education secured funding from the Ford Foundation for dissertation support for Chicano graduate students. Their work simultaneously stimulated archival efforts to salvage, inventory, and make usable long-languishing document collections, like the Paul Taylor and the Manuel Gamio Papers at the Bancroft Library of the University of California at Berkeley, collections at the newly-created Chicano Research Library at UCLA, and the Midwest collection spearheaded at the University of Notre Dame.

The confluence of available sources, more funding, and eager scholars produced an impressive array of historical research. New studies were completed on the early history of Mexican Californians, New Mexicans, and nineteenth-century Texans. These studies refined understandings we had gained from Carey McWilliams's *North from Mexico*, published originally in 1949.[1] The study of the urban history of Mexicans in the United

States was also a large beneficiary of those events. Several studies of Mexican immigration and settlement in early-twentieth-century Los Angeles, El Paso, San Antonio, and Chicago documented the similarities as well as the differences Mexicans encountered as they urbanized.[2] These studies noted the ways that Mexican immigrants followed the path and patterns of earlier European and African-American migration to cities. Yet they also chronicled the uniqueness of barrio formation in areas that had been originally Mexican. They told us a lot about local community institutions and organizations; intraethnic conflicts, as well as accomplishments; work experiences; and demographic change, especially during the 1920s.

Other topics that received special attention included the history of farm and industrial labor in the Midwest, as well as the southwest; women cannery workers; bracero contract labor; the Chicano Movement of the late 1960s and early 1970s; police-community relations; and repatriation during the Great Depression.[3] Additional articles and books were published which told us much about steelworkers and domestic workers, families and migration, and Mexican consulates and American labor unions.[4]

This was a good beginning. In only a decade at least a dozen colleges and universities had started Chicano studies programs, hiring Chicano historians along with Chicano social scientists, literary critics, writers, and artists. At least another dozen history departments had opened positions in Chicano and Chicana history by the mid-1980s. Most of these faculty members would gain tenure in their respective departments and programs and become well established in their disciplines.

A consortium of Chicano and Puerto Rican studies was formed by some of these professors in the Inter-University Program, which, funded once again by the Ford Foundation, supported an emerging Latino research agenda by providing some support to specific projects and a few specific scholars. UCLA, Stanford, the University of Texas, and the City College of New York formed the nucleus of a collaboration that successfully encouraged interdisciplinary and interuniversity investigation.

Where We Are Now

Despite expanded financial support, however, the number of Chicano historians had become more or less static by the 1980s. The pioneers aged and were only very slowly joined by younger colleagues. Not many graduate students were entering the field. What was happening in Chicano studies mirrored, in many respects, the state of higher education as a whole, especially the growing attacks on affirmative action and multicultural education that universities and colleges were receiving from Ronald Reagan and the political Right. Still, in recent years we have learned a great deal about the Mexican-American political generation and, more generally, about Mexicans during and after World War II.

Now, despite a changing climate, there are signs that a new generation of graduate students is rising, with interests in community histories ranging from new studies of Los Angeles to original looks at rural Nebraska, and to innovative peeks at Mexican life in Chicago during World War II. Others have shown an interest in such cultural topics as music, film, poetry, and literature, and the celebration of rites of passage from adolescence to adulthood. They, too, are slowly entering the Academy.

This has happened in part because in recent years, some traditional archival depositories have shown an interest in the recovery and preservation of documents relating to significant local as well as national events—like the Bloody Christmas episode referred to in the movie *L.A. Confidential*—or to people like Emma Tenayuca who are important to the history of Mexicans in the United States. Besides collecting statistical data sets, government documents, and other pubic records, libraries and special collections have made an effort to obtain and preserve oral history collections derived from the work of previous scholars and from specially commissioned bids to help with projects jointly sponsored by scholars and local historical societies and museums. In addition, personal records from a variety of local Mexican community members have increasingly been assembled and collected. The internet has made historical sources much more widely known and accessible. These preservation efforts, along with those of Chicano and Latino research centers around the country, have begun to make historical research easier and more rewarding.

The state of support for Chicano and Latino research—fellowships, dissertation support, seminars—is in flux. In California, the historic home of Chicano studies, faculty, and research, support for affirmative action has been withdrawn. This threatens to slow the flow of students eligible for graduate study and the support for these students. Faculty have retired in record numbers, but often they have not been replaced, making the addition of Chicano faculty problematic—whether they are studying traditional areas like French or English history or more contemporary Chicano history. It will be difficult for such scholars to become eligible for hiring in the new competitive job markets.

At the same time, there is evidence than many institutions—particularly private universities and colleges in the Midwest and East—are serious in their wish to add Chicano history to their curricula and, when possible, to add Chicanos and Chicanas to their faculty. Some of them still provide graduate student support for travel, archival searches, and dissertation research. For many untenured faculty, research stipends, protection from undue committee work, and sabbaticals spell the difference in their quest for tenure. The Rockefeller Foundation, which provided funds in the 1980s, has ended some of its support. The National Endowment for the Humanities, which has had a spotty record with respect to support of projects in Chicano history, has seen its own support decline in recent years and cannot be counted on for future funding.

This is a transitional period. Some historians are being well supported in their work; some graduate students will be able to complete their work on time and with great success. There are still some positions to be filled. But these are exceptions to the rule.

It is clear that the number of faculty mentors is limited. Few departments will try to fill more than one position in Chicano or Chicana history, making future appointments uncertain. In fact, many departments will try to fill the need for Chicano historians with untrained adjunct or part-time faculty. And while more research collections have been assembled in recent years, the range of their documents is still limited in a way that confines research to some of the more well traveled paths.

What Needs to Be Done

Planning for the future requires that thought be given not only to important areas of research yet to be done, but also to some of the means by which that research might be accomplished under the new circumstances in which we find ourselves. This assumes that the collection of important data and new sources of support for research on the history of Chicanos (and more generally Latinos) will continue.

As for research still needed, many community studies have yet to be undertaken and will be important to any new synthesis of Chicano history. Even most community studies already completed—about Los Angeles, El Paso, San Antonio, and Santa Barbara—need to take into account migration and settlement since 1960, since that is when the majority of Mexican immigrants arrived in the United States. In the last generation and a half, migration patterns have, in many instances, altered in response to fundamental and global economic shifts away from industry and toward service economies; away from either farms or central cities to suburbs and edge cities. Some recent studies have focused on Mexican migration from metropolis to outlying small town industrial centers. More studies like this should tell us a great deal about the latest migration generation and how it compares to those who came earlier.

Similarly, recent transnational research has been undertaken on new patterns of migration and settlement, and on cultural transfer between Mexican cities, towns, and villages and their American urban, suburban, and rural counterparts. For example, investigations into the rapid dissemination of and change in music forms and clothing can tell us a great deal about how change takes place over time. We know and have heard about the re-creation of the small towns of Michoacan or Guanajuato in suburban American apartment complexes. What does this mean for the sojourners on their return to Mexico? What about the Oaxacan immigrants who have found their way to Orange County? Many of them do not speak either Spanish or English, but rather the language of the ancient Zapotec. How do their lives change, and how do we change along with them?

Studies like these, individually and collectively, will help us compare representations of Mexicans across time as well as across space. For example, while migration theorists have told us a great deal about the migrants' universal characteristics, there is still much to be learned about immigration and emigration as a specific place and moment in time. Can this research help us measure, in a concrete way, characteristics that distinguished the first migration generation of the twentieth century from the most recent immigrants? What can these new studies tell us about the nature of leadership in the new environment, as compared with the 1920s, and about community development as well as sustenance in the 1960s, 1970s, and 1980s? And while we have some knowledge of rural migrant farmers, farm workers, and cannery workers, there has not yet been much work done on those who have settled in places as different as Watsonville, California; Schuyler, Nebraska; Tacoma, Washington; or even Boston, Massachusetts.

While much of this research will focus on economic factors, such as labor markets, entrepreneurialism, and income distribution, more work should be done on political life in Mexican-American settlements and communities since the Chicano Movement. There are now elected Chicano officials at the local and school board level as well as at the state and federal levels. How has this been accomplished? What has been the national as well as local significance of organizations such as the United Neighborhood Organizations, the Southwest and Midwest/Northeast Voter Registration Projects, and the Mexican-American Legal Defense and Education Fund? What are the major features common to successful organizations? Why have other efforts resulted in failure? How have Mexican Americans succeeded politically in towns and cities that do not have a Mexican majority: towns like Denver, Colorado, and Hutchinson, Kansas, which have elected Mexican-American mayors. What can all of these stories tell us about being "American" or about being Mexican or Mexican American?

Work on the development of important other local and national institutions has only recently begun. What do we know about the evolution of faith among Mexican Catholics or even Mexican converts to Protestantism? How has religion affected the way communities develop, or their definitions of themselves? What about the schools? In the late 1960s young Chicanos throughout the country participated in a movement to change schools, so that they could have better opportunities. There were the famous "blowouts" in Los Angeles, but there were also activities in Denver and south Texas, as well as in Chicago, where a decrepit old school in Mexican-American Pilsen neighborhood was replaced with the new Benito Juarez High School—but only with the active pressure of the community. Nevertheless, schools in these places, particularly in urban settings, seem to have taken a backward step in the last thirty years, with even more students dropping out of high school and proportionately fewer reaching college. How can they become historians if they don't finish high school, much less college?

At the same time there has been a mushrooming of organizations in support of Latino and Mexican professionals: for example, the Hispanic Bar Association, the Society for Hispanics in the Engineering Profession, and the National Association of Latino Elected Officials.

Each has attempted to meld the need for individual professional advancement with recognition of dependence on the group as a whole. How have these organizations formed, sustained themselves, and advanced? Have they changed much over time? How does a coalition of "Hispanics" or "Latinos" fare in comparison to organizations based on specific ethnicities? In fact, what has been the impact of increased immigration from Central and South America on Mexicans and Mexican Americans?

There are, of course, more focused topics yet to be covered. How has the *quinceañera*—the celebration marking a young woman's fifteenth birthday and coming of age—changed over time? In some places a debutante cotillion has replaced it, with some changes in its religious as well as social significance. Has the military changed in importance over time in the role it plays in the advancement of young people? If so, how? If not, why not? I recently met a young naval officer who had advanced through his career because of his bilingual facility, first as a translator of Spanish, to language school for training in Chinese and Russian, and finally to work as a cryptographer in national security—at least one instance in which bilingualism has been perceived as a distinct asset.

While institutional history is important and still very much needed, there are dozens, if not hundreds, of biographies—individual and sometimes group portraits—that would be not only inherently important and interesting, but of further value in helping us to understand events and the way they have evolved. The stories of some of the more prominent members of the community have already been taken on: Congressman Edward Roybal of Los Angeles; Bert Corona, the great organizer and labor leader; Emma Tenayuca and Luisa Moreno, labor leaders in their own right; Cesar Chavez and Jose Angel Gutierrez. But there are individuals in every community who have provided important leadership, and there are great stories to be told, like that of Hero Street in Silvis, Illinois, where a large group of young Mexican-American men went off to World War II, never to return.

As my students have discovered, some of the best stories are those told by parents and grandparents, seemingly ordinary people who have had extraordinary experiences and who have survived travail in the face of tremendous obstacles, usually unheralded and without fanfare, but with great importance to our collective history. What has been the story of childhood among Mexicans and Mexican Americans? How has it changed over time? And what about senior citizens? How have they fared?

Finally, there is an overriding theme that needs to be pursued whenever and however possible—the stories of women and the individual and collective contributions they have made to our history and the difference they have made over time. This requires that the perspective of women be included in every study of migration, settlement, or organizational history. It also demands that the unique qualities of women's lives also be investigated as important. The long-lasting tapestry of Chicano history can only be complete if each of these strands is strong and completely realized.

How We Can Best Facilitate the "Making" of New History

Now, more than ever, the study of our history is important to our further development as a community. But now more than ever, public and private support for historical research is diminishing, or unstable. How can we insure that the progress that has been made will continue and increase? This conference provides one answer—by raising consciousness about the importance of history and its role in community development. More concretely, however, these and other current efforts represent the need for collaboration, cooperation, and mutual support.

The number of academic consortia supporting Mexican-American research has been increasing and should be given our blessing, not only because funding, when it is available, will more likely go to collaborations than to individuals, but also because we and our research will benefit from exchanges and interchanges with others sharing our interests in historical investigation and analysis. Collaborative consortia, like the Midwest Consortium for Latino Research, could provide support for fellowships, seminars, travel and publications subvention that can supplement—not supplant—institutional, foundational, and governmental endorsement.

More than just offering financial and collegial support, however, collaboration on the research itself offers the promise of a wider net. While it is not traditional for historians to work in teams, the science and social science models have shown that group research can sometimes very productive. For example, to study Mexicans in the rural economy, it might be important as well as useful to simultaneously study the history of rural economic development (or lack thereof) in

Michigan, Illinois, Nebraska, California, Florida, and Arizona. A team approach would enable researchers to study not just the economy but corollary cultural developments, such as gender differences, community formation, impact on various sectors, and inter- and intra-ethnic interactions. Similar group projects might be envisioned in the areas of migration research and transnational research. One additional advantage of this approach is that it also promises interdisciplinary and cross-disciplinary perspective on these issues.

The Uses and Abuses of History

None of these suggestions would prohibit traditional approaches to the study of the history of Mexican Americans. Yet they are some of the same questions that were raised almost thirty years ago, when the Chicano political movement spawned Chicano studies. Because traditionalists in the various disciplines—sociology, psychology, and economics, as well as history—did not think of research on Mexicans and Mexican Americans in the United States as "legitimate," activists felt that a new discipline needed to be developed to ensure that this new scholarship would be undertaken with the goal of including it in curricula across the university. Thus Chicano studies was born.

But Chicano studies, as envisioned by its founders, was not simply study or research for its own sake—although that clearly could be undertaken by those who wished it. The study of Mexicans and Mexican Americans was undertaken to fill the void in information that existed. The original premise was that knowledge was the key to advancement of the community: both self-knowledge and universal knowledge. The knowledge the field's founders envisioned was consciously applicable, even when not applied. The dearth of knowledge at the time required that priority be given to urgent and perceived needs. This was not so that the result of research would be altered, but in the knowledge that information was used—consciously or unconsciously—to mold understanding. Ignorance, about Mexicans, for example, entered politics in the way of inaction as well as in the deliberate strategies that were developed.

Today our knowledge is still incomplete, although it is not as sparse as it was a generation ago. But questions about knowledge—how and why it is derived, if it is gathered at all—are still relevant. While our instincts and uses of knowledge might not be the same as they were, the demands of *this* moment are not that different. We are required to have a conscious understanding of the meaning and importance of our work, however we go about it.

Conclusion

Our discussion here was made possible by idealistic but pragmatic young scholars who created a new discipline and paved the way for the study of Mexicans in the United States to be accepted by departments across the country. However we define our task, we must remember *that* history, and acknowledge its centrality to the tasks we have at hand.

So-called pure or basic research is seen as a hallmark of a free society that respects knowledge for its own sake and with the understanding that it is for the ages. We have no quarrel with that. Research on Mexicans in the United States, however, must also continue to meet the demands of the moment for information. There are not yet many doing this research, so the obligations for each of us are different and greater than those of the historians of the European Middle Ages or of the German Renaissance. Our discipline is still in formation.

Notes

1. Carey McWilliams, *North From Mexico: The Spanish Speaking People of the United States.* New ed. (Westport, Conn.: Greenwood Press/Praeger, 1990).
2. See, for example, Richard Griswold del Castillo, *The Los Angeles Barrio, 1850–1890: A Social History* (Berkeley: University of California Press, 1979); Ricardo Romo, *East Los Angeles: History of a Barrio* (Austin: University of Texas Press, 1983); Mario T. Garcia, *Desert Immigrants: The Mexicans of El Paso, 1880–1920* (New Haven, Conn.: Yale University Press, 1981); Louise Año Nuevo Kerr, "The Chicano Experience in Chicago, 1920–1970," Ph. D. diss., University of Illinois at Chicago, 1976.
3. Dennis Nodin Valdés, *Al Norte: Agricultural Workers in the Great Lakes Region, 1917–1970* (Austin: University of Texas Press, 1991); Mark Reisler, *By the Sweat of Their Brow: Mexican Immigrant Labor in the United States, 1900–1940* (Westport, Conn.: Greenwood Press, 1976); Vernon M. Briggs, Walter Fogeland, and Fred H. Schmidt. *The Chicano Worker* (Austin: University of Texas Press, 1977); Vicki L. Ruiz, *Cannery Women, Cannery Lives: Mexican Women, Unionization, and the California Food Processing Industry, 1930–1950* (Albequerque: University of New Mexico Press, 1987).
4. Francisco Balderama, *In Defense of La Raza: The Los Angeles Mexican Consulate and the Mexican Community, 1929–1936* (Tuscon: University of Arizona Press, 1982); John C. Hammerback, *A War of Words: Chicano Protest*

in the 1960's and 1970's (Westport, Conn.: Greenwood Press, 1985); Carlos Muñoz Jr., *Youth, Identity, Power: The Chicano Movement* (New York: Verso, 1989).

CHAPTER 7

CITIZEN, IMMIGRANT, AND FOREIGN WAGE WORKERS: THE CHICANA/O LABOR REFRAIN IN U.S. LABOR HISTORIOGRAPHY

Zaragosa Vargas

CHICANO HISTORIANS HAVE BEGUN to refocus their attention on the histories and experiences of Chicano and Chicana workers, who comprise two-thirds of the twenty-five million Latinos in the United States and one of America's largest and fastest growing racial minority groups. Once peripheral to the dominant concerns of American historians, the study of Chicana/o workers is emerging together with the study of America's other racial minority laboring classes as a new and vibrant area of research. The reconstruction of the everyday lives of these wage workers, their worldviews, values, and habits provides a critical assessment of the rich diversity of their experiences. Much of this history of working-class struggle and action unfolded in Texas.

Historically, Texas has been the largest contributor of Chicana/o labor to other states, and Tejano (Texas Mexican) workers have played an integral role in the regional and national economies of the United States, from the turn of the century to well into the post–World War II years. Tejanos have undergone repression, discrimination, segregation, and integration. This is the historical perspective of David Montejano's prize-winning book, *Anglos and Mexicans in the Making of Texas*.[1] Using a sociological approach to history that borrows from the world systems of Immanuel Wallerstein and the excellent studies on peasant formations by Barrington Moore Jr., Montejano attempts a sweeping and interpretative history of race relations in South Texas from the Texas Revolution of 1836 to the present.

Montejano divides this history into four periods: incorporation (1836–1900), reconstruction (1900–1920), segregation (1920–40), and integration (1940–86). During the incorporation period (1836–1900), the Texas economy was transformed from Mexican hacienda/ranching to Anglo capitalist-based agriculture and trade.[2] The loss of economic dominance that led to the political subordination and eventual proletarianization of Tejanos sets the context from which Mexican and Anglo relations would evolve along the Texas border region. In this survey of the social and economic changes that followed the Texas Revolution, Montejano has pushed back the origins and growth of a Mexican wage labor force in one important sector of the Southwest to the early nineteenth century.

The Texas economy went through expansive "reconstruction" from 1900–1920 and an attendant recomposition of the Spanish-speaking working classes took place. Responding to market conditions, Anglos inaugurated commercial farming, which soon employed vast numbers of agricultural wage laborers composed of Mexican immigrants entering the United States illegally, legally, and under government-sanctioned labor contracts. Commercial farming in Texas would be built on the backs of these Mexican workers, especially the cotton industry, which had previously relied on white sharecroppers and blacks. Through formal and informal law making, government agencies in Washington began assisting Anglo Texan farmers and cotton growers in the maintenance and control of this virtually inexhaustible supply of labor from Mexico.[3]

The context for Jim Crow in Texas was state-sponsored coercion, legal fiat, and indiscriminate violence as Anglo agricultural interests transformed, organized, and disciplined the Tejano and Mexican labor force. Montejano states that workers "escaped" from Texas by crossing back into Mexico or by migrating out of the Lone Star State. Though Montejano points out that labor repression was never complete, there is a lack of focus on the kinds of spontaneous, informal, and organized actions taken by Mexican wage laborers in South Texas to maintain control over their labor. This subject is taken up in the prize-winning book *The World of the Mexican Worker in Texas* by Emilio Zamora.[4] While Montejano has analyzed how the structural contours of the South Texas economy were shaped by the transition to American capitalism, *The World of the Mexican Worker in Texas* is the first definitive historical account of the various collective struggles that unfolded in the South Texas border region against the rise of industrial development and commercial agriculture.

Mexican unions based in fraternal organizations and mutual aid societies included both Tejanos (Texas Mexicans) and Mexican nationals. The quest for self-identity as a Mexican working class underlined the response to radical politics in South Texas. Workers belonged to the anarcho-syndicalist Partido Liberal Mexicano (PLM) or were active in radical causes initiated by the Texas Socialist Party. The PLM offered a nationalist message and a combination of trade unionism and anarchism as an answer to labor's predicament. The Texas Socialist Party attracted thousands of Mexicans who perceived their struggles for worker equality along socialist lines. The Industrial Workers of the World and the Western Federation of Miners similarly drew large numbers of Mexican workers into their ranks.

According to Zamora, an "ethic of mutuality" formed the basis for collective action and a political strategy to fight against racism in the workplace and in the larger South Texas border community. The various mutual aid societies, patriotic clubs, and the Masonic orders helped strengthen the cultural bonds between Tejanos and Mexican nationals, as well as mold the foundation of an emergent Mexican-American working-class identity.

Unfortunately, Tejana and Mexicana working women do not figure prominently in *The World of the Mexican Worker in Texas*. Industrialization, high unemployment rates, seasonal work, and the rising cost of living were forcing Mexican women into the Texas labor market. Feminists, socialists, and to a lesser extent, working-class women lent their support to the men at the grassroots level, in strikes, and in other actions against worker and racial exploitation. The integration of the history of such notable women of Texas's borderland as Jovita Idar and Sara Estela Ramírez with that of Tejano and Mexicano men would have enhanced the overall accounts of the struggle for equality and labor unity in *The World of the Mexican Worker in Texas.* Nonetheless, Zamora's book is a richly detailed and solid account of a significant moment in the early history of Mexican-American wage laborers in South Texas. It is the first comprehensive history of Chicano working-class formation in the Southwest.

By the beginning of the twenties, Mexican and Tejano workers had established and shaped a "new labor frontier" in Texas that extended into and beyond the Southwest. As the 1930s ended, a depressed agricultural economy, race segregation, and the accompanying employment barriers were pushing Tejanos out of the Lone Star State. The Agricultural Adjustment Administration eliminated hundreds of thousands of acres from cotton production. Federal land reclamation projects also forced many Mexicans off the land. Of equal importance, however, was technological displacement—the mechanization of crop production and crop harvesting. Texas led the Southwest in this mechanization of agriculture. The Tejano migrants moved from as far south as the Río Grande Valley all the way across the intervening states into the agricultural sectors of the upper Midwest, the Mountain States, and the Pacific Northwest, with branch routes extending out to states on either side of the main routes.[5]

From 1940–86, the political and economic influence of agriculture in Texas declined. Urban commercial interests now dominated, creating a new social order that was less racially segregated and politically repressive. The civil rights activism of Tejanos and Tejanas notwithstanding, large-scale legal and undocumented immigration from Mexico deeply affected class and race relations in both rural and urban Texas. Montejano's world system approach thus overlooks the impact of international and national events on Tejano-Anglo relations, the extreme poverty along the border, and the simultaneous rise of a Spanish-speaking underclass. Still, Montejano provides crucial insights into the composite dynamics of race and class in South Texas.

On the eve of World War II, Tejanos and Chicanos from New Mexico, Colorado, and Arizona were part of the exodus of American workers to cities with war-related industries, such as Los Angeles, Chicago, and Detroit, in search of high-paying defense jobs. As the leading economic and commercial center of California, Los Angeles would serve as a magnet, pulling Tejanos out of the Lone Star State, and Chicanos out of the Mountain States, and Arizona. These men and women found employment in service occupations; construction; in airplane, iron, and steel production; and in vehicle assembly. With their families, the newly arrived Chicano migrants provided the labor necessary to specialized agriculture. Yet this time, the United States was deeply divided by race. A "color line" separated racial minorities politically, socially, and economically from other Americans. Mexican Americans began organized efforts to secure their share of jobs being created through war mobilization. In the summer of 1941, A. Philip Randolph and other black leaders planned a mass march on Washington to protest discrimination in the defense industry and by the armed services. In response, President Franklin D. Roosevelt's Executive Order 8802 set up the Committee on Fair Employment Practice (FEPC). In his book *Chicano Workers and the Politics of Fairness*, Cletus Daniel argues that by calling for an end to discrimination in hiring, the FEPC tried to assure that all workers could participate fully in defense industries, without the burdens of discrimination based on race, creed, color, or national origin. In an unprecedented move, the U.S. government established equal employment as official public policy.[6]

Daniel contends that from the very beginning, President Roosevelt saw the FEPC not as a vehicle to achieve equality in the workplace, but rather as a tool to appease the growing threat by southern Democrats trying to thwart the New Deal agenda, including programs like the FEPC. Rather than pursuing an active course, the Roosevelt administration thus opted for an accommodationist approach. Moreover, public hearings on job and pay discrimination against Mexican-American workers were canceled, since the U.S. government did not want to jeopardize its Good Neighbor Policy in Latin America. As a result, the longtime and widespread employment discrimination experienced by Mexican-American workers in the Southwest was never fully addressed or challenged.

Mexican-American organizations and individuals advocated on behalf of workers seeking to gain employment in war industries and to end racist hiring policies. The work of Ernesto Galarza for the Pan American Union made the federal government aware of the plight of the Mexican-American rank and file. New Mexico Senator Dennis Chavez played an active role in the Senate subcommittee hearings on the FEPC and helped place Mexican-American workers in the war industries in his home state. In the Midwest, the Spanish Speaking People's Council of Chicago focused on fair employment in the defense industries.[7]

Embroiled in jurisdictional disputes, AFL and CIO affiliates provided little assistance to Mexican-American union organizers. The United Cannery, Agricultural, Packing, and Allied Workers of America (UCAPAWA) which became the Food, Tobacco, Agriculture, and Allied Workers of America, the militant International Union of Mine, Mill, and Smelter Workers (MMSW), and the International Longshoremen and Warehousemen Union were the exceptions. Reflective of the purge of left-led unions within the CIO and the mass blacklisting that would mark the Taft-Hartley postwar years, Mexican-American labor organizers faced red-baiting as the federal government attempted to link communism with the work of the CIO along the border and with Mexican nationals entering the United States.[8] Unfortunately, the commitment of the national CIO to civil rights for its minority and female members was not shared as a whole by the Anglo rank and file, nor did it extend to the contracts the CIO bargained and signed with employers. Along with blacks and women, Mexican Americans would pursue alone their struggle to achieve equal rights in the workplace and within the CIO unions.[9]

At this time, Chicanas donned pants, put their hair up in bandannas, and went to work in the defense plants. Chicanas performed almost every kind of job, even those previously typed "men's work." "Rosita the Riveter" became the familiar symbol of the Chicana war worker, "making history working for victory." However, like their Chicano counterparts, Chicanas faced discrimination in employment. Despite federal rules requiring equal pay for equal work, Chicanas earned about 65 percent of what men did for the same work, and along with African-American women, were confined to the worst war production jobs. This inequality notwithstanding, Chicanas gained unprecedented employment opportunities, self-esteem, and a new sense of their potential.

Daniel provides only a partial history of the struggles of Mexican Americans to gain entrance into defense work. Examination of additional FEPC files will shed light on the extent of the failure of this government body to correct the condition of inequality among Mexican-American workers during the World War II years. *Chicano Workers and the Politics of Fairness* nonetheless chronicles one important though unfamiliar chapter in the history of the Mexican-American rank and file's struggle to achieve civil rights. Scholars will want to examine the full path that Mexican-American working-class identity took during the World War II years and after.

During World War II, a short-term solution to labor shortages in agriculture led to the Bracero Program. Over the next twenty-two years, approximately five million Mexican nationals were brought into the United States for seasonal employment in agriculture, the majority working in Texas, Arizona, and California. These temporary workers thus provided American agri-business interests (as well as some railroad companies) with a cheap and abundant source of labor.

The bounty of cheap Mexican labor increased during the postwar years through the influx of undocumented Mexican workers. Northern Mexican agri-business brought large numbers of Mexicans to the border to offset the equally great numbers of Mexican workers who, drawn by the higher American wages, crossed clandestinely into the United

States. Smuggling of undocumented workers was the other factor contributing to the growing numbers of Mexican workers entering the United States illegally. About 4,300,000 undocumented Mexican workers were apprehended between 1947 and 1955.

The dynamics of state-sponsored recruitment of bracero workers are illuminated in Kitty Calavita's excellent book *Inside the State*.[10] It offers a detailed and theoretical analysis of how, over a span of twenty-three years, Bracero Program guidelines were circumvented to fully exploit the contract labor system to benefit southwestern agricultural employers. Calavita correctly asserts that the goal of the Bracero Program, developed and administered by the Immigration and Naturalization Service (INS), was to legalize and control Mexican migrant farm workers for the benefit of large-scale farmers along the U.S. border.

The growing presence of undocumented Mexican workers threatened to imperil the Bracero Program. To counter this massive flow of undocumented workers, the Department of Labor intervened and on 9 June 1954 initiated a repatriation drive code-named "Operation Wetback." Through a massive deportation drive organized by the INS, the United States repatriated about one million undocumented Mexican workers. Operation Wetback was a public relations coup for the U.S. Border Patrol. Actually, the repatriation drive institutionalized and stabilized the Bracero Program, gaining greater control over and streamlining a highly profitable farm labor system for American agribusiness.

Bracero workers were not without allies. The proindustrial union and labor-oriented Asociación Nacional México Americana (ANMA), led by longtime trade union organizer Alfredo Montoya, actively campaigned against the deportation raids. Although critical of the Bracero Program, ANMA protested the mass deportations of Mexican immigrant workers. Veteran labor activist Ernesto Galarza organized undocumented Mexican workers as part of the efforts by progressive elements of the labor movement to establish unions among farm workers. Through the Community Service Organization (CSO) and ANMA, Bert Corona played a prominent role as an organizer in the ethnic communities of working-class Los Angeles.[11]

Calavita concludes her book with a fine assessment of the strengths and weaknesses of theories of the state. To analyze the Bracero Program, Calavita opts for a "dialectical model of the state" that identifies and traces the links between structural factors and the interactions among government officials, and between these officials and "clientele" (agri-business employers). Anyone interested in the uses of state power will find *Inside the State* a convincing and original study of the intricate relationship between immigration policies and practices and contract labor in the postwar era.

In his well researched and documented book *Al Norte,* Chicano historian Dennis Valdés analyzes the history of agricultural labor in the upper Midwest.[12] This history traces how the introduction of sugar beet production in the Great Lakes region in the late-nineteenth century triggered the emergence and eventual transformation of agriculture from subsistence farming to a labor-intensive corporate industry.

Valdés presents a detailed history of farmworker resistance to exploitation formed from mutually profitable relations between corporate farms, land-grant colleges, and the government agencies that regulated and protected these workers. With the departure of the earlier European immigrants from the migrant stream to become farmers or factory workers, African Americans and Puerto Rican Americans briefly served as sources of labor. Eventually, however, Mexicans and Mexican Americans came to comprise the majority of the agricultural workforce in the northern region. By 1938, ten thousand Tejanos migrated yearly to the beet fields of the Midwest. By 1940, more than sixty thousand Tejano workers annually entered the Great Lakes region for employment in agriculture, the majority migrating to Michigan. As Valdés notes, the entry of Tejanos into midwestern cities added diversity to the extant Mexican communities, flavoring them with Tejano culture, food, and music.

Organized labor neglected and opposed the farmworkers, who as early as the 1930s established their own unions. According to Valdés, this would become a missed opportunity to link the demands of agricultural workers to those of industrial workers. In 1965, Chicano farmworkers, organized by Cesar Chavez as the United Farm Workers of America, attained union representation after nearly fifty years of unsuccessful efforts. Farmworkers would make major organizational gains during this era of social and political upheaval. The farmworker victory of Cesar Chavez inspired farm labor activism and organization in other parts of the Southwest. As Valdés explains, this union movement soon spread to the Midwest. Farmworkers in the Great Lakes once again launched a concerted union drive, which was helped significantly by the termination of the Bracero Program in 1964. The labor organizing efforts of the eighteen to twenty thousand farm workers in northwest Ohio were particularly notable. Through the Farm Labor Organizing Committee (FLOC), individual farmers signed twenty-two contracts in 1968. These attempts at unionization by FLOC came to fruition again in the 1970s. Valdés has brought attention to agricultural labor relations in the Great Lakes region, a previously neglected section of the country.

The history of Mexicans in the entire Midwest was inextricably tied to the outmigration of Tejanos from farm work toward the need for unskilled factory labor. Corporations like General Motors, Ford, Chrysler, and United States Steel hired Mexican workers for their auto plants, mills, and foundries. The seasonal and cyclical fluctuations of the diversified industrial sector of the Great Lakes region continued to determine the patterns of the migration to and from Texas. The economic changes in Texas, along with the migration of Puerto Ricans and Mexican nationals, influenced the demographic composition of the Midwest following the end of World War II. These factors inaugurated a new era in the history of Spanish-speaking people in the Midwest.

As it did for blacks, the 1960s civil rights movement raised the expectations and hopes of Chicana and Chicano workers for increased job and wage opportunities and workplace equality. Despite persistent discrimination, Chicano wage workers continued to reduce the income gap. Throughout the 1950s and 1960s, the sustained increases in the productivity of American industrial workers paid for their annual increases in real wages. Union contracts improved the standard of living for America's workers as a form of business unionism gained prominence. Persistent racial discrimination, however, prevented rank-and-file Chicanos, blacks, and women from reaching wage parity with their white male counterparts. Local union affiliates excluded minorities and women from membership or did not fully address issues of racial and gender equality in the call for democratic working-class solidarity. By the 1970s, the downward shift of the American economy was beginning to undermine the vaulted status of America's workers. The inroads in wages, offset by an upsurge in the cost of living, were occurring during a downturn in the profitability of American corporations. For the nation's auto makers, this precipitous decline coincided with the large-scale assault by the Japanese to gain control of the world car market.[13] Autoworkers responded to the loss of their livelihood and status by staging wildcat strikes, but this worker insurgency was checked by the 1974–75 recession, the nation's worst economic crisis since the Great Depression era. Unemployment among factory workers climbed to nearly 14 percent but was twice this percentage for Chicanos and other blue-collar minorities, who were often the first workers let go. The recession ushered in a new economic order, one that would have severe and long lasting implications for America's heretofore privileged wage workers. Next, deindustrialization led to the massive displacement of autoworkers. Chicano autoworkers would lose their recently won middle-class status through plant closures, downsizing, and consecutive wage concessions.[14]

In the past five years, Chicana and Chicano workers, drawing on a long tradition of struggle and using well-developed organizing strategies, have played a prominent role in the growing resistance to the employer offensive. The 1990 Justice for Janitors victory in Los Angeles, led by the progressive Service Employees International Union Local 399; the strike by Chicana and Mexicana high-tech workers in Sunnyvale, California; and the recent strike by Mexicano and Latino immigrant carpenters in southern California demonstrate that Spanish-speaking workers will organize if they believe they can hold on to their jobs. Last April, the UFW launched a major organizing campaign to rebuild the union to its membership levels of one hundred thousand achieved in the 1970s. Over thirty thousand farmworkers and their supporters marched from Delano, California, to the state capitol in Sacramento. At issue were wages, job security, benefits, and protection against toxic workplace conditions. Through the mobilization committee of the Multiracial Alliance, the mostly Central American and Mexican immigrant membership of SEIU Local 399 are waging a movement for democratic reform and greater worker participation within the local union. Indeed, Chicano and Latino workers, both citizens and recent immigrants, are leading the reemergence of rank-and-file unionism in America, a fact acknowledged by many employers, union leaders, and labor experts. According to labor journalist Kim Moody, "Far from undermining U.S. labor, Latino workers are on the front lines fighting to defend them."[15]

There has been an increase in arrests of undocumented workers. In 1990, the number of these arrests rose above one million for the first time since 1987. Undocumented immigrants are a boon for agri-business and increasingly for the industrial and service sectors of the

American economy because these fearful workers are easily exploited. For example, in the Los Angeles garment industry, 41 percent of undocumented Mexican women receive less than the legal minimum wage.[16] Yet Chicano workers continue to wage resistance against their exploitation in the workplace, the NAFTA, and against the current wave of immigrant bashing. Ignored for the most part by organized labor, Latino workers seek support from within their own ranks by creating and forming alternative labor movements. For example, through the newly emerging community-based "Worker Centers," Latino workers are organizing in the agricultural, garment, restaurant, and commercial food processing sectors. The Asociacíon de Trabajadores Latinos (Latino Workers Association), the Union de Trabajadores Agricolas Fronterizos (UTAF), La Mujer Obrera (Woman Worker), and other community-based worker centers stress worker abuse, anti-immigrant sentiment, and discrimination.[17] The strong racial-ethnic identity attached to Latino working-class consciousness will spur these minority workers to gain recognition and acceptance as Latinos, and as important members of the American working classes. Along with blacks and women, Latinos and Chicanos will continue the struggle to achieve equal rights in the workplace and within the unions.

The new directions in historical research represented by the books reviewed in this chapter focus attention on the importance of Chicano workers in American history. The process of historical revision of scholarly work is ongoing, and its beginnings can be traced back to Victor S. Clark's *Mexican Labor in the United States,* produced over eighty years ago for the U.S. Bureau of Labor Statistics.[18] Chicana/o workers share a legacy of labor exploitation and special forms of oppression. However, the many dimensions of this labor history, much of which remains unexplored, illustrate that along with common differences of race, ethnicity, and gender among American workers there are also common patterns of resistance and struggle. Chicano and non-Chicano labor scholars need to introduce methods and concepts to provide new historical perspectives and insights about workers generally slighted by American history. More important, labor historians need to relate these histories to other sets of events and issues that confront the larger American society.

Notes

1. David Montejano, *Anglos and Mexicans in the Making of Texas, 1836–1986* (Austin: University of Texas Press, 1987).
2. Migration of Mexican workers into the south Texas area was already evident by 1854. Entire Mexican villages were recruited as ranch hands by Anglo Texan cattlemen like Captain Richard King. Hubert J. Miller, "Mexican Migration to the U.S., 1900–1920: With a Focus on the Texas Río Grande Valley," *Borderlands* 7 (spring 1984): 184.
3. Gregory DeFreitas, *Inequality at Work: Hispanics in the U.S. Labor Force* (New York: Oxford University Press, 1991), 16. The border region would become a "deconstitutionalized zone" where government interest, police authority and abuse, and repression subordinated Mexicans to Anglo employers. María Jiménez, "War in the Borderlands," *Report on the Americas* 26 (July 1992): 30.
4. Emilio Zamora, *The World of the Mexican Worker in Texas* (College Station: Texas A & M University Press, 1993).
5. Mario T. García, *Mexican Americans: Leadership, Ideology, and Identity, 1930–1960* (New Haven, Conn.: Yale University Press, 1989), 176.
6. Clete Daniel, *Chicano Workers and the Politics of Fairness: The FEPC in the Southwest, 1941–1945* (Austin: University of Texas Press, 1991).
7. Juan Gómez-Quiñones, *Chicano Politics: Reality and Promise, 1940–1990* (Albuquerque, N.M.: University of New Mexico Press, 1990), 35–40.
8. García, *Mexican Americans,* 182.
9. Richard White, "It's Your Misfortune and None of My Own," in *A New History of the American West* (Norman, Ok.: University of Oklahoma Press, 1991), 592–93; Kim Moody, *An Injury to All: The Decline of American Unionism* (New York: Verso Books, 1987), 23–24.
10. Kitty Calavita, *Inside the State: The Bracero Program, Immigration, and the I.N.S.* (New York: Routledge, 1992).
11. Gómez-Quiñones, *Chicano Politics,* 51; García, *Mexican Americans,* 204–12; Mario T. García, "Working for the Union," *Mexican Studies/Estudios Mexicanos* 9 (summer 1993): 242. ANMA was dedicated to gaining civil and economic rights for Mexican Americans, and toward this end developed coalitions with other racial and ethnic minorities and with progressive organizations like the Civil Rights Congress. In light of the anticommunist hysteria and resulting domestic repression, ANMA appealed to the United Nations Commission on Human Rights to investigate the dismal plight of Mexican immigrant farm workers, and publicly opposed the Korean War conflict, U.S. support for Latin American dictatorships, and interventions in Guatemala and the Middle East. Red-baited as a subversive group, ANMA soon lost credibility.

    In the post–World War II years, farm workers faced particular problems because of the growth of the corporate farm; with investments in cattle, petroleum, and other nonagricultural goods, factory farming was twice as productive as industry. Restricting and eventually eliminating the contract system would be a greater challenge than factory farming faced by farm workers. In 1946, the National Farm Labor Union was granted a charter by the AFL and targeted the Di Giorgio Fruit Corporation ranch in California's San Joaquin Valley. Three years later, the NFLU organized a strike by over twenty thousand cotton pickers in the region. The use of bracero workers helped defeat this strike.

12. Dennis Nodin Valdés, *Al Norte: Agricultural Workers in the Great Lakes Region, 1917–1970* (Austin: University of Texas Press, 1991).
13. Moody, *An Injury to All,* 72–75; J. Holmes, "The Continental Integration of the North American Automobile Industry: From the Auto Pact to the FTA and Beyond," *Environmental and Planning* A 24 (January 1992): 99–100.
14. Moody, *An Injury to All,* 87–92.
15. Kim Moody and Mary McGinn, *Unions and Free Trade: Solidarity vs. Competition* (Detroit, Mich.: A Labor Notes Book, 1992), 41; "Immigrants Unite in the Silicon Valley," *Labor Notes* 167 (February 1993): 9; David Bacon, "Immigrant Carpenters Battle Contractors and the 'Migra,'" *Labor Notes* 195 (June 1995): 2, 14; Sue Johnson, "Farm Workers' March Kicks Off New Organizing," *Labor Notes* 183 (June 1994): 5–6; "What? The Members Want to Run the Union?" *Labor Notes* 197 (August 1995): 3–4; Moody, *An Injury to All,* 287–88.
16. Kitty Calavita, *Inside the State: The Bracero Program, Immigration, and the I. N. S.* (New York: Routledge, Chapman and Hall, 1992), 167. The Human Rights Commission in San Francisco found one garment sweatshop in which undocumented workers had not been paid for eight months and had lodged no complaints. So valuable is this cheap labor that throughout the 1970s the chambers of commerce of U.S. border cities advertised its availability in an attempt to lure industry to the area. Exploitation of sweatshop workers is endemic.
17. Mary Hollens, "Worker Centers: Organizing in Both the Workplace and Community," *Labor Notes* 186 (September 1994): 8–9; Cahti Tactaquin, "What Rights for the Undocumented?," *Report on the Americas* 26 (July 1992): 27.
18. V. S. Clark, *Mexican Labor in the United States* (Washington D.C.: Government Printing Office, 1908).

CHAPTER 8

HISTORY AND ANTHROPOLOGY: CONDUCTING CHICANO RESEARCH

Martha Menchaca

History and Anthropology

This paper examines my historical research on Chicanos and illustrates the type of historical methods used in anthropology. My approach differs from that of a historian, as my intent in conducting historical research is to understand cultural change. In this paper I plan to: first, explain what the subspecialization of history and anthropology is; second, discuss the relationship between Chicano studies and anthropology; and third, close with two examples of my research.

Within the discipline of anthropology there are four subspecializations: sociocultural anthropology, linguistics, archaeology, and physical anthropology. The study of history and anthropology comes under the subfield of sociocultural anthropology. In my view, the study of history within anthropology is associated with a more critical and reflexive academic discourse because anthropologists argue that culture must be understood from a historical perspective in order to determine how the structure of a society was formed, to identify who controls power in a community, and to discern how cultural relations have evolved. In his book entitled *Anthropologies and Histories: Essays in Culture, History, and Political Economy* (1991), William Roseberry also asserts that without studying culture from a historical perspective, the researcher may unwittingly misinterpret a people's behavior or misunderstand how a society's economy impacts the social relations of a community.

The idea of historically contextualizing an ethnography was popularized by Franz Boas, who is credited today with being the father of American anthropology (Jackson 1986). Boasian thought emphasized the importance of understanding each culture on its own terms, and part of the mission of Boasian anthropology was to give to groups that did not enjoy a sense of antiquity the equivalent of a classical past by collecting texts of myths and folklore and by preserving their artifacts. Many of his students sought to understand a society's social structure from a diachronic perspective. For a moment let me explain what the term *diachronic* is, as it is based on the concept of structure. As you know, the term *structure* refers to studying a society's formal and informal institutions. (The formal institutions include the political, economic, legal, and educational domains; the informal institutions of a society include the family, the neighborhood, and the friendship networks). By the term *diachronic*, Boasian anthropology referred to the study of the social relations of a society over time. This diachronic approach was based on the perspective that when anthropologists enter the field, the culture they observe has been influenced by past events.

Thus, my point is that when an anthropologist writes a historical ethnography, the individual examines a contemporary society from a diachronic or historical perspective. I would like to add, however, that anthropologists also conduct historical research that does not include the ethnographic component. This type of historical research focuses on archival records, yet its intent is similar to the historical ethnography, in that the researcher's goal is to understand the evolution of a society's cultural relations, and not necessarily to present a chronology of events.

Canons

There have been many historical anthropologists, and their work has been very critical of racism and the economic exploitation suffered by people living in poverty. Some of the most important works of this genre are discussed here. One of the earliest ethnographies that I have been moved by was Philleo Nash's monograph entitled *The Place of Religious Revivalism in the Formation of the Intercultural Community on Klamath Reservation* (1937). This is an account based on archives and oral histories collected from the children of Native Americans who survived the Indian extermination campaigns in California. Most of the remembrances of Nash's informants dealt with their history of survival and the nativistic religious revival movements that surfaced between

1871 and 1878. The doctrine and ritual of the Ghost Dance were used as forms of ethnic resistance and spiritual empowerment.

Classic studies within the field of history and anthropology include works by Clifford Geertz, Sidney Mintz, Marshall Sahlins, Eric Wolf, and Américo Paredes. These scholars critically propose that the interpretation of cultural symbols often necessitates historical contextualization, particularly when the subjects of study deal with interethnic relations and colonial domination. One specific historical approach employed by Eric Wolf in *Europe and the People Without History* (1982) and Sidney Mintz in *Sweetness and Power* (1986) is the application of a macroeconomic method, or what is often called the metaeconomic narrative. Within their historical approach, both authors argue that the world economy must be closely analyzed before we can understand the culture and structure of a society.

In contrast to this macroeconomic historical approach are the classic works produced by Clifford Geertz, such as his book entitled *Negara: The Theatre State in Nineteenth-Century Bali* (1980). Geertz has been highly criticized for his narrative style, in which the voices of his informants are solely filtered through his monologue. Although I concur with Geertz's critics, his narratives are excellently researched and descriptively thick. Geertz also applies a "historical particularism" approach to the study of culture. When anthropologists use this approach they do not contextualize their community study by examining the world economy. Rather, in the analysis of data anthropologists focus on the particular history, economy, and social relations of the community or region under study.

Américo Paredes has also influenced the field of history and anthropology, with his classic study *With His Pistol in His Hand* (1958). Unfortunately, it was only a few years ago that the American Anthropological Association officially recognized Dr. Paredes's contributions to the discipline of anthropology. Paredes is another anthropologist who supports the position that cultural studies need to be historically contextualized. Likewise, he has advanced methods to verify this theoretical orientation. For example, in many of Paredes's writings he has demonstrated that community histories and important events germane to Mexican Americans can be reconstituted through evidence found in archives. In particular, legal archives offer great value as informative documents. That is, judicial court records contain narratives that have documented many social injustices committed against racial minorities, and these narratives also contain the ideological rationalizations used by Anglo-Americans to justify such practices. Paredes has also demonstrated that events can be reconstituted or verified through the use of newspaper articles and by collecting oral histories.

Contemporary works

More current research conducted by historical anthropologists is voluminous. However, I consider the works of Renato Rosaldo, James Clifford, and Richard Fox to be representative of an anthropology that is more political and critical of the economic and racial inequities that exist in the societies they study. These scholars have also attempted to integrate the theoretical writings of racial minority anthropologists into their narratives, in order to begin making the discipline of anthropology a field that is not solely dominated by whites. Like Paredes, Renato Rosaldo was one of the first Mexican Americans to break into the field of anthropology and to prove to mainstream anthropologists that, "Yes, Mexican Americans have valuable and sophisticated narratives to tell." Rosaldo has numerous books and articles dealing with such topics as: social theory, multicultural education, history and society, rethinking ethnographic methods, oral history, Chicano studies, and research on MesoAmerica and the Philippines (Rosaldo 1980, 1993). In my analysis, one of Rosaldo's main contributions to anthropology has been his ongoing call to anthropologists to stop making "people of color" appear exotic—for when they are represented in such a manner, they are represented as different, inferior, and as the objectified other.

James Clifford and Richard Fox concur with Rosaldo's critique regarding issues of representation. These two anthropologists are also very critical of the field of anthropology for its insistence on representing people of color rather than allowing them to speak for themselves (Clifford 1988; Clifford and Marcus 1986; Fox 1991). The problem that currently exists is that anthropologists solely seek to represent the "other," rather than developing an academic agenda to encourage people of color to become anthropologists so that they may represent themselves. This academic practice has resulted in the social formation of a shallow discourse that exoticizes subaltern cultures. The existence of poverty, exploitative relations, and patriarchal domination in nonwhite communities have been documented excellently by anthropologists. Yet, anthropologists have done little to liberate their subjects or to make them seem less exotic (see Comaroff and Comaroff 1992; Taussig 1992). "Giving voices to the voiceless" and using polyphonic writing styles that attempt to represent other cultures through the lenses of the "other" are revolutionary ethnographic techniques that are practiced by anthropologists who support Clifford's school of thought. The problem that persists, however, as expressed by Rosaldo, Clifford, and Fox, is that the field of anthropology refuses to allow the "other" to speak. This results in the treatment of people of color as objects. The most blatant example of muting the voice of the other is when anthropologists refuse to integrate the academic discourses of racial minority scholars within the core of anthropological theory. It appears that most anthropologists are content with studying people of color, but are not prepared to study the theories developed by racial minority anthropologists.

Anthropology and Chicano Studies

In 1985, Renato Rosaldo wrote an article entitled "Chicano Studies, 1970–1984." This article was very significant, for it was the first article on Chicanos published in the *Annual Reviews of Anthropology*. The journal is very prestigious and one of the most respected within our discipline. This article was also significant because it revisited the Romano-Madsen debate, a controversy that was ignited by the words of two anthropologists and which to a large measure led to the forging of the theoretical characteristics of Chicano studies. The debate focused on two opposing anthropological interpretations of the nature of Chicano culture, and on the issue of whether the Chicanos are at fault for the poverty they experience in South Texas.

On the one hand, in 1968 Octavio Romano wrote an article, "The Anthropology and Sociology of the Mexican Americans: The Distortion of Mexican-American History" criticizing social scientists (Romano-V 1968). Here Romano asserted that Anglo-American scholars were generating a "deficit thinking" discourse in an effort to blame Chicanos for the social and economic problems that Anglo-American racism had generated. Romano brilliantly charged that Anglo-American scholars, particularly anthropologists, had failed to analyze how racism (and more specifically social segregation) had been used by the majority population to obstruct the social, economic, and political mobility of the Mexican-origin population. Romano urgently called Chicano students—and all people who opposed racism—to contest the stereotypes and racist propaganda that were being perpetuated about his people. These stereotypes, Romano argued, were dangerous because this was the ideological discourse used in the United States to blame Chicano culture for the social problems they were experiencing.

In the opposing camp was William Madsen. Madsen and Romano knew each other well, as they had worked together on the "Hidalgo-Camaron Ethnographic Health Project," which resulted in the production of Madsen's highly controversial book entitled *Mexican Americans of South Texas* (1964). Madsen was the project director and Romano was a member of the ethnographic field research team. In his book, Madsen argued that Mexican American's culture was the root cause of their inability to succeed in America. That is, their inability to become socially mobile was intrinsic to their culture. Allegedly, the Mexican Americans' cultural core—which was composed of familism, Catholicism, honor, and machismo—led these people to behave dysfunctionally, and thus obstructed their ability to move forward in society. The mother, in particular, was identified as a prime cause of this dysfunction, for she taught her children to be passive, fatalistic, suspicious, and lazy, and to seek immediate gratification. If her children were male, she also taught them to disrespect women and to commit violence against them.

Having worked in Madsen's research team, Romano clearly knew that these were ethnographic distortions. He charged that Madsen was a racist who was perpetuating false stereotypes of Chicano people without considering how a history of discrimination had impacted them. The debate was ignited, and Romano used this context to introduce a Chicano theoretical agenda. He proposed that the study of Chicano culture should be historically contextualized in order to understand how institutional discrimination affected Chicanos. Romano's recommendations significantly contributed to the future direction of Chicano studies and also influenced anthropologists. It became quite clear to anthropologists that, if they studied American culture, they must be careful because their informants would read their research and counter with more reasonable interpretations.

My main point in reminding you about this account is that

Chicano studies and anthropology have a long and intertwined history. Also, I provide this setting to briefly address Edward Said's critical assessment of anthropology (1989). He states that although the discipline of anthropology has produced countless studies that treat people with respect, white anthropologists continue to dominate the representations of people of color. Furthermore, these scholars have done very little to recruit people of color into the discipline (in efforts to change its discriminatory racial hierarchy). Said views this to be a critical problem, as the "other" continues to be represented by those in power. He offers an analysis similar to that of Paredes, who states that people of different cultures have the right to study each other (Paredes 1978). However, Paredes cautions, when those in power refuse to allow the other to speak, the structures of domination are reinforced. I concur. Although anthropologists no longer endorse a discourse a la Madsen, it is unfortunate that the academic power relations that existed between Madsen and Romano still persist. White male anthropologists continue to control most departments and disciplinary journals, while racial minorities have been largely excluded from these academic social circles.

Historical Ethnography and Archival Approaches

My own research reflects the theoretical influence of the field of anthropology and the theoretical agenda set by Romano. Using two of my studies, I would like to illustrate two different types of histories anthropologists reconstruct. They are (1) historical ethnographies and (2) histories reconstructed on the basis of archives. I will first speak about my book entitled *The Mexican Outsiders: A Community History of Marginalization and Discrimination in California* (Menchaca 1995) as an example of an ethnographic history. This book provides an ethnographic history of the prejudice and discrimination experienced by the Mexican-origin people of Santa Paula, California. In this book, I attempt to write about their untold local community history and their memories of marginalization and discrimination. In writing their oral histories and verifying their accounts with written documents, I describe how unequal interethnic relations were structured and reproduced through the use of coercive social mechanisms.

I also illustrate how anthropologists use ethnographic histories to explain how the past and the present are related. Specifically, I demonstrate how present cultural relations are impacted by past events. I clearly show how past events of social injustice have affected Santa Paula's contemporary interethnic relations.

Santa Paula is a biracial agrarian community in Ventura County, located sixty miles northeast of Los Angeles. Currently, Santa Paula is an ethnically balanced Anglo-American and Mexican-origin community that is politically and socially dominated by Anglo-American families who owe their wealth to the citrus industry (Belknap 1968; Menchaca 1989; Triem 1985). The city has a long and unpleasant history of social segregation, which has evolved into an interethnic system that I refer to as "social apartness." My conception of "social apartness," a construct developed for this analysis, refers to a system of social control in which Mexican-origin people are expected to interact with Anglo Americans only on Anglo-American terms. Anglo Americans determine the proper times and places in which the two groups can come into contact. There are clear social boundaries that define where the Mexican-origin population is unwanted and displaced. This system is maintained by enforcing interethnic norms of correct social comportment. In other words, there is a set of prescribed and proscribed interethnic rules that serve to maintain cordial, yet socially distant relations. Indeed, this system is a manifestation of modern racism and ensures a type of privilege enjoyed by the Anglo Americans of Santa Paula.

Social apartness is manifested in (1) the perpetuation of school segregation, (2) the unbalanced urban development of the Mexican neighborhoods in comparison to the predominantly Anglo-American neighborhoods, (3) the forced social isolation of Mexican-origin people with respect to social clubs and churches, and (4) the belief of racist Anglo Americans that Mexican-origin people can be humiliated when the groups come into contact. This system of social apartness cannot be labeled "segregation," because neither laws nor violence are used to confine Mexican-origin people in particular social spaces. Social apartness is different from segregation, because segregation against people of color was sanctioned by federal law (*Robinson and Wife v. Memphis and Charleston Railroad Company* 1883; *Plessy v. Ferguson* 1896) and enforced by local police departments. Violence was also used by white Americans to terrorize people of color and thereby prevent them from breaking segregationist laws. Today, in many rural communities of the United States, segregation still exists because violent and coercive actions are practiced by white Americans against people of color in order to ensure that they remain within their ethnic neighborhoods (see Feagin 1989). In Santa Paula, however, social segregation in its traditional form evolved into a system of social apartness. As in the past, Anglo Americans continue to determine the community's social space, but now they use new methods of enforcement. The problem with this system is that it is a subtle type of oppression, in that it serves to humiliate, debase, and marginalize people of Mexican descent. It also leads to unbalanced economic rewards that favor the Anglo-American community.

An examination of Santa Paula's history can help to illustrate how this community's interethnic social relations evolved and how this behavior was conditioned by past events.

Santa Paula was founded by Chumash Indians and subsequently colonized and settled by Spanish and Mexican colonists. Many of the residents of Santa Paula are of bicultural ancestry—Chumash and Mexican. The Chumash and Mexican populations built an irrigation system, planted the first orchards, and established ranchos and *rancherías*. (*Rancherías* were Indian villages that retained close contact with the Spanish or Mexican colonists in exchange for agricultural knowledge or military assistance. Legally, the Spanish incorporated the Indian villages as part of their colonial municipalities). Following the Mexican-American War of 1846 to 1848, the U.S. government dispossessed the former inhabitants of their land ownership rights and transferred legal title of the land to Anglo-American homesteaders and eastern capitalists. In 1867, Santa Paula experienced a tremendous influx of Anglo Americans and they became the majority population. They immediately took over the land by employing both legal and illegal means. Only one wealthy Mexican land owner—Julio Peralta—was able to successfully defend his property rights by taking the homesteaders to court. In three court cases, Julio Peralta was deemed to be the rightful owner and the squatters were ordered to leave his land. However, since the Anglo-American population outnumbered the Mexicans, they used violence against Julio Peralta and forced him to leave town. By the turn of the century, all Mexicans in Santa Paula were converted into farm labor and only eight families were able to subsist by other means.

By the early 1900s, a system of social segregation had also been institutionalized throughout Santa Paula. Mexicans were allowed to live only in the Mexican East Side. All of their social activities were confined to their neighborhoods, and when schooling was finally extended to Mexicans it was also provided in a segregated and inferior manner. By 1925, 950 Mexican elementary students attended a wooden schoolhouse composed of eight classrooms, while 667 Anglo-American elementary students attended a modern school composed of more than twenty-one classrooms.

In addition to social segregation, Mexican Americans in Santa Paula were also paid substandard farm labor wages. Over the course of Santa Paula's history, its Mexican-American residents fought back several times against the economic inequities by organizing labor unions. However, every time they formed a union their resistance was met with hostility and violence. Labor strikes were repeatedly broken by the use of police brutality and the labor leaders were imprisoned. Worst of all, from 1910 to the mid-1930s, the Ku Klux Klan was used against Mexicans to frighten and to force them to conform to Santa Paula's segregation and labor wage norms.

After World War II, when Mexican Americans returned from serving in the war, the veterans and the Mexican-American merchants launched a civil rights movement to desegregate Santa Paula. They formed coalitions with other Mexican community members. Several times they attempted to take over the city council, to desegregate the neighborhoods and the local theater which forced Mexicans to sit on one side of the theater. It was not until 1959, however, that social segregation began to be dismantled, after Mexicans insisted on sitting wherever they wanted in the theater and entering any store that they wanted. Residential segregation disappeared gradually, but it was difficult to abolish. It did not break down on a large scale until businessmen built a new residential district and decided that it was a profitable venture to sell houses to Mexicans.

It was not until after the termination of the Bracero Program in the mid-1960s that gradual improvements began to occur for Mexican-American farm labor. When the Mexican national contract laborers returned to Mexico, the domestic farm labor force of Santa Paula was able to launch several massive strikes, demonstrating to the growers that if their company's production was to run smoothly, wages needed to be raised and housing conditions improved. By the mid-1980s, the majority of the farmworkers had launched a judicial court battle against the growers in order to improve the housing conditions in the labor camps. The courts ruled in favor of the farmworkers, and within a few years the dilapidated labor camps were converted into modern working-class neighborhoods.

Today, although farm labor conditions and Santa Paula's interethnic relations have improved, the Mexican-origin community continues to be subjected to racist practices. The schools have not been desegregated, although the California State Office of Education has asked the Santa Paula School Board of Education to do so. The Mexican Americans have also not been able to dismantle the at-large electoral system which consistently favors Anglo Americans during city council elections. In turn, the city council continues to disproportionately fund urban improvement projects (e.g., repairing of streets and drainage systems, maintenance of parks, erecting of youth recreation centers) in the Anglo-American neighborhoods despite the demographic reality that more people live in the Mexican neighborhoods. The city council has also failed to relocate a pesticide company and an oil tank farm that are located next to the largest Mexican school.

One area where Mexican-origin people have been able to fight back is in their shared interethnic public places. Although the norm of social apartness serves to maintain the separate Mexican and Anglo-American communities, Anglo Americans know that they can no longer spit at Mexican-origin people. Furthermore, Anglo Americans are now aware that if they humiliate a Mexican national—and a Mexican American observes this—it will not be tolerated.

Now, I return to my initial point about how past events have influenced Santa Paula's current interethnic relations. I have found that a history of discrimination has allowed Anglo Americans to consider Mexican-origin people to be inferior. Examining Santa Paula from a historical perspective elucidates why there is so much social distance between Mexican-origin people and Anglo-American citizens. It also helps to explain how Anglo Americans achieved the political power and social privileges they enjoy today. Social segregation, dominant group violence, the prohibition of collective bargaining for farmworkers, and racism have been effective means used to control and dominate people of Mexican descent.

Archival History Applied

A large part of my archival research focuses on using legal archives to reconstitute American history. A section of an article I recently published illustrates this point. The article entitled "The Treaty of Guadalupe Hidalgo and the Racialization of the Mexican Population" (1999), presents a cultural and legal history of the impact of the Mexican-American War of 1846 to 1848 upon the inhabitants of what today is the U.S. Southwest. Theoretically, it has been influenced by Eric Wolf's (1982) macrosystem approach and by Pierre Bourdieu's (1992) analysis of the influence the legal domain has upon the culture of a people.

One of the theoretical aims of this article is to delineate how laws and government policies transformed the public culture of the mission and Christian *ranchería* Indians. The legal literature I review ranges from 1528 to 1872 and covers Spanish, Mexican, and U.S. periods. This article concludes that, after the Southwest became part of the United States, many former mission and Christian *ranchería* Indians were pressured to claim Mexican citizenship in order to survive. Those who claimed Mexican citizenship and passed as Mexican were exempt from the Indian Intercourse Act of 1834, which decreed that Indians were to be placed on reservations or exterminated.

After the Mexican-American War of 1846 to 1848, the U.S. government recognized that among the conquered Mexican population of the Southwest there were many detribalized Indians who had been previously accorded Mexican citizenship. The problem the U.S. government officials now encountered was: should mission and Christian *ranchería* Indians be treated like the rest of the conquered Mexican population, or should they come under the laws governing Indians such as the Indian Intercourse Act of 1834? Government officials acknowledged that the mission and Christian *ranchería* Indians were culturally part Mexican, and therefore should be distinguished from the nomadic Indians and possibly be given some of the political rights of Mexicans. In response to these issues the U.S. Congress gave each territory and state government of the Southwest the right to decide if their mission and Christian *ranchería* Indians should be exempt from the laws governing Indians. In Texas, since the Indians had been nearly exterminated prior to the end of the Mexican-American War, the surviving mission and Christian *ranchería* Indians no longer posed a political threat. In 1849, therefore,

Texas passed liberal legislation with respect to mission and Christian *ranchería* Indians and exempted them from the Indian Intercourse Act. In other words, if these types of Indians wanted to remain in Texas rather than relocating to the reservations, they were required to prove either that they were culturally Mexican or that they were detribalized Indians in the process of becoming Mexican. Furthermore, the state government decreed that if mission Indians could document that they were culturally Mexican, their land claims would be validated by the U.S. government. The legal procedure that Indians had to follow was stipulated in the Texas State Supreme Court ruling *McMullen v Hodge and Others* (1849). Under this legislation, former mission Indians would be able to retain titles to the land they were granted under Spanish and Mexican property laws and be exempt from federal Indian legislation if they followed set procedures. To be eligible for such consideration, they had to prove that they or their ancestors: (1) were released by missionaries, (2) spoke Spanish, (3) had passed a two-year secularization probationary period where they were observed to have practiced Mexican traditions, (4) had been Spanish subjects or practicing Mexican citizens (e.g. voted, ran for office, practiced the holy Catholic Sacraments), (5) had obtained property alienation rights releasing their land from the tutelage of the church or government, and (6) had had their land surveyed according to U.S. law.

Under *McMullen v Hodge and Others,* the state also ruled that in the case of the Christian *ranchería* Indians, they would be allowed to live among non-Indians if they could prove that they had adopted a Mexican lifestyle. However, the Christian *ranchería* Indians would not be given property rights, unless they could prove that their village had been formally incorporated into a Mexican township before the Mexican-American War. As a result of this legal process, many mission and Christian *ranchería* Indians survived and were pressured to lead a Mexican cultural lifestyle.

My research on mission and Christian *ranchería* Indians shows how law and culture historically have been intertwined. That is, those in power enact laws that impact peoples' behavior and culture. In the case of the Indians of Texas, if they preferred to not be placed in reservations they needed to prove that they were culturally Mexican. This was a way of coercing their public culture to change by the use of legal mandates.

Conclusion

In closing, I have illustrated the type of research anthropologists who specialize in history and the study of Chicano people conduct. I have also attempted to illustrate the influence Octavio Romano has had in my research, for I concur with him that the study of culture needs to be historically contextualized.

References

Belknap, Michael. 1968. "The Era of the Lemon: A History of Santa Paula, California." *California Historical Quarterly* 47, no. 2: 113–40.

Bourdieu, Pierre. 1992. *Outline of a Theory of Practice*. Cambridge: Cambridge University Press.

Clifford, James. 1988. *The Predicament of Culture: Twentieth Century Ethnography, Literature, and Art.* Cambridge, Mass.: Harvard University Press.

Clifford, James, and George E. Marcus. 1986. *Writing Culture: The Poetics and Politics of Ethnography*. Berkeley, Calif.: University of California Press.

Comaroff, John, and Jean Comaroff. 1992. *Ethnography and the Historical Imagination*. Boulder, Colo.: Westview Press.

Feagin, Joe. 1989. *Racial and Ethnic Relations*. Englewood Cliff, N.J.: Prentice Hall.

Fox, Richard G., ed. 1991. *Recapturing Anthropology: Working in the Present.* Santa Fe: School of American Social Research.

Geertz, Clifford. 1980. *Negara: The Theatre State in Nineteenth-Century Bali.* Oxford: Princeton University Press.

Jackson, Walter. 1986. "Melville Herskovits and the Search for Afro-American Culture." In *Malinowski, Rivers, Benedict and Others*, George W. Stocking Jr., ed., 95–127. Madison: University of Wisconsin Press.

Madsen, William. 1964. *Mexican Americans of South Texas*. New York: Holt, Reinhart and Winston.

McMullen v Hodge and Others, 9 Texas Reports 34–87 (Texas State Supreme Court, 1849).

Menchaca, Martha. 1995. *Mexican Outsiders: A Community History of Marginalization and Discrimination in California*. Austin: University of Texas Press.

———. 1989. "Chicano-Mexican Cultural Assimilation and Anglo-Saxon Cultural Dominance." *Hispanic Journal of Behavioral Sciences* 11, no. 3: 203–31.

———. 1999. "The Treaty of Guadalupe Hidalgo and the Racialization of the Mexican Population." *The Elusive Quest for Equality: 150 years of*

Chicana/o Education, Jose Moreno, ed., 3–30. Cambridge, Mass.: Harvard Educational Review.

Mintz, Sidney. 1986. *Sweetness and Power: The Place of Sugar in Modern History.* New York: Penguin Books.

Nash, Philleo. 1937. *The Place of Religious Revivalism in the Formation of the Intercultural Community on Klamath Reservation*. Chicago, Ill.: University of Chicago Libraries.

Paredes, Américo. 1978. "On Ethnographic Work Among Minority Groups." In *New Direction in Chicano Scholarship*, Ricardo Romo and Raymund Paredes, eds., 1–32. San Diego, Calif.: Chicano Studies Monograph Series, University of California.

———. 1958. *With His Pistol in His Hand*. Austin: University of Texas Press.

Plessy v Ferguson, 163 US 537–64 (1896).

Robinson and Wife v Memphis and Charleston Railroad Company, 109 US 3–62 (1883).

Romano-V, Octavio. 1968. "The Anthropology and Sociology of the Mexican Americans: The Distortion of Mexican-American History." *El Grito* 2, no. 1: 13–26.

Rosaldo, Renato, Jr. 1993. *Culture and Truth: The Remaking of Social Analysis*. Boston, Mass.: Beacon Press.

———. 1985. "Chicano Studies, 1970–1984." *Annual Reviews of Anthropology* 14: 405–27.

———. 1980. *Ilongot Headhunting 1883–1974: A Study in Society and History*. Stanford, Calif.: Stanford University Press.

Roseberry, William. 1991. *Anthropologies and Histories: Essays in Culture, History, and Political Economy.* New Brunswick, N.J.: Rutgers University Press.

Sahlins, Marshall. 1985. *Islands of History*. Chicago, Ill.: University of Chicago Press.

Said, Edward. 1989. "Representing the Colonized: Anthropology's Interlocutors." *Critical Inquiry* 15, no. 2: 205–25.

Taussig, Michael. 1992. "Culture of Terror—Space of Death: Roger Casement's Putumayo Report and the Explanation of Torture." In *Colonialism and Culture*, Nicholas B. Dirks, ed., 135–74. Ann Arbor: University of Michigan Press.

Triem, Judith. 1985. *Ventura County: Land of Good Fortune*. Northridge, Calif.: Windsor Publications.

Wolf, Eric. 1982. *Europe and the People Without History*. Berkeley: University of California Press.

CHAPTER 9

BEYOND INTERNAL COLONIALISM: CLASS, GENDER, AND CULTURE AS CHALLENGES TO CHICANO IDENTITY

María E. Montoya[1]

I HAVE A CONFESSION TO MAKE: I was born in 1964. I was not alive when Oswald shot President John F. Kennedy. I was one year old when Cesar Chavez led his first strike. I was two years old when Reis Tijerina occupied Echo Amphitheatre in New Mexico. And I was five years old when Neil Armstrong walked on the moon. What difference do these events make to my particular life? And more importantly, what do these historical milestones and personal history have to do with the future of Chicana/o history? For me, every one of those events is history—I have no direct memory or relationship to any of them. Take, for example, events that occurred in my own hometown of Denver. The only memory I have of Corky Gonzales and the Crusade for Justice is attending an event sponsored by the crusade (I have no direct memory of him) when I was about five years old. We went with my "radical" (radical because he wore a Nehru jacket) uncle, who was younger than my parents and who had become involved with the crusade while attending the University of Denver Law School. That evening remained a clear and powerful memory, and in the end shaped much about how I think and live my life today. Yet, it is a memory that made sense only after I had left home and *read* about the crusade and Corky Gonzales while in college.

I suspect that for many of the scholars in the field of Chicano/a history who are older than I am, the shooting of JFK, Armstrong's walk on the moon, and, more particularly, the movements led by Cesar Chavez, Corky Gonzalez, and Reis Tijerina are not merely historical events. For most, they are part of a personal history and, in many cases, part of a personal memory. I, however, lived my childhood, received my education, and became politically aware in the early years of the Reagan era and the Republican revolution. The rhetoric of "equality" espoused by the far Right, who were eager to eliminate affirmative action programs, and not the liberal radicalism of the previous decade, shaped by youth. My role models were not liberals like Dolores Huerta and Corky Gonzalez, but conservatives like Linda Chavez and Manuel Lujan.

I came from a family that was far from radical and embraced the American Dream as we made our home in the very white and quietly hostile world of suburban Denver. During their childhood and education my parents had been criticized by well-meaning Presbyterian missionaries for speaking Spanish and practicing anything that vaguely resembled Catholicism. So I grew up without learning my parents' native language and rarely setting foot into the Catholic Church. I suspect that this is a very different experience from most scholars writing in the field to date. Yet, I doubt that my experience is that unique among the Chicana/os of my age cohort or among the graduates and undergraduates I currently teach. It is not an experience that we have written about, and it is one we have rarely discussed publicly.[2] In fact, it is a very unromantic, apolitical coming-of-age tale that cannot compare, in terms of drama and hardship, with the radical youth of the 1960s and 1970s, or even with the struggles of my parents in the 1950s, or my grandparents' experiences during the Depression. I do think, however, that my experience reflects the diversity of people and points of view that are beginning and will continue to shape this field we call Chicana/o history.

For those who fought the battles to establish Chicano studies in the early 1970s, this changing demography among scholars may not come as welcome news. Many older scholars do not trust a new generation to carry on the vision that guided them in the creation of the Chicano Movement. Today, Chicana/o history stands at a crossroads. For the first time, this "new," but really remade, Chicano history will be told and retold by people who were not there at the inception of the field and who will barely be able to muster up a historical memory to go along with the history they write. Moreover, this "new" history will come from a diverse set of scholars trained in a variety of disciplines and schools across the country. This difference will have a profound effect on the field.

As more scholars enter the field, there will be such diversity of thought that it may become difficult to define exactly what we mean by

Chicana/o history. The new generation of scholars will create their own methodology, voice, and even definition of the field, and will continue to borrow from other forms of academic discourse, such as postmodernism, postcolonial studies, and transnationalism. Rather than looking for methodologies that separate Chicano history from the fields of U.S., Mexican, and Latin American historiographies, the trend will be for scholars to look for ways to connect Chicana/o history to other methodologies and theoretical frameworks. The political urgency that marked so many of the early writings and the revisionist spirit in which those texts were written will begin to fade away as younger scholars search for a more academic voice in which to place their work. As the field stands at this crossroads it is appropriate to ask: Is it possible to combine the earlier political agenda of writing Chicano history with what will be a very lucid and constantly redefined field of Chicana/o history in the coming decade?

I want to challenge the very notion of "Chicano" and ask what use the term and historiography hold for us as scholars in academia and activists in the world in which we live. In preparing this paper, I was surprised at the relatively small amount of self-critical examination of Chicano history that has been written.[3] I was trained in the history of the American West, where people make their writing careers by doing nothing else but critiquing the field and others in it.[4] It is my sense, however, that Chicana/o historians have been too busy producing actual knowledge. Since relatively few monographs and textbooks about Chicanos and Mexican Americans exist, we have consequently spent the better portion of our time digging through archives, taking oral interviews, and poring over government documents in order to tell the stories of people who have never had their stories told, much less had their lives reexamined by revisionist historians. Chicana/o historians have not had the luxury of the longevity in the field that allows for the kind of self-reflection inherent in a field like western history, which originated over one hundred years ago with an essay by Frederick Jackson Turner.

What troubles me most as I continue to do research and teach in the field of Chicana/o history is that I find it difficult to define the field as a discipline. I have become even more overwhelmed in the last few years because of my move from Colorado to Michigan. At least in Colorado I could delude myself into thinking that geographical boundaries defined Chicana/os and their history—particularly the southwestern states of California, New Mexico, Texas, Arizona, and portions of Colorado and Utah. Now, I come to find out that Chicanos have spread out across the entire Midwest.[5] Speaking with students at both Michigan State University and the University of Michigan, I have been constantly amazed and comforted by the many similarities we share, despite the vast differences in geography, landscape, and economic bases. Nevertheless, there is something unique to the midwestern Chicano experience that defies complete categorization with Chicanos of the American Southwest. Not only do Chicano scholars need to contend with the diversity within the Chicano community, but as the field moves toward a pan-ethnic identity of Latino we will need to look for ways to incorporate the experiences of Cubans, Puerto Ricans, and other Latin American immigrants. Although this is a topic for another paper, it is a concern we should keep within our sights as we move into a twenty-first century that will bring more immigrants and link us all through technology and mass media. Nevertheless, several factors, other than geographical diversity, separate and distinguish the myriad of Chicano experiences. I would like to discuss three issues that I think challenge our community of interest, in terms of both academia and our activism. They are issues centering around class, gender, and what I will broadly label as culture.

In terms of class, diversity among the Mexican-American population has always marked the Chicano experience, but this is becoming even more prevalent as more Chicanos slowly make their way into the middle and even upper classes of American society. I will limit my remarks, as this is already fairly well traveled territory in the historiography.[6] Internal colonialism, the early model prevalent in Chicano history, tended to subordinate class divisions and differences between Mexican Americans to the common ethnicity, which marked Chicanos as the "other" in U.S. society. Internal colonialism sets up an "us versus them" model of Anglos against Chicanos. In this model there was little room for examining how income, neighborhood, or class divisions affect the unity of Chicanos as a group. Early scholarship in the field focussed primarily on the working-class and economically struggling Mexican Americans, and studies tended to dismiss those persons and experiences that did not fit into that model. For example, among scholars of the Chicano generation it fell out of fashion to study the Spanish conquest of the New World. Part of this was a periodization choice, as most Chicano histories began with the U.S. conquest of Mexican territory in

1848. Nevertheless, the conquest certainly offers spectacular examples of domination and conquest when we think about the how the Spanish government, soldiers, and priests subordinated native peoples. Including the Spanish conquest, however, complicates the internal colonial model significantly. The prospect of thinking about Spanish-speaking men dominating Native Americans simply muddies the picture of Anglo-Mexicano relations too much for the internal colonial model to embrace. Internal colonialism, in fact, has never been able to satisfactorily explain how to deal with the complex problem of *mestizaje* between Spaniards and Native Mexicanos. By picking up the story in 1848, internal colonialism avoids the problem and can simply label all the inhabitants of the recently conquered territory as Mexicans.[7]

Yet, class has been one of the most divisive issues in the community and in scholarship. In particular, those who have moved into the middle class, and seemingly have forgotten their roots, have been singled out for criticism by Chicano scholars.[8] Only with Mario Garcia's work, *Mexican Americans*, has the middle class become a viable and acceptable research topic.[9] Yet, while Garcia's work has been well received and much appreciated, few have followed his lead and pursued other middle-class-based analysis of Mexican Americans: there is virtually no study of post-1960s middle-class Mexican Americans. It is as if there were no conservative, middle-class Mexican Americans during or after the Chicano Movement.

Certainly this is not considered a "hot," or even a viable, topic within the canon of Chicano history, which has preoccupied itself with telling stories that are not based on assimilation or acceptance of the dominant society. Chicano historians' monographic replies to the assimilationist stories of an earlier generation have led the discipline to focus narrowly on tales of resistance and victimization. Consequently, those historical actors who did not particularly interest Chicano historians in the early years have been lost in our historical memory. As a profession and a discipline, we have to cast our net more broadly and look at Mexican Americans of all classes and working backgrounds if we are to truly understand the total Chicana/o experience. It is not enough to label members of our own community as "other" or "Hispanics," implying that the middle class were sellouts to the Chicano Movement. Instead, we need research that examines forces that lead to assimilation and asks why people make the choices they do about identity, citizenship, and political affiliation.

Even more divisive than class, however, has been the failure of the majority of Chicano (not Chicana) historians to incorporate gender as a meaningful category of analysis in their work.[10] Very little of the early historiography even marginally integrates women into the stories male scholars have told about conquest, resistance, and adaptation.[11] As a community of scholars, the field has readily accepted the one-paragraph excuses of scholars like Mario Garcia in *Mexican Americans* who exempt themselves from writing about women because it takes them too far afield from their main interest of study or because there is seemingly not enough primary source material. Garcia writes, "Finally, although I considered writing a separate chapter on women within the Mexican American Generation, I decided that such a chapter might be construed as patronizing and incorrectly suggest the women did not participate in the larger movement such as those of the Left."[12] In the book, however, there is relatively little of discussion of women as actors within the roles that Garcia defines as "leadership." Perhaps a more fruitful way of examining the experiences of women in this generation would have been for Garcia to critique the idea of "leadership" using gender analysis in the same way that he critiqued the category of "leadership" by looking through the lens of ethnicity. Furthermore, Garcia merely accepts the patriarchal system that kept women out of nationally prominent leadership positions without examining the ideological underpinnings of the men in these groups. I do not mean to single out Professor Garcia; there were many scholars before him and even after his book appeared who simply never examined the role of women or the construction of patriarchy within their work.

Scholars in Chicano studies, unintentionally and subconsciously, have created a gendered division of labor that assigns the telling of women's tales to women, while men get to study and write about everything else. Despite this gendered division, some of the most interesting work in Chicano history has been done by women and in the study of women, particularly the work of Vicki Ruiz, who has been a mentor to a lucky handful of graduate students.[13] Moreover, when women complained (whether in the Chicano Movement, in academia, or even in today's local MECHA organizations) about the inequality of treatment within the community or within the existing scholarship they were told to stop causing division in the field and to go along with the main movement: racial over gender loyalty is always preferred.[14]

Chicana historians find themselves in a precarious and often lonely position. Mainstream (white) women's historians are often blind to the class, racial, or ethnic diversity that marks the experiences of women of color as different from their own experience. Consequently, Chicana historians have found an uneasy home in the world of women's history.[15] To make matters worse, the field of Chicano history, with less than twenty (and here I suspect I am being generous) women Ph.D. historians, has not been an inviting or nurturing place for women and their work. Men should not be so surprised or hurt when these scholars reject the male-dominated paradigms in favor of finding their own voice apart from the often chauvinistic world of Chicano scholarship as well as from the ethnocentric views of women's historiography. Only when women of color scholars are accepted on an equal footing within the Chicano academic community can a bridge be built to cover this gap that threatens to divide our discipline. We simply must cease to have this gendered division of academic labor: women should be encouraged to pursue topics outside of Chicana history and men should naturally reach for gender as a viable and enlightening category of analysis in their work. Just imagine what the work of David Montejano would have looked like if he had looked at women's work and their place in the world economy. How would Mario Garcia's book have changed had he challenged and refined the idea of leadership?

In the final analysis, what and who defines Chicano culture may help us to define what Chicano history is and what it will be in the future. The problem for Chicano historians, however, is how to come to terms with the diversity of interests, both academically and personally, within the Chicano community. If historians want to study and analyze Chicano ethnicity and the role it plays in American society, then we must treat it simply as one category of analysis. Ethnicity is only one of the myriad of ways that people define themselves and their community of interest. We have got to break away from the idea that there is a monolithic, hegemonic ideal that we label "Chicano." More importantly, we must be aware of excluding those, whether scholars, neighbors, or historical figures, who do not fall completely under a strident and unyielding definition of "Chicano."

Let me explain my point by using one example. My own particular confrontation with how diversity of interests affects our definition of Chicano came while looking at the difference between urban and rural Chicanos in the state of Colorado. I am particularly interested in comparing the people of the San Luis Valley, an extremely rural and poor section of the state, with those of the city of Pueblo, a union town that historically has found its economic base in the steel industry, which today struggles to revive its economy. The Chicanos who live in these two places, divided by 150 miles and a mountain range, share the same ethnicity, same familial backgrounds, same religion, and same social customs.[16] Yet, because of where they live, either rural or urban, they often have very different interests that put them at odds with one another and have them allying with other ethnicities and classes in their own region. One particular issue that they differ over is the issue of water. The San Luis Valley sits on possibly one of the largest untapped aquifers in the American Southwest. Cities like Denver, Albuquerque, Pueblo, and even Los Angeles have been eyeing the water for years. The litigation within the state of Colorado over the last five years about who "owns," needs, and ultimately gets to use the water, however, has the possibility of pitting rural and urban Chicanos against each other as both strive to preserve their jobs, community, and homes.

The discipline, and particular models such as internal colonialism, give us few tools with which to analyze this problem. How do we decide which group is more "Chicano" and consequently more deserving of the water and our historical understanding ? Is it the traditional Hispano farmers who maintain their own farms in the valley? Is it the recent immigrant farmworkers from Mexico who work for the agribusinesses and larger farm owners in the valley? Or is it the urbanized, out-of-work steelworkers who need the water to help their fledgling community survive and expand? I would argue that all three groups have a viable claim to the resource and to the political power embedded in the term Chicano? As "new" Chicano historians, our job should be to create a paradigm and a discipline that incorporates all of these groups and explains their conflict, as well as their cooperation, with one another. This rural/urban diversity is just one area that needs exploration. Chicano historians should also find a way to accommodate and explain the differences in region, migration patterns, and countries of origins, and determine how these diverse influences shape the Chicana/o experience.[17]

Despite my previous comments, I would like to suggest that in fact there is something we can define as Chicano History and that there is a community that somehow, despite all of our differences, we manage to see as Chicanos. Most of the criticism of the recent Chicano history by scholars of a previous generation focuses on how the younger generation has forgotten the past—forgotten the Chicano Movement of the 1960s and 1970s and, more specifically, the goals set forth by the Plan de Santa Barbara. The plan, written by young scholars in the field at the time, outlined a program for scholarship, scholars and their relationship to the community, and activism.[18] The critique by the older generation of Chicano scholars is that: young scholars are so concerned with the rules of academia, their careers, and their own personal attainment that they have forgotten about their past and their community. The problem with this critique, however, is that it is based on a static notion of what Chicano history is, or should be. The critique harkens back to the past, when it might be more productive to look to the future.

The first and second generations of Chicano scholars may have done their job too well. They opened the doors and allowed younger scholars access into the best schools of California and into Ivy League institutions. They said that Chicanos were equal to the task and could succeed in this white-dominated environment, if only given the chance through affirmative action programs. And, in fact, young scholars thrived. My generation of scholars is a product and a result of the radicalism of the 1970s and we are the beneficiaries of all that hard work. These results are not only evident in academia. Undergraduates who came into contact with Chicano professors, MECHA, and other organizations designed to help them survive the difficult world of university life graduated and took their place in America's middle class. So rather than complaining about how unradical this most recent generation has become, we should examine their experiences and understand why they seem to have no need to embrace radicalism. In fact, I suspect that fewer and fewer of our undergraduates want to fight the old battles of the 1960s and 1970s. They, moreover, face new and difficult challenges posed by the anti-immigrant movement and the affirmative action backlash.

Instead, in this new world of multiculturalism and race and ethnicity requirements in college curriculums, it seems to me that our task as teachers goes way beyond the goals outlined by the Plan de Santa Barbara. I agree wholeheartedly that part of our obligation as scholars in the Academy is to provide a safe, inviting, and nurturing environment in which Chicano and Chicana students can learn and thrive. I, however, see a second obligation to the wider community, which I address through my own teaching. By placing myself in a mainstream department and by teaching such mainstream courses as history of the American West, environmental history, and particularly the U.S. history surveys, I have access to many students that I would not if I were to teach only courses in Chicano history. By reconceptualizing how the U.S. history courses are taught I am able to put the history of women, Chicanos, and all people of color in their correct and proper context. I believe that not only do we have an obligation to teach young Chicana/os about their own history, but we have an even greater obligation to enlighten other students with whom we come into contact about the history of other people—people with whom they will work and live for the rest of their adult lives.

In fact, it may be time for us to reconsider what our goals are as Chicana/o historians who want to live in the community and work within the confines of academia. We may have to abandon documents like the Plan De Santa Barbara and other manifestos written in that unique and radical time period. Instead, I think the time has come to step back and marvel at the numbers we have in our field and the diversity of those scholars. Only then can the field honestly evaluate the political and academic climate in which we live and work, and determine how we can make the best contribution to the field, our students, and to ourselves as scholars and activists.

Notes

1. María E. Montoya is an assistant professor at the University of Michigan in the Department of History and the Program in American Culture. Her book, *Translating Property: The Maxwell Land Grant and the Conflict over Land in the American West, 1840–1920* is forthcoming. She would like to thank Natalia Molina, Estevan Rael y Galvez, Tom I. Romero II, and Sonya Smith for their comments.
2. As an example of this middle-class narrative, see Ruben Navarette Jr., *A Darker Shade of Crimson: Odyssey of a Harvard Chicano* (New York: Bantam Books, 1993). Probably the best known set of these coming-of-age biographies from a middle-class perspective are Richard Rodriquez's *Hunger of Memory* (New York: Bantam Books, 1982) and *Days of Obligation: An Argument with my Mexican Father* (New York: Penguin Books, 1992).

3. The notable exceptions are Tomas Almaguer, "Ideological Distortions in Recent Chicano Historiography: The Internal Colonial Model and Chicano Historical Interpretation," *Aztlán* 18 (1989): 7; Ignacio M. Garcia, "Juncture in the Road: Chicano Studies since 'El Plan de Santa Bárbara,'" in *Chicanas/Chicanos at the Crossroads: Social, Economic, and Political Change* David R. Maciel and Isidro R. Ortiz, eds. (Tucson: University of Arizona Press, 1996), 181; Richard Griswold del Castillo, "Southern California Chicano History: Regional Origins and National Critique," *Aztlán* 19 (spring 1988–90): 109; David G. Gutiérrez, "The Third Generation: Reflections on Recent Chicano Historiography," *Mexican Studies/Estudios Mexicanos* 5 (summer 1989): 281; David G. Gutiérrez, "Significant to Whom?: Mexican Americans and the History of the American West," *Western Historical Quarterly* 24 (November 1993): 519–39; Alex M. Saragoza, "Recent Chicano Historiography: An Interpretive Essay," *Aztlán* 19 (spring 1988–90): 1.
4. As an example of this self-reflection of a field see the critiques of Patricia Nelson Limerick's *Legacy of Conquest* (New York: W. W. Norton, 1988), who, herself, was critiquing Frederick Jackson Turner and his frontier thesis. See, for example, Larry McMurtry, "How the West Was Won or Lost," *New Republic* 22 (October 1990): 32–38. See also the most recent reflections of the field in the collection edited by Clyde Milner, ed., *A New Significance: Re-envisioning the History of the American West* (New York: Oxford University Press, 1996).
5. See the work of Dennis Nodín Valdés, *Al Norte: Agricultural Workers in the Great Lakes Region, 1917–1970* (Austin: University of Texas Press, 1991); and Zaragosa Vargas, *Proletarians of the North: Mexican Industrial Workers in Detroit and the Midwest, 1917–1933* (Berkeley: University of California Press, 1993). The work of the Julian Samora Center at Michigan State University also has provided valuable documentation about Mexican migrants and Mexican Americans in the Midwest.
6. See, for example, Almaguer, "Ideological Distortions," 11; and Garcia, "Juncture in the Road," 192. One of the best monographs that does use class as a basis of analysis is David Montejano's *Anglos and Mexicans in the Making of Texas, 1836–1986* (Austin: University of Texas Press, 1987). Richard Garcia in *Rise of the Mexican-American Middle Class: San Antonio, 1929–1941* (College Station: Texas A&M Press, 1991) also looks at the Mexican-American community through the lens of class. Certainly the works of David Gutiérrez, *Walls and Mirrors: Mexican-Americans, Mexican Immigrants, and the Politics of Ethnicity* (Berkeley: University of California Press, 1995); and George J. Sanchez, *Becoming Mexican American: Ethnicity, Culture, and Identity in Chicano Los Angeles, 1900–1945* (New York: Oxford University Press, 1993) take into account how class influences issues of identity.

7. Early Chicano scholars dismissed, rather than revised, the work of earlier scholars like Carlos Casteñeda, who wrote about the Spanish experience in North America in rather glorious terms. See, for example, Carlos Castañeda, *Our Catholic Heritage: The Finding of Texas*, vol. 1 (Austin: University of Texas Press, 1936).
8. In particular, see Rodolfo Acuña, *Occupied America: A History of Chicanos*, 3d ed. (New York: Harper and Row, 1988), chapters on the post-Chicano generation years. For a particularly, and needlessly, harsh critique see Garcia, "Juncture in the Road," 192.
9. Mario T. Garcia, *Mexican Americans: Leadership, Ideology, and Identity, 1930–1960* (New Haven: Yale University Press, 1989). Younger scholars like Cynthia Orozco and her work on women in LULAC, however, offer new and gendered interpretations of the middle class.
10. I mark the exceptions of more recent scholarship like Ramón Gutiérrez, *When Jesus Came the Corn Mothers Went Away*, (Palo Alto: Stanford University Press, 1989); Sanchez, *Becoming Mexican-American*; and Neil Foley, *The White Scourge* (Berkeley: University of California Press, 1997). While Chicana feminists may not agree with their methods and interpretation, nevertheless, these three scholars have sought to incorporate the history of women, and particularly Chicanas, on an equal footing with their male historical subjects.
11. For a particularly good critique of the field and its lack of gender analysis see Cynthia Orozco, "Chicano Labor History: a Critique of Male Consciousness in Historical Writing," *La Red/The Net* 77 (February 1984): 2.
12. Garcia, *Mexican Americans*, 3.
13. In particular, articles by Antonia Casteñeda and Deena Gonzales have been important influences in the field. See also Vicki Ruiz, *Cannery Women, Cannery Lives: Mexican Women, Unionization, and the California Food Processing Industry, 1930–1950* (Albuquerque: University of New Mexico Press, 1987) and *From Out of the Shadow: A History of Mexican Women in the United States, 1900–1995* (New York: Oxford University Press, 1997).
14. See Garcia, "Juncture in the Road," 190–92; Vicki L. Ruiz, "Texture, Text, and Context: New Approaches in Chicano Historiography," *Mexican Studies/Estudios Mexicanos* 1 (winter 1986): 145; Denise A. Segura and Beatriz M. Pesquera, "Beyond Indifference and Antipathy: The Chicano Movement and Chicana Feminist Discourse," *Aztlán* 19 (fall 1988–90): 69; Ramón Gutiérrez, "Community, Patriarchy and Individualism: The Politics of Chicano History and the Dream of Equality," *American Quarterly* 45 (March 1993): 44.
15. Antonia Castañeda, "Women of Color and the Rewriting of Western History: The Discourse, Politics, and Decolonization of History," *Pacific Historical Review* 61: 4 (November 1992): 501. Recent collections of essays have also been extremely helpful in filling the gaps of Chicana history. See,

for example, Cherrie Moraga and Gloria Anzaldúa, eds., *This Bridge Called My Back: Writings by Radical Women of Color* (New York: Kitchen Table/Women of Color Press, 1983); and Adela de la Torre and Beatríz M. Pesquera, eds., *Building with Our Hands: New Directions in Chicana Studies* (Berkeley: University of California Press, 1993).

16. See Richard L. Nostrand, *Hispano Homeland* (Norman: University of Oklahoma Press, 1992).
17. The recent work of David G. Gutiérrez, *Walls and Mirrors,* looks at the diversity of communities within the Chicano community and how those differences have played themselves out in politics and the immigration debate.
18. For a rather strident critique see Garcia, "Juncture in the Road"; Acuña, *Occupied America,* 363–412. Regarding the *Plan de Santa Barbara* see Carlos Munoz Jr., *Youth, Identity, and Power: The Chicano Movement* (London: Verso, 1989), 84–90.

CHAPTER 10

MAKING HISTORY: THE CHICANO MOVEMENT

Lorena Oropeza

I WAS VERY HONORED TO receive an invitation from Dr. Refugio Rochín and the Julian Samora Institute to present my work at this conference. The title of my presentation today is "Making History: The Chicano Movement." The title is a not too subtle play on words meant to underscore a pattern: most scholars who have written about the Chicano Movement were Chicano Movement participants themselves. Nearly thirty years ago, this generation captured national attention as activists. In the years since, a handful of these activists have recorded and constructed—that is, made—this history as scholars.[1] I therefore represent a break from tradition. Like Professor Maria Montoya, whose birth year I share, I did not participate in movement events of the 1960s and 1970s. For example, one key interest of mine, and a major focus of my talk today, is the origins of the National Chicano Moratorium March Against the War In Vietnam on 29 August 1970. On that day between twenty thousand and thirty thousand Chicanos marched down East Los Angeles' Whittier Boulevard in one of the largest Mexican-American demonstrations the country has ever seen.[2] During the late summer of 1970 in Tucson, Arizona, I was preparing for my own triumphal march, but it was to walk four blocks—all by myself—to Rogers Elementary and the first grade.

This morning I want to discuss the development of the Chicano Moratorium March as well as address the significance of my work—and my working—within the broader field of Chicana/o studies. Specifically, I wish to respond to Ignacio M. García's article, "Juncture in the Road: Chicano Studies Since 'El Plan de Santa Bárbara,'" a recent essay by a Chicano Movement scholar and former movement participant that critiques young scholars entering the field and mentions me by name.[3] My discussion thus moves from historical inquiry to contemporary debate. Along the way, however, similar themes prevail: unity, diversity, and political purpose.

As "Juncture in the Road" makes clear, Chicano Movement debates that arose a generation ago continue today. Engaged in a widespread and multifaceted struggle for social justice, many Chicano Movement participants were inspired by the belief that cultural pride and ethnic unity were together the raw stuff of political mobilization and empowerment. In striving toward ethnic and political solidarity, however, movement participants constantly grappled with a series of difficult problems, among them: cementing a movement marked by considerable regional and ideological differences; gaining recruits among nonmovement Mexican Americans; and recasting the ethnic minority's relationship with majority U.S. society. Inclined to dismiss the preceding generation's civil rights efforts as the "politics of accommodation," activists sought nothing less than, in the words of one key movement proclamation, "total liberation from oppression, exploitation and racism."[4] Certainly members of the Chicano Moratorium Committee were eager to build a broad-based ethnic campaign not just against the war in Vietnam, but also against a host of social injustices that Mexican Americans faced on the home front. For their part, the drafters of *el Plan de Santa Bárbara,* the founding document of Chicano studies, chose higher education as their arena of operation. As originally conceived, Chicano studies was going to politicize Mexican Americans—students and nonstudents alike—as well as dismantle the marginalization of the ethnic group through illuminating research. Unfortunately, the determined quest for social justice that was an integral part of the moratorium campaign and that helped inspire the formation of Chicano studies was only partially rewarded. The decades since the Chicano movement have brought political and educational progress for some people of Mexican descent and continued economic inequality for many more.[5] Not surprisingly, within the field of Chicana/o studies, many of the same questions over which activists pondered a quarter-century ago—questions of unity, diversity, and political purpose—remain. Indeed, these questions may be more pressing than ever.

The Making of the Moratorium and the History of the Movement

Before examining the present-day state of Chicana and Chicano studies, I wanted to share a portion of my historical research on Chicano antiwar activism. The two topics are not so far removed: like scholars within Chicana and Chicano studies today, members of the National Chicano Moratorium Committee Against the War In Vietnam confronted issues of unity, diversity, and purpose. They had to decide how to build their campaign, whom to include within it, and what their overall aim was. Indeed, one good way of appreciating the diversity within the Mexican-American population during this time period is to trace the emergence of Chicano antiwar activism. Mexican Americans traditionally had taken tremendous pride in the ethnic group's military service record, yet the Chicano Moratorium Committee succeeded in putting together the largest antiwar demonstration by any minority group in the history of the United States. They did so by tapping into powerful ethnic group notions of legitimacy, soldiering, and citizenship.

I thought I might first briefly summarize the origin of my own interest in Chicano antiwar activism. In 1988, I went to Cornell University to study the history of U.S. foreign relations. I was particularly interested in U.S.-Central American relations. During my first year in graduate school, however, I took a course taught by Professor Felix Masud-Piloto on the political history of Hispanics in the United States. At that point, my aim became to research some topic that lay at the intersection between U.S. foreign policy and Chicano history. As the Chicano Movement and the years of most intense fighting in Vietnam were roughly coeval, this particular juncture seemed the most promising. Still, when I picked this topic, I was unaware of the moratorium effort. I had never heard the name Ruben Salazar.[6]

Which is to say the history of Chicano protest against the Vietnam War was, for me, a blank slate. I therefore had a lot of questions. When did it arise? Why? Was it stronger in some places than in others? How did Mexican Americans who were not in the movement react to antiwar activism on the part of Chicanos?[7] I quickly found that accounts of the antiwar movement during the Vietnam era did not have much to say about the Chicano Moratorium.[8] Fortunately, during the course of my initial research, Carlos Muñoz Jr. and Juan Gómez-Quiñones both published works that provided important overviews of the Chicano

Movement.[9] Combined, their work not only answered some questions but raised others. How did Chicano antiwar activists interact with the national peace movement? What was the relationship between the moratorium effort and other Chicano issues?

As a means of sharing my research, I will address just one question this morning: what prompted so many people to join the Chicano moratorium antiwar demonstration in East Los Angeles on 29 August 1970?

Of course, one of the most commonly cited reasons for the Chicano antiwar effort, cited by activists then and scholars since, was evidence of disproportionate casualty rates.[10] In early 1967, Rafael Guzmán, a political scientist who was working on a massive data collection project for the Ford Foundation, looked at casualty rolls from the five southwestern states of Texas, New Mexico, Arizona, California, and Colorado. Examining the names of war dead from 1 January 1961 to 28 February 1967 in conjunction with data from the 1960 census, Guzmán concluded that, "American servicemen of Mexican descent have a higher death rate in Vietnam than all other GIs." According to Guzmán, while Spanish-surnamed men of military age made up only 13.8 percent of the Southwest's total population, Spanish-surnamed soldiers during the time period accounted for 19.4 percent of the war dead.[11] In 1969, Guzmán released a second study that had produced similar findings.[12] Nevertheless, a nearly three-year gap exists between the initial circulation of Guzmán's statistics and the emergence of a Chicano antiwar crusade in Los Angeles. Thus, evidence of disproportionate casualty rates alone does not explain the creation of a Chicano moratorium.

In fact, Guzmán's work in 1967 and 1968 was at least as likely to be mentioned by Mexican Americans eager to work with the administration of President Lyndon B. Johnson than by Chicanos protesting the war. During the early years of massive U.S. troop involvement in Vietnam, many older Mexican Americans took it as a point of honor that members of their ethnic group were fighting and dying overseas and not—at least not in any greatly visible numbers—marching down the streets. One such person eager to highlight the sacrifices of young Mexican-American men was the state chairman of the California G.I. Forum, a branch of the American G.I. Forum, which was a leading Mexican-American veterans and civil rights organization. In 1967, state chairman Mario R. Vasquez obtained and decided to forward to

President Johnson the last letter written by a slain Marine from San José, California. The Marine's name was Patrick Vasquez Jr., although he was apparently no relation. In a spring 1967 letter, the soldier Vasquez reassured his "Pop" that he was risking his life in a good cause: to save the "Free World" from the "Red Empire." Already twice-wounded, the doomed Vasquez wrote, "God will lead me to my destiny....If I should die over here, I'll be proud to know that I died for my country and I hope that you'll be proud of me too, for I am a *Marine*."[13] Forwarding Patrick Vasquez's words to the president, Mario Vasquez reminded Johnson that, "Mexican Americans have died in many wars in our fight to preserve freedom. If the people who are now rioting in this country had the same thoughts as Patrick, I am sure we could go about making the United States the country that it should be."[14]

Implicitly, Vasquez was reminding Johnson that service on the battlefront merited the recognition of Mexican Americans on the home front. Since at least as early as World War II, Mexican Americans had sought to further their civil rights struggle by calling attention to their battlefield performance. The argument, put forth by other minority groups before and since, was that military service merited first-class citizenship. In other words, those who risked death on behalf of a country should be granted legitimacy within it. Supporting this set of ideas in the Mexican-American case was the particularly commendable service record established by members of the ethnic group during World War II. Not only did some statistics suggest that Mexican Americans served and died in disproportionate numbers, veterans came home with medals on their chest—including eleven Congressional Medals of Honor.[15] If wartime service was a way to gain equality as citizens, Mexican Americans were eager for others to know that, considering their fighting capacity as soldiers, they were more than deserving of fair treatment.

The patriotic legacy of the Second World War and again Korea, where Mexican Americans, according to one popular author, fought valiantly, worked to curb Chicano antiwar activism in some areas of the Southwest.[16] At the forefront in muting criticism against the war amongst Chicanos was the Mexican American Youth Organization (MAYO), a Texas group that became the precursor of the state's Chicano political party, La Raza Unida. Wary of alienating potential sympathizers and voters, the organization initially deemed antiwar protest counterproductive. As MAYO cofounder Mario Compean later defended the group's reluctance to address the issue, "if MAYO would have spoken out against the war in the barrios it would have been run out immediately."[17] In the neighboring state of Arizona, refusing the draft in 1968 did indeed earn Chicano activist Salomón Baldenegro a chilly reception from older Mexican Americans in his hometown of Tucson. That same year, moreover, Baldenegro was ejected from the University of Arizona's Mexican American Students Association—a group he helped form—because he continued to speak out at campus antiwar rallies.[18] Elsewhere—Denver and the San Francisco Bay Area stand out—opposition to the war among Chicanos was less a matter of debate. Yet nowhere during the early years of massive U.S. troop involvement in Vietnam was antiwar activism a top priority for most movement participants. Instead, the young Chicano Movement tended to be more concerned with educational reform, the farm workers' struggle, and gaining political control of the barrios.

Nevertheless by November 1969, Chicano antiwar activism had begun to flourish in even previously resistant quarters. At an antiwar rally in San Antonio that month, Mario Compean of the Mexican American Youth Organization had abandoned his cautionary stance. Compean told the student crowd that it was high time for "all Chicano brothers to manifest themselves in opposition to the Vietnam War and to give up all this patriotic . . ." (The newspaper report contained ellipses rather than repeat Compean's apparently profane word choice.)[19] In the more liberal environment of California, the war issue was not just on the Chicano agenda but had moved to the forefront of movement activism. In late 1969, a uniquely Chicano antiwar effort was born in Los Angeles with the coming together of a group that became the National Chicano Moratorium Against the War in Vietnam. The group's idea of holding Chicano antiwar demonstrations quickly took hold in towns throughout the Southwest: by the spring of 1970 more than a dozen local Chicano moratoriums were on the planning board. So how can we explain this shift in attitude and priorities?

One necessary piece of the puzzle was that activists were taking their cue from national events. Across the country, Vietnam protest had become impossible to ignore. In the fall of 1969, massive antiwar demonstrations took place in cities across the country. In San Antonio, Compean was speaking at a local event that was one of many coordinated across the country by the Vietnam Moratorium Committee, a national group. The next month, enormous antiwar rallies took place in San Francisco and Washington, D.C. Perhaps as many as a quarter of a million people participated on the West Coast, half a million on the East.[20] These demonstrations were an inspiration to Chicanos. According to David Sanchez, founder of the Brown Berets (a Los Angeles-based militant youth organization), and one of the original members of the Chicano Moratorium Committee, antiwar protest was "a trend, a national trend, and we just made it into a Chicano trend."[21] In the same manner, Ramsés Noriega, a man who was a key behind-the scenes director of the entire moratorium effort, explained that organizing around the war among Chicanos began because "the war was very hot and people were willing to talk about it and deal with it."[22]

Chicanos saw the mainstream peace movement organize rallies and reached the conclusion: we can do that. Yet Chicano Vietnam protest was not just a matter of mimicry. Along with inspiration came motivation. Clearly, one stated goal of Chicano antiwar protest was the immediate withdrawal of U.S. troops from Southeast Asia. The main emphasis, however, was to use Vietnam as a kind of springboard to reach out to those Mexican Americans who were not part of the Chicano Movement. To repeat the words of Noriega, if people were willing to talk about the war and deal with the war, maybe they would also start talking about and dealing with issues closer to home. Most emphatically, moratorium members wanted to mobilize the Mexican-American population not just against the war but against domestic problems confronting the ethnic group. The war proved a good candidate for this mobilizing mission for three reasons.

First, the war was an excellent entry into a whole array of domestic issues. The Moratorium Committee shrewdly used the war in Southeast Asia to highlight problems Mexican Americans faced in the southwestern United States. Suddenly the statistics compiled by Guzmán were of prime importance. As moratorium members sought support for their cause among the membership of Mexican-American civic and political organizations, they routinely began their presentations with a simple statement: Mexican Americans are dying in Vietnam in numbers disproportionate to their population in the United States. Then they would ask: "Why?" In the answers they put forth, they addressed a whole host of domestic inequalities afflicting the Mexican-American population. One fundamental problem, for example, was education. As antiwar Chicanos explained, in elementary school, children of Mexican descent were stripped of their cultural background; in high school, they were tracked in vocational classes. The result was that few Chicanos were on college campuses and thus few were eligible for college draft deferments. Moratorium volunteers also linked the casualty rate to the problem of poverty. They argued that a degrading welfare system plus a lack of job opportunity pushed young Mexican-American men toward military service. Even police brutality was labeled a "push" factor. As Rosalío Muñoz, chair of the Chicano Moratorium Committee, contended when he refused the draft in September 1969, "I accuse the law enforcement agencies of the United States of instilling greater fear and insecurity in Mexican youth than the Viet Cong ever could, which is genocide."[23] Finally, all of these problems, and thus the casualty rate itself, were rooted in a fundamental lack of Mexican-American political clout.

As they recited these injustices, moratorium organizers were pleased to find a generally receptive audience. Here was the second reason the August moratorium march attracted widespread support: by 1970 a substantial amount of antiwar sentiment already existed among Mexican Americans. Although in the earliest years of widespread U.S. military involvement some key Mexican-American elites had endorsed the endeavor, the general Mexican-American population apparently was less firm in its support of the war. Just as in the rest of the country, hawkish attitudes among Mexican Americans may have dissolved in the face of mounting casualties.[24] The last letter written by Patrick Vasquez to his father is telling in this regard. Apparently father and son did not see eye-to-eye on the war. The junior Vasquez's letter was a reply to an earlier missive from his father, who had noted that many parents whose sons had died in Vietnam had turned against the war. Much of the reply reads as if the younger Patrick was trying to convince his father that U.S. military intervention in Vietnam was just and necessary.

By 1970, Mexican Americans may have been even more opposed to the war than the general U.S. population. Unfortunately, only one poll specifically targeted Mexican-American attitudes on the war. Taken in Santa Barbara, California, a few weeks before the August moratorium in Los Angeles, the survey of three hundred Spanish-surnamed area residents showed strong antiwar opinions among the survey group. Asking similar questions to those found within national Gallup polls, researchers found a substantial amount of antiwar sentiment. For example, while Americans as a whole still rejected immediate withdrawal from Vietnam in favor of Vietnamization, the measured substitution of Vietnamese troops for U.S. combat units, nearly two-thirds of the Santa Barbara group favored an immediate U.S. withdrawal over Vietnamization. Also interesting given the career ladder provided by the military, a majority of those polled said that they would discourage any sons they had from entering the army.[25] By linking the war issue to domestic problems, moratorium members were also able to tap into widespread Mexican-American discontent over the war's continuation.

The final reason the committee was able to construct a winning appeal was that members put the patriotic legacy of World War II to good use. Rather than permitting the legacy of World War II to be a stumbling block, committee members appropriated these ideas, but with a twist. They mentioned familiar themes of Mexican-American bravery at times of war and Mexican-American validation through military service, but they put these ideas toward antiwar ends.

In a newspaper interview, Rosalío Muñoz, chairman of the Moratorium Committee, summarized the traditional formula and then explained the Chicano moratorium's departure from it. In his words, "Chicanos came back from World War II and. . . they put on their uniforms and medals, and they'd say, 'We served; you can't call me a wetback, you can't tell me where to go.'" But the result, Muñoz said, was that "we developed this cultural and psychological thing. You prove yourself . . . by going through the service." The Chicano's machismo was channeling Mexican Americans toward military life. Rather than accept this situation, Muñoz argued, the Moratorium Committee, as he put it, "had to go directly the other way against it."[26] Specifically, Muñoz was suggesting that moratorium members cast antiwar protest as an honorable, courageous cause and, in particular, present resisting the draft as an act of bravery.

Under these circumstances, Muñoz contended that the moratorium committee's "first priority was educating the community" to abandon the traditional high value Mexican Americans presumably had placed upon military service.[27] By criticizing the Vietnam War, the Moratorium Committee rejected the military as an avenue of social advancement and personal glory for Mexican-American men. Yet nothing in the moratorium's message went directly against the conception—and acclamation—of Mexicanos as *muy machos,* as very manly.

The difference was that now machismo was imbued with a specific political and social consciousness, one that was pro-Chicano and antiwar. As one young scholar, who spoke highly of the moratorium effort, contended, "To resist, is in the strongest sense of the word a test of manhood, personal courage, and honor, *machismo*."[28]

Neither was praising the machismo of draft resisters a phenomenon restricted to men. While the handful of students who headed the moratorium effort were mainly men, women who wrote articles in support of the antiwar effort offered similar arguments to those of the men who spoke to audiences from up on stage. In fact, Corinne Sánchez, a writer for *El Alacrán,* the Chicano student newspaper at California State Long Beach, placed a special burden upon Chicanas to recognize that machismo began at home. Because of their "cultural upbringing," Chicanas valued manly acts of courage and so, indirectly, put pressure upon Mexican-American men to go to war, she contended. Sánchez did not ask that Chicanas forsake their cultural values, just that they redirect them on behalf of the movement. She implored Chicanas to "become educated on the total Vietnam War," and so recognize that "manliness is a beautiful cultural concept that should be utilized for the betterment of our people, and not for the destruction of other people."[29]

By mentioning casualty rates and by referring to the ideas of World War II, moratorium members anchored their appeal to the same grave injustice that Mexican Americans had noted since World War II: they were dying overseas for the United States while still subject to discrimination at home. The main thrust of the moratorium demonstration remained clear enough to one Mexican-American woman, who explained that she had marched on 29 August because she wanted her son, a soldier in Vietnam, to come home. But Cora Barba continued to use her son's military service to validate her own reach for equality. As she understood the purpose of the demonstration: "If my boy has a right to be out there...and has to be suffering...I demand my rights and I want justice done."[30]

Barba's comments indicated that the moratorium campaign had achieved, in part, what it set out to do. Organizers had convinced many Mexican Americans, even those not involved in the Chicano Movement, that the "batalla," the battle, for Chicanos was not in Vietnam, but, as one newspaper advocated, "in the struggle for social justice in the U.S."[31] That accomplishment was incomplete, however.

A violent clash instigated by law enforcement on the day of the march ultimately cost three people—including journalist Ruben Salazar—their lives. Successive moratorium marches were never able to capture the numerical strength or the widespread optimism of the August demonstration. Harassed by police authorities and suffering a reputation damaged by repeated clashes between law enforcement and Chicanos, the moratorium effort gradually lost support and direction.

Historical accounts of the moratorium effort have emphasized the tragedy and violence that took place on 29 August 1970, and the subsequent unraveling of the Moratorium Committee.[32] Such an emphasis, however, obscures the Moratorium Committee's central accomplishment: the massive display of ethnic solidarity that was the march itself. Eager to take advantage of the attention commanded by the war in Vietnam, activists in Los Angeles used the war issue to build support for the Chicano cause; they reached out to a broad sector of the Mexican-American population by carefully crafting an appeal that emphasized domestic inequities and praised Mexican-American soldiering ability; they also promoted political mobilization. For a short while, they achieved tremendous unity in the face of quite remarkable diversity. The Moratorium Committee, however, never developed a political program beyond marching, beyond mobilization. In that respect, the moratorium effort fit a broader movement pattern: coming together in marches and conferences as proud and militant Chicanos was always easier than agreeing upon what path Chicano militancy should take.

Just as Chicano antiwar activism offers insight into the broader Chicano Movement, so the study of this activism offers some suggestions about movement history. Before turning to a discussion of the present-day state of Chicana and Chicano studies, I would like to briefly mention the historiographical implications of the history I've shared. In terms of scholarship on the movement, I think my research makes three recommendations: to examine movement history in conjunction with the history of the broader Mexican-American population; to place movement history within the greater context of U.S. history; and to develop a more detailed knowledge of movement history through additional research.

First, the work argues for exploring the movement in tandem with nonmovement Mexican-American politics. For example, I was interested to find that one of the earliest Vietnam demonstrations organized by Mexican Americans was a march in support of LBJ's policies.[33] As Professor Gómez-Quiñones has suggested, movement activists were a minority within a minority.[34] In that case, what was their relationship to the greater Mexican-American population? Activists often labeled Mexican Americans who did not agree with them "vendidos," or sellouts, yet Mexican-American opposition to movement politics undoubtedly had more than just one source. Clarifying the relationship between activists and the broader Mexican-American population is critical if we are to understand not just what inspired young people to join the Chicano Movement, but also what motivated many Mexican Americans to stay away.

Second, as my work is at the crossroads of antiwar and Chicano protest, the very conception of the project advocates studying the Chicano Movement within the broader context of U.S. history. Yesterday we heard some reasons from Professor Ramón Ruiz why Chicano history should be placed within the field of Mexican history. For the Chicano Movement, the context of the 1960s and early 1970s within the United States is just as important. For instance, although I did not expand on this point today, one of the reasons movement activists in Los Angeles decided to stage their own protest march was that they felt mistreated by West Coast peace activists at a massive San Francisco demonstration in November 1969.[35] While scholars readily acknowledge that the emergence of the Chicano Movement coincided with a swirl of protest activity across the country, they have not pressed the point. Thus the apparent influence of Black Power ideas upon the movement philosophy of Chicanismo has been mentioned only in passing. Instances of collaboration between the Chicano and American Indian movements likewise await investigation.

Granted, the number of works on the Chicano Movement is still relatively small. Yet only by looking at the Chicano Movement as part of the social movements of the 1960s and 1970s do the precise ways in which Mexican-American activism of the era was unique become apparent. For example, scholars have cited the moratorium effort and its "international orientation" as evidence that the elements within the Chicano Movement were moving toward a more explicitly ideological framework, presumably Marxism.[36] Certainly the national peace movement included a substantial radical wing. Yet within the Moratorium Committee, the guiding inspiration was cultural nationalism, which was hardly new and, according to at least one disappointed

Chicano activist, hardly an ideology.[37] Seemingly fearful of impugning the distinctive quality of the movement, of diminishing its contribution, many scholars have failed to explore areas of overlap—and divergence—between Chicanos and non-Chicano activists. In this regard, Armando Navarro's 1995 work on MAYO, which breaks down the causes of the movement into endogenous and exogenous categories may mark an important turning point.[38]

Third, although my research examines what might be called the Chicano antiwar movement, I think my work strongly lobbies for continued in-depth study of the Chicano Movement overall. I use the war issue as a way to understand the development of the Chicano Movement over time. You could repeat this exercise using the issue of feminism and the woman's struggle, for example, and perhaps at the end you might begin to learn more about the story of the Chicana movement.[39] Likewise, the role of class within the movement needs to be explored. Muñoz asserted that the movement was a fundamentally working-class project.[40] Gómez-Quiñones lamented that it wasn't working class enough.[41] Neither investigated the relationship between class status and movement participation with any specificity. Still another unknown is what happened to most participants after the heyday of the movement. Easiest to trace are those in academia, but they are few in number.

Fortunately, numerous sources exist to help scholars compile a more comprehensive history of the Chicano Movement. Although scholars have used newspaper accounts and oral history interviews, neither avenue has been fully explored. While more than fifty alternative Chicano newspapers were printed during the time of the movement, only a fraction of these publications—Los Angeles media figure prominently—have appeared in works on the movement.[42] Similarly, the recollections of Chicanas have received less attention from historians than the musings of their male counterparts. Other sources, moreover, are available. Despite an abysmally slow response time, the Federal Bureau of Investigation has been known to surrender files, albeit frequently censored, requested under the Freedom of Information Act.[43] Overlooked almost entirely are the papers of elected officials ranging from the president of the United States to the local city council member.[44] In addition, personal archives of activists await scholarly scrutiny, as probably no more than a dozen have been deposited at university libraries.[45]

Exploring these still relatively untapped sources may provide a more nuanced picture of the movement. Until now, scholarship on the movement has been marked by an air of disappointment. *Youth, Identity, Power* by Carlos Muñoz Jr., for example, presented *el Plan de Santa Bárbara,* the master plan of Chicano studies, as one of the foremost accomplishments of a movement dominated by young people. Reserving a survey of the development of Chicano studies for another chapter, however, Muñoz had little else to say about youth activism at its peak: the following section was labeled "The Decline of the Student Movement."[46] For his part, Juan Gómez-Quiñones in his book *Chicano Politics* included a section called "The Movement's Insufficiencies," but did not include one labeled "The Movement's Accomplishments." Gómez-Quiñones furthermore expressed regret that the 1969 Plan de Aztlán, the movement's foremost political pronouncement, was so loosely written as to allow "its language concerning issues to degenerate into reformism."[47] Indeed, although the alternative was never made explicit, mere "reformism" appeared to be his indictment of the Chicano Movement overall. Somewhat more optimistically, Ignacio M. García titled his work on La Raza Unida Party *United We Win*. While a statement of aspiration and a call to action, the title inevitably was also an ironic commentary on what the party failed to accomplish.[48]

The Chicano Movement never did achieve "total liberation from oppression, exploitation, and racism." Nor did the movement secure enduring unity—cultural or political—for all Mexican Americans. Within the movement itself, activists disagreed on how to advance Chicano liberation and also disagreed as to what exactly constituted Chicano liberation. Given the enormity of the task, however, the vision and willingness to struggle were remarkable. The widespread, complex, passionate explosion of cultural expression and political challenge that was the Chicano Movement deserves further study. Additional research may further a more detailed and textured understanding of the movement, perhaps a greater appreciation of the Chicano Movement's accomplishments in union with its limitations. Undoubtedly, however, the continued making of movement history, just like the movement itself, will have to address the substantial diversity found among Mexican Americans in general and among Chicano activists in particular.

The Making of Chicano Studies and the Future of the Field

When I was first placed on a panel entitled "Positions," charged with exploring various positions on Chicana/o and ethnic studies, I thought at first I had no right to speak, and, to be brutally self-revealing, perhaps little worthwhile to contribute. This is my first year at the University of California in Davis. My position, moreover, is within the history department. Still, I am exceedingly proud to serve on the Chicana/o Studies Program Committee at Davis and I did spend a year at the University of California in Santa Barbara as a Chicana Dissertation Fellow. Since being invited to this conference, moreover, I also find myself in the middle of a debate about the future direction of the field.

As I now turn to a discussion about Chicana and Chicano studies, the themes I have discussed so far remain important. Just as the Chicano Movement struggled to forge unity amidst diversity for a greater political purpose, so Chicano studies was conceived in the hope of accomplishing the same task, specifically through institutions of higher education. *El Plan de Santa Bárbara,* collectively authored in 1969 by students, staff, and faculty, was the original statement of purpose and aspiration for the nascent field. A groundbreaking reconception of what higher education might mean for Mexican Americans, the plan sketched out not only what Chicano studies hoped to achieve, but also for whom and by whom. Along the way, the plan attempted to reconcile a specific notion of community, the barrio, and a specific ethnic identity—the Chicano—with the inherent diversity of the Mexican-American population. More than a quarter of a century later, as social injustices remain even as the number of Mexican Americans with doctorates has increased, the field of Chicana and Chicano studies continues to confront questions of purpose and, equally important, of participation. A generation after the plan was written, who belongs in the field, and to what avail?

I propose that the future vitality of Chicana and Chicano studies depends upon an inclusive vision of the field and of who may rightfully claim membership within it. The dangers posed by the opposite approach are revealed in Ignacio M. García's "Juncture in the Road: Chicano studies Since 'El Plan de Santa Bárbara.'" A former Raza Unida Party activist in Texas who is now an assistant professor of history at Brigham Young University, García wishes to recapture what he believes the field has lost with the passage of time, namely "the spirit of *el Plan de Santa Bárbara*."[49] Surveying the history of the field since its inception, García closely echoes the plan in his understanding of the emergence of Chicano studies and its purpose. As a historian, however, he neglects to address a central dilemma that arose in 1969 and remains today: juggling the triad of unity, political purpose, and, especially, diversity. Instead, even more so than the authors of *el Plan de Santa Bárbara,* García embraces the notion of a single, authentic Chicano community as both the source and beneficiary of Chicano studies activism. The ironic result is that the article, while raising some interesting questions about the future direction of the field, ultimately prescribes political and academic stagnation.

The impetus of "Juncture in the Road" is clear. Chicano studies programs today, García laments, are in a deplorable condition, "stepchildren of the academy, with few resources, a limited staff, and often, a marginal reputation."[50] Eager to spur a revitalization of the field, García enumerates the challenges confronting Chicano studies. He mentions the decline in student activism since the late 1970s and the conservative backlash that began in the 1980s.[51] Yet by far the greatest threat to the field, according to García, is largely a product of the 1990s. Thirty years after *el Plan de Santa Bárbara* was crafted, he writes, people working within Chicano studies lack dedication to—or, worse, knowledge of—the field's founding document. Wishing to curb such apparent waywardness, García offers a solution: to reinvigorate Chicano studies by moving it closer to "what the authors of el Plan de Santa Bárbara had in mind."[52]

Although García was not among these authors, to fully appreciate his concerns, an overview of what the plan means to him is helpful. As García notes, *el Plan de Santa Bárbara* endorsed a myriad of assignments to make the university a more hospitable and pertinent place for Chicanos. These included advancing the recruitment and retainment of students and faculty alike; politicizing Mexican Americans on campus and off to the goals of the movement; and conducting research on the plight of the ethnic group. From the start, García explains, "Chicano Studies had a responsibility beyond instructing students about their history and culture and helping them to meet their degree requirements."[53] At peril today, he argues, is this greater, essential mission: "to reach out toward the community to assist in resolving the problems that *la raza* faces daily."[54]

Unlike the present-day situation, the initial years of Chicano studies, according to García, were a time when *el Plan de Santa Bárbara* was in full force. When young, García recalls, "the field was slanted toward activism," and Chicano studies programs were important vehicles of student politicization. Therefore no matter how embryonic the courses were, he fondly remembers, "in Chicano Studies everyone became a philosopher, a political scientist, and a reformer, and those roles were often taken beyond the classroom."[55] Professors in the field, moreover, faithfully attended to the plan's mandate to conduct "action-oriented analysis" and research.[56] Starting in 1970, scholars promoted the theory that Mexican Americans constituted an internal colony within the United States. García describes this initial "Chicano paradigm" as revolutionary: in one swift blow, he writes, the internal colonial theory "relieved the burden that self-victimization brought to many Mexican Americans."[57] Extolling what Chicano studies accomplished in the early 1970s, García hopes that the field once again will become infused with a pioneering sense of purpose and militancy.

Perhaps that is why his vision for the future of the field so liberally borrows from the past. Specifically, García uncritically appropriates specific notions of community and, more implicitly, identity, that flourished during the time of the movement. Particularly revealing is his description of the origins of the field. As García explains, "Chicano Studies emerged out of a need to legitimize the Chicano experience and to provide the people in the barrio with a collective identity." Lacking access to the university and, partly as a consequence, lacking historical knowledge about themselves, he continues, "Chicanos suffered not only exploitation and poverty, but also an identity crisis that divided the community."[58] To summarize García's analysis, identity problems plagued the barrio and the community. A familiar movement assumption repeatedly found within *el Plan de Santa Bárbara* evidently still carries weight with him: to García, notions of barrio and community are closely intertwined. Both ideas, moreover, tend to exclude a specific subset of the Mexican-American population. As García explains, one segment of the ethnic group had by the birth of Chicano studies all but forfeited their claim to barrio or community membership. "Those who sought economic stability, upward mobility and acceptance," he declares, "often found themselves moving toward assimilation and away from the community."[59] Without repeating the movement's familiar distinction between the militant "Chicano" and the assimilationist "Mexican American," García nevertheless reprises an assertion found within *el Plan de Santa Bárbara*. As the plan put it, assimilation, as evidenced by a "turning away from the barrio and la colonia," was the "ultimate cost" some ethnic group members had paid to achieve social mobility.[60]

Upon close inspection, however, García appears to have exceeded "what the authors of el Plan de Santa Bárbara had in mind." Advocating greater fidelity to the plan, García fails to note that the Santa Barbara document incorporated a certain leeway in its definitions. The supposedly sharp divide between two archetypal ethnic identities is one example. On the one hand, the plan did contrast the assimilationist, middle-class, and politically ineffective Mexican American with the politically committed, culturally proud, and barrio-based Chicano.[61] On the other hand, the plan expressed the fervent hope that all Mexican Americans were "potential Chicanos."[62] Similarly, the opening lines of the plan's manifesto clearly equated "our people, the community," with "el barrio, la colonia."[63] Yet the plan also held out the possibility that the concept of community could be, perhaps should be, "all-inclusive."[64] This occasional relaxing of definitions and categories at the height of the movement is revealing. Even as the authors of *el Plan de Santa Bárbara* embraced a specific ethnic identity emerging from a particular community as the building blocks of the movement, they acknowledged the inherent diversity of the ethnic group. In 1969, they also harbored the hope that their crusade might someday appeal to virtually all Mexican Americans.

In contrast, García refuses to address fundamental issues of achieving unity amidst diversity. The result is that he can only maintain his idea of community by tossing people out. Convinced that the original crusading spirit of Chicano studies has been lost, García questions the legitimacy of those he believes are responsible for detrimental deviations. In essence, he denies them community membership. Furthermore, because García upholds his narrow definition of community as both the wellspring and guarantor of activism, he denies their work any social or political relevance. Indeed, García accuses many of these suspect scholars of willfully divorcing themselves from a "passion for progressive scholarship."[65] Consequently, García's perception of who belongs in the field and what their work may entail is a narrow one. Such a circumscribed vision, however, ultimately undermines whatever potential Chicana and Chicano studies has to effect meaningful politi-

either in Borderlands history or in Texas history but not in Mexican-American history.

Before World War II, the few published works dealing with Mexican Americans were mainly sociological or anthropological studies of labor immigration, works on "home missionary work" by Protestant missionaries, or educational studies focusing on Mexican educational deficiencies. Some of these works contained useful historical overviews or regional material, much of which was used by Carey McWilliams in *North from Mexico: The Spanish Speaking People of the United States.* (1949).

Published in 1949, McWilliams's *North from Mexico* was the first general history of Mexican Americans in the United States. Works by other authors such as Manuel Gamio, Emery Bogardus, and George I. Sanchez provided secondary sources for McWilliams's work. *North from Mexico* was a seminal accomplishment. Indeed, immigration historian Arthur Corwin Jr. actually went so far as to claim that McWilliams "invented Mexican-American history."[4]

After World War II and the Korean War, the GI Bill provided significant numbers of Mexican Americans some access to universities. Scholars from this generation, including Manuel P. Servin, Ramón Eduardo Ruiz, and, slightly later, Rodolfo Acuña, were to play a critical role in either prefiguring or establishing Chicano history. By the 1960s, Servin, Ruiz, and a few others had attained doctoral degrees in Latin American history, and taught courses in Mexican history. Works such as Ramón Eduardo Ruiz's reader, *The Mexican War: Was It Manifest Destiny?* (1963) were viewed as beacons of scholarship by young Mexican-American students.[5] The works of Borderlands social historians, such as Leonard Pitt's *The Decline of the Californios* (1966), Alan C. Hutchinson's *Mexican Settlement in Frontier California* (1969), and David J. Weber's *Foreigners in Their Native Land: Historical Roots of Mexican Americans* (1973) provided a major stimulus to Chicano historians.[6]

In the 1960s, the field of Chicano history arose as a result of the rise of a new social history and the influence of the Chicano Movement of the 1960s and 1970s. The first courses in Chicano/a history were established in the 1960s, and by the 1980s courses were created in Chicana history, labor history, and historiography, as well as Texas, New Mexico, and California Mexican-American history.

Mexican Perspectives of Mexican Americans

The understanding of Mexican-American history requires an understanding of its relationship to Mexican history and Mexican historical research. Prior to the mid-twentieth century, however, there were few published Mexican histories of the former Mexican territories of Texas, New Mexico, Alta California, and La Mesilla/Arizona. Spanish and Mexican historical literature for the colonial period has been discussed by Juan Gómez-Quiñones and David Weber. [7]

In the 1980s, the focus of the work of Chicano historians shifted, with increasing recognition and publication in Mexico. Research on immigration also focused attention on the history of Mexican Americans in the Midwest, Plains States, and Pacific Northwest. Important works include Mercedes de Carreras de Velesco's *Los Mexicanos que devolvio la crisis, 1929–1932* (1974).[8]

Mexicans in Western and Borderlands History

Prior to the 1960s, United States histories referring to Mexican Americans reflected developmentalist perspectives of the "Western Expansion" and "Spanish Borderlands" schools of historiography, or the evolutionist conquest and cultural conquest perspectives in the cultural conflict school of Texas history. [9]

Borderlands history treated Mexicans indirectly as objects of institutional and political themes. These themes emphasized a perspective of the Southwest as being concerned primarily with the Spanish colonial period. Otherwise Mexicans were viewed through the history of the Anglo-American West, as a barrier to be overcome by the Anglo pioneer settler, as twentieth-century immigrants, or as a colorful and touristic Mexican Indian backdrop to the Sun Belt of the late-twentieth century.

In addition, the history of Mexicans was obscured by a widespread convention among scholars of Western, California, and Borderlands history that pre-1900 settlers were "Spanish Americans."[10] This convention was characterized by Carey McWilliams in *North From Mexico* as the "Spanish Myth." While McWilliams was not the first scholar to recognize this major defect in the treatment of the pre-1848 Mexican Far West and Southwest, he was the first to provide a comprehensive reexamination and rebuttal. [11] Unfortunately, McWilliams's challenge received little immediate serious attention because historians underrated his book as social journalism rather than scholarly work. It was not until the 1960s brought new developments in the discipline of history and the reemergence of a critical ethnic consciousness that *North from Mexico* received critical acclaim.

Rise of Chicano History and Historiography

Since the 1960s, social historians, Chicano historians, and other scholars have initiated an extensive reexamination and reinterpretation of the Mexican presence in United States history. Numerous studies now reveal the complexities and contributions of Mexican society in California and the Southwest during the colonial period and the nineteenth and twentieth centuries. Early contributors to the development of Chicano history in the 1960s included Manuel P. Servin of the University of Southern California and folklorist Americo Paredes at the University of Texas, Austin. At the very end of the 1960s they were joined by Rodolfo Acuña at California State University, Northridge; Juan Gómez-Quiñones at the University of California, Los Angeles; and Matt Meier and Feliciano Rivera at the University of Santa Clara and San Jose State University. [12]

Theoretical and Philosophical Influences

Because Chicano/a historiography is new, any discussion of theoretical and philosophical influences must be both tentative and fluid. The brief time frame and small numbers of Chicano/a historians must also be considered.

The field is only now nearing the end of its formative phase. The size of the first generation of Chicano/a scholars, who received Ph.D.s between 1970 and 1980, is quite small. Almost all are still in midcareer and are continuing to develop their perspectives. Their students, who received degrees between 1980 and 1990, are in early to midcareer. Compared to the historical discipline in the United States as a whole, even the most senior Chicano/as have barely entered their mature phase. Only a few scholars who began in the middle to late 1950s, prior to the existence of a Chicano history field, are at a career phase comparable to senior American historians. [13]

Individual Mexican-American scholars are open to and influenced by multiple philosophical perspectives and change their viewpoints over time. It would be both inaccurate and dogmatic to associate an individual historian exclusively with one point of view, unless they so identify in their writings.

A discussion of influences must consider the immediate context at the time of the formal establishment of the Chicano/a field, as well as the prior context of Mexican-American history writing and American historians' treatment of Mexicans. The immediate context in the 1960s was the rise of social history as a major catalyst in the legitimization of histories of American peoples of color, including Chicanos. Obviously, the rise of social history paralleled changing political and social attitudes. Other influences were the developing revisionist perspectives in Spanish Borderlands history, United States immigration history, and Mexican history.

Prior to the 1950s, Mexican-American history writing was carried out by regional, local authors; university-affiliated scholars such as Carlos Castañeda, Arthur Campa, and George I. Sanchez were rare exceptions.[14] Earlier influences on historical interpretation include those from both Mexican and American ideological and philosophical perspectives. Mexican American regional and local history to the mid-twentieth century reflected both Mexican and American ideological influences. Some accounts were *costumbrista* (attempting to present a literary folkloric archtype of a particular area or community), antiquarian (presenting a isolated incident or antecedotal case or event), or moralistic (presenting a moralist or nostalgic view of a lost past) in being concerned with local and regional tradition. Other manuscripts reflected the successive and competing influences of Mexican liberalism, clerical conservatism, revolutionary populism, and institutionalized revolutionary symbolism.[15] Folklorists such as Arthur Campa and Ameríco Paredes pioneered in developing a broader concern with the relationship between regional Mexican-American cultural history and Mexican cultural history. Western American and Borderlands history reflected a philosophical range between American and Latin American conservative (Whig or Catholic clerical) and liberal traditions. By the 1940s, developmentalist perspectives such as those of Arnold Toynbee were influencing some Western Borderlands scholars, while Texas history remained influenced by an evolutionist cultural conflict school.

While Carey McWilliams did not invent Mexican American history, he did bring to it a new ideological interpretation. McWilliams broke with regional accounts, social science, and radical overviews of

Mexican Americans to reflect the American radical traditions of Upton Sinclair-style populism and social democracy. In style and tone, *North from Mexico* combined the radical side of muckraking tradition with New Deal reformist concerns.

Important to the development of Chicano history was the convergence of influence from several related fields within history. Chicano history emerged as a new field affected by various philosophical and ideological perspectives, including the new social history; European and Latin American progressive and radical traditions; and Whig and liberal American historical traditions.

The field was dominated by the theoretical and methodological concerns of the new social history with its predominantly progressive and radical perspectives. In the 1960s and 1970s prominent new social historians included Herbert G. Gutman, Eric Foner, Gabriel Kolko, Alexander Saxton, Eugene Genovese, Gary Nash, Gerda Lerner, and Lawrence Levine.[16] Scholars and theorists from outside the discipline of history provided critical perspective, including Ernesto Galarza, Harold Cruze, Octavio Romano, Tomas Almaguer, Robert Allen, Mario Barrera, Ralph Guzman, Carlos Muñoz, Henry Louis Gates Jr., Rosaura Sanchez, Renato Rosaldo Jr., and Martha P. Cotera.

International, European, and Mexican influences came from such scholars and theorists as E. P. Thompson, Raymond Williams, Eric J. Hobsbawn, Pierre Villar, Franz Fanon, Antonio Gramsci, Albert Memmi, Leopoldo Zea, Fernand Braudel, Luis Gonzalez, Enrique Semo, Josefina Zoraida Vasquez, and Enrique Florescano. Concerns included labor history, movements of the dispossessed and social change, nationalism, education and ideology, the history of racially and sexually excluded groups, and the domination and co-optation of excluded groups.

In the American historical tradition, influential liberal historians included Oscar Handlin, Norris Hundley Jr., and Matt Meier. Among the Whig, conservative historians were Arthur Corwin Jr., Phillip W. Powell, Paul Horgan, and Walter Prescott Webb. A small number of Mexican-American historians were shaped by their traditional training in Whig and liberal American historical interpretations. Most conservative Mexican Americans steered clear of Chicano history, yet a few iconoclasts, such as Manuel A. Machado (*Listen Chicano!,* 1978), represented a faint Whig voice. A much larger influence has been that of the liberal interpretation, which has continued to exercise a potent influence over a larger sector of Mexican-American historians. This influence was early reflected in the group of scholars associated with the *Journal of Mexican American History* and in the works of Matt Meier and Feliciano Rivera. [17]

Theoretical and Philosophical Developments

It is too early for more than a tentative discussion of the theoretical and philosophical development of Chicano historiography from the 1970s through the 1990s. Any attempt at interpretation also inevitably has ideological association with the development of the directions of national and Mexican-American/Latino/Hispanic politics from the 1970s through the 1990s. As noted, a major limitation in identifying philosophical/ideological schools in Chicano historiography is quite simply the very small number of Chicano/a historians in the 1970s. Indeed, prior to 1970 there was not a single Chicana with a Ph.D. in history who was primarily engaged in teaching and research on Chicana/Mexicana history.[18] Because of this, the period from 1970 to 1980 was a formative one in which key historians such as Manuel P. Servin, Rodolfo Acuña, Juan Gómez-Quiñones, and Louise Año Nuevo Kerr acted as pioneers in striking new directions. Often it was scholars from disciplines like anthropology, sociology, and political science—among them Americo Paredes, George I. Sanchez, Ernesto Galarza, Tomas Almaguer, and Fred A. Cervantes—who took the lead in charting theoretical and philosophical directions.

Because of the small numbers, it is more accurate to speak of theoretical/philosophical clusters and affinity groups rather than schools or groups. By the end of the 1970s, Chicano/a/Mexican-American history had developed several theoretical and philosophical clusters.[19] These can be characterized as internal colonial, colonial and labor resistance, Chicana feminist, labor assimilation, liberal, and conservative (Whig).

It must be emphasized that the degree of theoretical and philosophical consistency was developing unevenly and did not necessarily imply a highly defined philosophical and theoretical unity. Rather, it reflected general interests in developing research agendas and some degree of commitment or reaction to the applied focus of Chicano studies. Individual scholars were open to and influenced by multiple philosophical perspectives, and few, if any, associated exclusively with one viewpoint. Because of this complexity, it would be a mistake to directly correlate philosophical perspectives with thematic approaches or subfields.

The internal colonial perspective was defined by the work of sociologist Tomas Almaguer, political scientist Mario Barrera, and the major historian who employed it was Rodolfo Acuña, while many graduate students, including Ramón A. Gutiérrez, adopted it in their early writings. Colonial and labor resistance had been defined in part by Carey McWilliams and culturally enriched by Americo Paredes.[20] The major historian associated with this perspective was Juan Gómez-Quiñones, who was also the most prolific historiographic essayist. The Chicana feminist perspective was initially defined by nonhistorians Martha P. Cotera and Rosaura Sanchez, and later by historian Louise Año Nuevo Kerr and sociologist Ana Nieto Gómez. [21]

The Chicano labor assimilation perspective was defined by historian Mario T. Garcia and influenced by U.S. immigration and labor historians. The liberal perspective was best represented by Matt Meier and Feliciano Rivera. A conservative (Whig) tendency was vocally represented by Manuel A. Machado, whose book *Listen Chicano!* opened with a preface written by Barry Goldwater.

By the late 1990s, this configuration had begun to shift as scholars reexamined and better defined their positions. Rodolfo Acuña shifted from use of the internal colonial perspective, and Juan Gómez-Quiñones from the colonial perspective, to a developing postcolonial perspective that was first defined in the critique of the internal colonial perspective by political scientist Fred A. Cervantes.[22] Another contributor to the postcolonial school and to the development of the field of subaltern studies is Jorge Klor de Alva.

Ramón A. Gutiérrez, a self-described early proponent of the internal colonial perspective, emerged as the first and leading Chicano historian proponent of a postmodernist perspective. The postmodernist perspective has been much enriched by scholars in cultural studies, comparative literature, and sociology, too numerous to be mentioned here. Key figures include Tomas Almaguer, Juan Bruce Novoa, Ramon Saldivar, Genaro Garcia, and Nicolas Kanellos.

A significant cluster of scholars have moved toward a vaguely defined liberalism and neoliberalism. These include several prominent scholars who appear to occupy an ambiguous space between the labor assimilation perspective and a neoliberal perspective. Their future work should clarify changes in their philosophical perspectives. Other scholars, including Matt Meier, appear to be positioned between liberalism and neoliberalism.[23] Finally, the underdeveloped conservative position has shifted to a neoconservatism and received a real voice from cultural commentator Richard Rodriguez. Richard Garcia, who has been influenced by Rodriguez, appears to represent a recent move in this direction by some Chicano historians.[24]

This tentative interpretation of philosophical influences on Chicano/a history can be confirmed or modified only by detailed analysis of the work of historians, their statements, and continuing changes and enrichment from many sources. Any characterization of colleagues must be tentative and subject to revision. In reality, historical scholars are dynamic and seek, receive, integrate, express, and debate multiple influences in a constant effort to advance the quality of historical theory, research, writing, and teaching.

Historiographic Issues

Major issues in Chicano history include (1) the periodization and degree of historical continuity between pre-twentieth-century Mexicans and twentieth-century Mexican Americans; (2) the stagnation or decline perspective of nineteenth-century Mexican society in the Southwest; (3) the origins of Mexican labor organizations and the influence on them of the American labor movement; (4) the role of women in the reproduction of Chicano/a identity and culture, and the lives and struggles of Mexican women as central in Chicano/a history; (5) the imagining of and changes in identities—i.e., national, ethnic, regional, local, gender; and (6) organization, politics, and political ideology.

Periodization

Periodization has been much debated and is linked to the debates on different paradigms of Chicana/Chicano history. Many periods have been proposed as the starting point of Chicano history. Among these periods and corresponding paradigms are:

Indigenista

1. Indigenous Native American Creation Origins. A native theological perspective of origins claimed by those Mexican, Chicano indigenistas

who accept the validity of indigenous theology as the origin of Mexicans as a people of fundementally indigenous identity. 2. Bering Straits theory, 15,000–100,000 A.D. Starting from the presence of prehistoric Asiatic migration, Mexicans are viewed as mainly indigenous, with the earliest scientifically proven presence of Native Americans viewed as their earliest origin. 3. Meso-American Pre-Classic to Classic. Olmecs, Teotihuacán, Toltecs, Mexicans indigenous with the earliest Meso-American civilizations viewed as the most significant starting point. 4. 1100 A.D. Arrival of eleven Chichimec tribes/clans led by Zolotl in valley of México from Aztlán, based upon the Chichimeca Nahua Mexica chronicles as a historical origin for the Mexican and Mexican-American people.

Colonial Period/Mestizaje

5. Early Conquest, 1521–1640. The period of early contact/conquest/colonization viewed as most formative in its subsequent influence on Mexican society, including Catholicism, the Spanish language, and the origin of the Virgin of Guadalupe as a symbol of Mexican identity. 6. Century of Depression, 1640–1750. The middle colonial period viewed as formative of criollo elite, large scale mestizaje among Criollos, Indians, Africans, mestizos, development of regional cultural identities. 7. Late-Bourbon Reforms, 1750–1810. A period of increasing colonial state power which displaced, and antagonized criollo elites, and intensified exploitation and local resistance by Indians and *castas,* including mestizos and mulattos.

Mexican Revolution/Independence

8. Hidalgo, Morelos, Guerrero Revolution. The outbreak of armed revolt and the mass proclamation of a Mexican national identity and liberal ideology. 9. Independence, 1821. The actual achievement of formal political independence and establishment of a Mexican national state.

War and Annexation by Anglo-Americans

10. Texas, 1836. The separation of Tejanos, (the five thousand Mexican inhabitants of Texas) viewed as the creation of a Mexican group outside of the Mexican state and dominated by non-Mexicans. 11. Mexico-U.S.

War, 1836–1848. Viewed as the creation of the first Mexican group within the United States, outside of the Mexican state, and dominated by non-Mexicans. 12. Transitional Period, 1850–1880s, viewed as the period when fundamental social, economic, and political conditions characterizing the Mexican-American/Anglo-American relationship were established. Viewed as formative period of either colonial, internal colonial, or other forms of domination of Mexican Americans within the United States.

Historical events in Mexico during the periods of the Reforma 1850s, the War of the French Intervention, 1860–67, and the Porfiriato, 1877–1910, can also be viewed as significantly influencing the Mexican community in the United States during the late-nineteenth century.

Twentieth-Century Mexican Immigration

13. Immigration of one million Mexicans to the United States between 1900 and 1920. The first large twentieth-century wave of immigration is viewed as a fundamental factor in the formation of Mexican-American identity and community. The Mexican Revolution, 1910–19, can be viewed as contributing not only to stimulating immigration but also as influencing Mexican ideology and self-images in the United States in the mid-twentieth century. Sometimes viewed from the Oscar Handlin immigrantion perspective that Mexican immigration can be explained by the same basic assimilation framework as that of other immigrant goups. A varient model holds that Mexican Americans are assimilating as working-class ethnics who are culturally and socially integrated but economically disadvantaged relative to other Americans.

The periods most often proposed as the start of Chicano/a history are pre-1521 A.D., 1836, 1848, 1850–80s (the transitional period), and 1900–1920. Several of these correspond to a particular paradigm or historiographic approach.

The pre-1521 A.D. period corresponds to several different perspectives, including an indigenous perspective that views Chicanos as Native Americans whose identity has been negated by Spanish, Mexican, and later Anglo-American domination. The conquest is thus viewed as initiating the colonization of the Mexican people. Gender approaches also view the Spanish conquest as a key point in the construction of a European-derived patriarchy, based upon a shame/honor system that subjugated women and men.[25]

The colonial transculturation perspective views the period from 1521 to 1821 as one of transculturation (a process of cultural change from an earlier culture to a new one), mestizaje (the intermixture of different ethnic and cultural groups), and development of a syncretic culture (a new culture evolving from the combination of elements of several earlier cultures). This perspective was developed by ethnohistorians like Eric Wolf in *Sons of the Shaking Earth* (1959) and revisionist historians like Jaime E. Rodriguez and Colin M. MacLachlan in *The Cosmic Race: A Reinterpretation of Colonial Mexico.* (1980).

The 1836 and 1848 dates place emphasis on the annexation and conquest of the native population that became the Mexican population within the United States. The Texas revolt in 1836 resulted in the separation of five thousand Tejanos from Mexico. The signing of the Treaty of Guadalupe Hidalgo in 1848 placed a Mexican population of nearly one hundred thousand within the United States. Rodolfo Acuña's masterwork *Occupied America* begins with the foreign settlement in Texas leading up to the 1836 revolt. [26]

Albert Camarillo characterized the period from 1848 to the 1880s as being the critical transitional period in the formation of the unequal set of relationships that have since prevailed between Mexicanos and Anglo-Americans in the Southwest. Pre-1848 Mexican regional identity in Mexico's far north, while reflecting a popular civic and cultural concept of Mexicano, lacked the institutional state-created cult of *Mexicanidad* that was characteristic of the development of Mexican elementary and secondary education beginning in the 1880s.[27]

Issues of Periodization and Complexity

The very complexity of Chicano history suggests that it has no single starting point, except in a formal sense. More productive is a multi-period approach recognizing that many or all of these periods are phases of Chicano history. Obviously, there will be continuing debate on their respective degrees and types of relevance, but it may be alleged that all are, in some respects, starting points or phases. Furthermore, these starting points in some degree correspond to particular ideological perspectives of Chicanos, whether or not that correspondence is recognized by historians. In this sense, 1900 may be as much an imagined beginning as 1100 or 1848. For example, in the imagining of the Chicano/a indigenista historian, the arrival of Xolotl in 1100 is more real than the beginnings of working-class ethnic assimilation in 1900. Thus, rather than closing off the field at a single, official date, it is more useful to view all of these dates or phases as an unending transitional research agenda being constantly redefined, debated, and reimagined.

Chicano historians quickly confronted the Spanish myth. Critics such as Arthur Corwin Jr. argued for a lack of continuity in which the earlier history of "Spanish people" was made distinct from that of post-1900 Mexican immigrants. While the early periods studies by Chicano historians provide a corrective of the Spanish Myth, they are not intended to and do not negate the influence of Spain and of European Spaniards. Rather, they effectively demonstrate that Spanish influence was primarily mediated and modified through the presence of Mexican settlers in Alta California and the Southwest. An increasing number of community studies, including those of Camarillo (1979) and Griswold del Castillo (1979), further show a continuity of community, culture, and identity among California's Mexican population, from the *pobladores* (settlers) of the eighteenth century to the Mexican immigrants and community of the 1980s. These demonstrate a changing, dynamic community formed by both its past and the influences of the present, as opposed to a static continuity.

Another difference in interpretation has been the nineteenth-century Mexican stagnation, or decline perspective, in which colonial and Mexican society are viewed as decadent or in decline. Contrary to the stagnation perspective, the colonial and Mexican national periods in far northern Mexico were periods of growth, adaptation, and change. Following Mexican independence, Nuevo México and Alta California society entered an even more dynamic period of change. While Tejas was devastated by the royalist military during the 1811–14 revolution, by the mid-1820s a recovery was stimulated by foreign trade.[28]

Theoretical and Thematic Approaches

There is an ever-increasing number of theoretical and thematic approaches and subfields of Chicano history. Newer approaches have developed from older ones. Some have resulted from the influence of other disciplines, such as sociology and comparative literature. Others have resulted from the application of new theories and methodologies. They sometimes overlap in varying degrees; for example, gender studies and the history of the family; intellectual history and postmodern cultural studies. New subfields are continuing to emerge. New paradigms may combine several approaches in new working synthesis.[29]

Thematic Approaches

The first thematic areas that developed were social, labor, immigration, and border history. Since then, many new theoretical and thematic approaches have been added, so that the list now includes:

1. *Labor History*. Chicano labor history was prefigured by the work of social scientists Manuel Gamio, Paul Taylor, Carey McWilliams, and Ernesto Galarza. Ernesto Galarza's works include *Merchants of Labor* (Santa Clara, Calif.: Rosecrucian Press, 1964); *Mexican Americans in the Southwest* (Santa Barbara, Calif.: McNally & Loftin, 1969); *Spiders in the House & Workers in the Field* (Notre Dame, Ind.: University of Notre Dame Press, 1970). The school of Chicano labor history developed around the journal *Aztlán*. Key works include Juan Gómez-Quiñones, "The First Steps," *Aztlán* 3, no. 1: 13–49; *Artisans and Laborers across the Rio Bravo 1600–1900* (Los Angeles: CSRC, UCLA, 1981); *Mexican American Labor, 1790–1990s* (Albuquerque: University of New Mexico Press, 1994). See also Luis Leobardo Arroyo, "Labor Issue," *Aztlán* 6, no. 2 (1974): 277–303; Luis Leobardo Arroyo, "The State of Chicano Labor History, 1970–1980" in *Chicanos and the Social Sciences: A Decade of Research and Development (1970–80)*, Isidro D. Ortiz, ed. (Santa Barbara: University of California, Center for Chicano Studies, 1983).

A major issue has been whether Chicano labor organization resulted primarily because of the influence of the American or Mexican labor movements, was an independent development, or was some combination of the two. Studies of agricultural labor include Richard Griswold del Castillo and Richard Garcia, *Cesar Chavez: A Triumph of Spirit* (Norman: University of Oklahoma Press, 1995); Mark Reisler, *By the Sweat of Their Brow: Mexican Immigrant Labor in the United States, 1900–1940* (N.Y.: Greenwood Press, 1976); Camile Guerin Gonzales, *Mexican Workers and American Dreams: Immigration, Repatriation, and California Farm Labor, 1900–1939* (Rutgers, N.J.: Rutgers University Press, 1994); Devra Weber, *Brown Sweat, White Gold* (Berkeley: University of California Press, 1995). Studies of industrial workers include Clete Daniel, *Chicano Workers and the Politics of Fairness: The FEPC in the Southwest, 1941–1945* (Austin: University of Texas Press,

1991). A comprehensive history is Juan Gómez-Quiñones. *Mexican American Labor, 1790–1990* (Albuquerque: University of New Mexico Press, 1994). An important regional study is Emilio Zamora, *The World of the Mexican Worker in Texas* (College Station: Texas A & M. University Press, 1993), which credits Mexican-American workers with the major impetus for their own organization. The essays in John Mason Hart, ed., *Crossing Borders* (New York: Scholarly Resources, 1998) examine the relationship of Mexican and Mexican-American labor.

2. *Immigration History.* Chicano immigration history reflected the influences of the Oscar Handlin school of immigration history and a new revisionist Chicano immigration history. Immigration historian Arthur Corwin stated that Mexican-American history began in the 1900s with large-scale immigration. This was challenged by Rodolfo Acuña and by Juan Gómez Quiñones. In the 1980s Ricardo Romo "Mexican Americans in the New West," in *The Twentieth Century West*, Gerald D. Nash and Richard W. Etulain, eds. (Albuquerque: University of New Mexico Press, 1989); and George J. Sanchez, *Becoming Mexican American* (New York: Oxford University Press, 1993) have developed a modified perspective that views the twentieth century as the primary focus of Mexican-American history.

The first seminal work was Manuel Gamio's massive study *Mexican Immigration to the United States* (Chicago: University of Chicago Press, 1930); and *The Mexican Immigrant: His Life Story* (Chicago: University of Chicago Press, 1931). A new synthesis of pre-1930 immigration was provided by Lawrence A. Cardoso, *Mexican Emigration to the United States, 1897–1931* (Tucson: University of Arizona Press, 1980). Immigration history is intertwined with the work of the labor school of historians, especially Juan Gómez-Quiñones, described above. This includes Antonio Ríos-Bustamante, ed., *Mexican Immigrant Workers in the United States* (Los Angeles: CSRC, University of California, 1981); Carlos Vasquez and Manuel Garcia y Griego, eds., *Mexican U.S. Relations: Conflict and Convergence* (Los Angeles: CSRC, UCLA, 1983); Mario T. Garcia, *Desert Immigrants: The Mexicans of El Paso, 1880–1920* (New Haven, Conn.: Yale University Press, 1981) examined El Paso as the main twentieth-century gateway. Studies of the 1930s repatriation include Francisco E. Balderrama, *In Defense of La Raza* (Tucson: University of Arizona Press, 1982); Francisco E. Balderrama, *The Decade of Betrayal* (Albuquerque: University of New Mexico Press, 1996); and Juan Garcia, *Operation Wetback* (Westport, Conn.:

Greenwood Press, 1980). More recently George Sanchez, in *Becoming Mexican American* (Oxford, New York: Oxford University Press, 1993), views Mexican Americans as culturally assimilating but economically lower-class American ethnics, similar to the experience of Polish, Czech, and Hungarian immigrants in the Midwest.

3. *Urban Rural History.* The development and growth of Mexican-American communities and neighborhoods has been a major focus of Chicano historians starting with Albert Camarillo, *Chicanos in a Changing Society* (Cambridge, Mass.: Harvard, 1979) and Richard Griswold del Castillo. *Los Angeles Barrio 1850–1890* (Berkeley, Calif.: University of California Press, 1979). While beginning with an urban emphasis, community studies are inherently both urban and rural, dealing with a transition from rural to urban communities. A key historiograpic essay is Albert Camarillo, "Chicanos in the American City" in *Chicano Studies: A Multidisciplinary Approach,* Eugene E. Garcia et al., eds. (New York: Columbia University, Teachers College Press, 1984).

Gilbert Gonzalez and Raul Fernandez, "Chicano History: Transcending Cultural Models," *Pacific Historical Review* 4 (1994): 469–97, have criticized Chicano urban historians for an overemphasis on urban communities and ignoring rural communities. In making this overdue criticism they have in fact exposed a dichotomy regarding what has actually been more a process of transition from rural to urban communities, within which the scale of what constitutes urban has also changed quantitatively and qualitatively.

Southern California and Texas communities have been more heavily treated than other areas. Arnoldo De Leon has written the seminal studies of San Antonio, Houston, San Angelo, and other Texas cities. Major works include: Richard Griswold del Castillo, "Tucsonenses and Angelenos: A Socio-Economic Study of Two Mexican American Barrios, 1860–1880," *Journal of the West* 18, no. 1 (January, 1979, 58–66); Ricardo Romo, *History of a Barrio: East Los Angeles* (Austin, Tex.: University of Texas Press, 1983); Antonio Ríos-Bustamante, *Mexican Los Angeles: A Narrative and Pictorial History* (Encino, Calif.: Floricanto Press, 1992); Antonio Ríos-Bustamante, ed., *Mexican Immigrant Workers in the U.S.* (Los Angeles: CSRC Publications, UCLA, 1981); Antonio Ríos-Bustamante and Pedro Castillo, *An Illustrated History of Mexican Los Angeles, 1781–1985* (Los Angeles: CSRC Publications, UCLA, 1981); Rodolfo Acuña, *A Community Under Siege: A Chronicle of Chicanos East of the Los Angeles River, 1945–1975* (Los

Angeles: CSRC Publications, UCLA, 1984); Rodolfo Acuña, *Anything but Mexican* (New York: Verso, 1996); Arnoldo De Leon, *The Tejano Community, 1836–1900* (Albuquerque: University of New Mexico Press, 1982); Arnoldo De Leon, *Mexican Americans in Texas: A Brief History* (Lawrence: University of Kansas, 1989); Gilberto Hinojosa, *A Borderlands Town in Transition: Laredo, 1755–1880* (College Station, Tex.: A & M University Press, 1983); Gilbert G. Gonzalez, *Labor and Community: Mexican Citrus Worker Villages in a Southern California County, 1900–1950* (Urbana: University of Illinois Press, 1994); and Martha Menchaca, *The Mexican Outsiders: A Community History of Marginalization and Discrimination in California* (Austin: University of Texas Press, 1995).

4. *Chicana History*. Chicana history of Mexican women is as wide-ranging as Mexican-American history as a whole. Women have participated in all aspects of life. Their lives, struggles, and contributions are essential to the recovery and writing of a comprehensive history. Major themes include the role of women in the reproduction of culture; changing female-male relationships; women at work and in labor organization; changing female and male gender roles and images; biographical studies and literary history; and political and cultural ideology in Mexican-American history. Important works include Rosaura Sanchez, "The History of Chicanas: Proposal for a Materialist Perspective," in *Between Borders: Essays on Mexicana/Chicana History*, Adelaida Del Castillo, ed. (Encino, Calif.: Floricanto Press, 1990), 1–29; Antonia Castañeda, "The Political Economy of Nineteenth Century Stereotypes of Californians" in *Between Borders: Essays on Mexicana/Chicana History,* Adelaida Del Castillo, ed. (Encino, Calif.: Floricanto Press, 1990), 213–36; Adelaida Del Castillo, *Between Borders: Essays on Mexicana/Chicana History* (Encino, Calif.: Floricanto Press. 1990): v–xv; Cynthia E. Orozco, "Sexism in Chicano Studies and the Community," in *Chicana Voices,* Theresa Cordoba, ed. (Austin: CMAS, University of Texas, 1986): 11–18; Cynthia E. Orozco, "Beyond Machismo—La Familia, and Ladies Auxiliares: A Historiography of Mexican Origin Women's Participation in Voluntary Associations and Politics in the United States, 1870–1990," *Perspectives* 5 (1995); Alma Garcia, "The Development of Chicana Feminist Discourse, 1970–1980." in *Unequal Sisters,* Ellen Carol DuBois and Vicki L. Ruiz eds. (New York: Routledge, 1990), 418–31; Antonia Castañeda, "Women of Color and the Rewriting of Western History: The Discourse, Politics, and

Decolonization of History," *Pacific Historical Review* 61, no. 4 (1992); Vicki L. Ruiz, *From Out of the Shadows: Mexican American Women in the Twentieth Century* (Oxford: Oxford University Press, 1998); *Chicana Feminist Thought: The Basic Historical Writings,* Alma M. Garcia, ed. (New York: Routledge, 1978); Alma Garcia, "The Development of Chicana Feminist Discourse, 1970–1980," in *Unequal Sisters,* Ellen Carol Du Boise and Vicki L. Ruiz eds. (New York: Routledge, 1990).

Works on women workers and labor organization includes Vicki L. Ruiz, *Cannery Women/Cannery Lives: Mexican Women, Unionization and the California Food Processing Industry, 1930–1950* (Albuquerque: University of New Mexico, 1987). Historiographic essays by Ruiz include: "Mascaras y Muros: Chicana Feminism and the Teaching of U.S. Women's History" (1994); and "Star Struck: Acculturation, Adolescence, and Mexican American Women, 1920–1940" (1992). Anthropologists such as Adelaida del Castillo and have contributed to the analysis of Mexican women's roles by examining Dona Marina Malinche and Tonantzin/Guadalupe, see Adelaida R. del Castillo, "Malintzin Tenepal: A Preliminary Look into a New Perspective" (Los Angeles: Chicano Studies Publications University of California, 1977). Other works include, Sara Deutsch, *No Separate Refuge: Culture, Class, and Gender on an Anglo-Hispanic Frontier in the American Southwest, 1880–1940* (1987); Elizabeth Salas, *Soldaderas in the Mexican Military* (1990); Shirlene Ann Soto, "The Mexican Woman: A Study of Her Participation in the Revolution, 1910–40" (Ph.D. diss. 1977); Raquel Rubio Goldsmith, "Seasons, Seeds, and Souls: Mexican Women Gardening in the American Mesilla, 1900–1940" (1994); Maria Lina Apodaca, "The Chicana Women: An Historical Materialist Perspective," *Latin American Perspectives* 4, nos. 1 and 2 (winter/spring 1977); Deena J. Gonzalez, "The Spanish Mexican Women of Santa Fe" (Ph.D. diss., U.C. Berkeley, 1985); Gilberto Garcia, "Beyond the Adelita Image: Women Scholars in the National Association for Chicano Studies, 1972–1992," *Perspectives* 5 (1995); George J. Sanchez. "Go After the Women: Americanization and the Mexican Immigrant Woman, 1915–1929," in *Unequal Sisters,* Ellen Carol DuBois and Vicki L. Ruiz eds. (New York: Routledge, 1990), 250–63; and Deena J. Gonzalez, "The Widowed Women of Santa Fe: Assessments on the Lives of an Unmarried Population, 1850–1880" (1990).

5. *Regional History.* Regions, regionalism, and regional identities have been primary influences in Mexican history from the pre-1521 Meso-American periods to the present. Early regional studies included works by amateurs Benjamin Read and Hubert Howe Bancroft, and professional works such as Dr. Carlos Castañeda's *Our Catholic Heritage in Texas* (1936). More recent monographs include Richard Griswold Del Castillo's *The Los Angeles Barrio, 1850–1890* (Berkeley: University of California Press, 1979); Thomas Sheridan's *Los Tucsonenses* (Tucson: University of Arizona Press, 1986); and Arnoldo De León's *The Tejano Community* (University of New Mexico, Albuquerque: 1982); Juan R. Garcia "Mid-West Mexicanos in the 1920s: Issues, Questions, and Directions."

General works include: Juan Gómez-Quiñones, *Development of the Mexican Working Class North of the Rio Bravo* (Los Angeles: CSRC, UCLA, 1982); Antonio Ríos-Bustamante, ed., *Regions of the Raza: Changing Perspectives of Mexican American Regional History* (Encino, Calif.: Floricanto Press, 1992); Carlos E. Cortes, "Mexicans," in *Harvard Encyclopedia,* Stephen Therstrom, ed. (Cambridge: Harvard University, 1980); and Thomas D. Hall, *Social Change in the Southwest, 1350–1880* (Lawrence: University Press of Kansas, 1989).

The works of Arnoldo de Leon and Richard Griswold del Castillo are of key importance. Newer regional historiographic surveys include Richard Griswold Del Castillo, "Tejanos and California Chicanos: Regional Variations in Mexican American History," *Mexican Studies/Estudios Mexicanos* 1, no. 1 (winter 1985); Arnoldo De Leon, "Tejano History Scholarship: A Review of the Recent Literature," *West Texas Historical Association Year Book* 59 (1985): 116–33; and Arnoldo De Leon, "Texas Mexicans: Twentieth Century Interpretations," in *Texas Through Time: Evolving Interpretations,* Walter L. Buenger and Robert A. Calvert eds. (College Station: Texas A&M University Press, 1991); Arnoldo De Leon, *Mexican Americans in Texas: A Brief History* (Arlington Heights, Ill.: Harlan Davidson, Inc., 1993); David Montejano, *Anglos and Mexicans in the Making of Texas, 1836–1986* (Austin: University of Texas Press, 1987); Andres Tijerina, *Tejanos & Texas under the Mexican Flag, 1821–1836* (College Station: Texas A & M. University Press, 1994); Sara Deutsch, *No Separate Refuge: Culture, Class, and Gender on an Anglo-Hispanic Frontier in the American Southwest, 1880–1940*; Richard Nostrand, *The Hispano Homeland*

(Norman: University of Oklahoma Press, 1992); and Ralph. H. Vigil, ed., *Spain and the Plains* (University Press of Colorado, 1994).

Also see Thomas E. Chavez, *An Illustrated History of New Mexico,* (University Press of Colorado, 1992); Albert Camarillo, *Chicanos in California: A History of Mexican Americans in California* (San Francisco: Boyd & Fraser, 1984); Antonio Ríos-Bustamante, "The Barrioization of Nineteenth Century Mexican Californians: From Landowners to Laborers," in *Anthropology of the Americas; Masterkey* 60, nos. 2 and 3 (summer/fall 1986): 26–35; Antonio Ríos-Bustamante, *Mexican Los Angeles: A Narrative and Pictorial History* (Encino, Calif.: Floricanto, 1992); Douglas Monroy, *Thrown Among Strangers: The Making of Mexican Culture in Frontier California* (Berkeley: University of California Press, 1990); Juan R. Garcia, "Mid-West Mexicanos in the 1920s: Issues, Questions, and Directions," *Social Science Journal* 19 (April 1982); Erasmo Gamboa, *Mexican Labor and World War II: Braceros in the Pacific Northwest, 1942–1947* (Austin: University of Texas, 1990); Erasmo Gamboa, "Chicanos in the Northwest: An Historical Perspective," *El Grito* 6 (summer 1973).

6. *Border History.* Border history developed as an offshoot of concern with immigration, folklore, and urban history. Folklorist Americo Paredes developed seminal cultural critiques of the border region and Mexican American culture. Juan Gómez-Quiñones led in developing a historiographic analysis of the border and border culture. Sociologists such as Jorge Bustamante and Raul Fernandez also influenced historiographic perspectives. See Raul A. Fernandez, *The United States-Mexico Border* (Notre Dame, Ind.: Notre Dame University Press, 1977). Major studies include those of historians Juan Gómez-Quiñones and Oscar Martinez. See Juan Gómez-Quiñones, "Mexican Immigration in the United States and the Internationalization of Labor, 1848–1980: An Overview," in *Mexican Workers in the United States,* Antonio Ríos-Bustamante, ed. (Los Angeles: CSRC, University of California, 1981); Juan Gómez-Quiñones, "Notes on an Interpretation of the Relations Between the Mexican Community in the United States and Mexico," in *Mexican U.S. Relations Conflict and Convergence,* Carlos Vasquez and Manuel Garcia y Griego eds. (Los Angeles: CSRC, University of California, 1983); Oscar J. Martinez, *Troublesome Border* (Tucson: University of Arizona, 1988); and Oscar J. Martinez, *Border People: Life and Society in the U.S. Mexico Borderlands* (Tucson: University of Arizona, 1991).

7. *Mexican/Mexican-American Relations.* Mexican Americans have always been concerned with Mexico and their relationship to it. The Mexican War and Treaty of Guadalupe created a changed relationship with Mexico. The Mexican Revolution, and cycles of anti-immigration hysteria, equate to important periods of political conflict. Key works are Juan Gómez-Quiñones, "Piedras contra la Luna, Mexico en Aztlan y Aztlan en Mexico: Chicano-Mexican Relations and the Mexican Consulates, 1900–1920." in *Papers of the IV International Congress of Mexican History,* James W. Wilkie, et al. (Los Angeles: University of California Press, 1976); Richard Griswold Del Castillo, *The Treaty of Guadalupe Hidalgo* (Norman: University of Oklahoma, 1991); Juan Gómez-Quiñones, "Notes on an Interpretation of the Relations Between the Mexican Community in the United States and Mexico," in *Mexican U.S. Relations Conflict and Convergence,* Carlos Vasquez and Manuel Garcia y Griego eds. (Los Angeles: CSRC, UCLA, 1983); David Maciel, "La Frontera historiografica: Mexico y Estados Unidos 1968–1988" (1989); Axel Ramirez, *Chicanos: El Orgullo de Ser* (Mexico: UNAM, 1992); Juan Gómez-Quiñones y Antonio Ríos-Bustamante, "La Comunidad Al Norte Del Río Bravo," in *La Otra Cara de Mexico: El Pueblo Chicano* (Mexico D.F.: El Caballito, 1977), 24–35; and Juan Gómez-Quiñones, *The Origins and Development of the Mexican Working Class in the United States: Laborers and Artisans North of the Rio Bravo, 1600–1900* (Los Angeles: CSRC, UCLA, 1977).

Relations during the Mexican Revolution are examined in Juan Gómez-Quiñones, *Sembradores Ricardo Flores Magon y el Partido Liberal Mexicano: A Eulogy and a Critique* (Los Angeles: CSRC, UCLA, 1973); John Mason Hart, *Anarchism and The Mexican Working Class, 1860–1931;* James A. Sandos, *Rebellion in the Borderlands: Anarchism and the Plan of San Diego, 1904–1923* (Norman: University of Oklahoma Press, 1992).

8. *Political History.* Richard Griswold Del Castillo, in *The Treaty of Guadalupe Hidalgo* (Norman: University of Oklahoma, 1991) examines the treaty which defined the political status of conquered Mexicans after 1848. The first general political history of Mexicans in the United States was by political scientist Ralph Guzman, "The Political Socialization of the Mexican American People" (Ph.D. Diss., UCLA, 1970). The major political histories are Juan Gómez-Quiñones, *Roots of Chicano Politics: 1600–1940* (Albuquerque: University of New Mexico, 1994); and Juan Gómez-Quiñones, *Chicano Politics: Reality*

and Promise, 1940–1990 (Albuquerque: University of New Mexico Press, 1990).

Works examining the development of political ideology include Rudolfo A. Anaya, ed., *Aztlan: Essays on the Chicano Homeland* (Albuquerque: University of New Mexico Press, 1989); Mario Barrera, *Beyond Aztlan: Ethnic Autonomy in Comparative Perspective* (Notre Dame, Ind.: University of Notre Dame Press, 1988); and Arturo Rosales, "Mexican Immigrant Nationalism as an Origin of Identity for Mexican Americans: Exploring the Sources," in *Mexican American Identity,* Martha E. Bernal, ed. (Encino, Calif.: Floricanto, 1992). An important concern has been the Chicano movement, Carlos Munoz Jr., *Youth, Identity, Power: The Chicano Movement* (New York: Verso, 1989); Juan Gómez-Quiñones, *Mexican Students Por La Raza;* Ignacio M. Garcia, *United We Win: The Rise and Fall of La Raza Unida Party* (Tucson: Mexican American Studies and Research Center, University of Arizona, 1989); and Armando Navarro, *Mexican American Youth Organization* (Austin: University of Texas, 1995).

Works concerning leadership and organizations include Richard Griswold Del Castillo and Richard Garcia, *Cesar Chávez: A Triumph of the Spirit* (Norman: University of Oklahoma Press, 1995); Cynthia Orozco, "The League of United Latin American Citizens and the American G.I. Forum," (Ph.D. diss., UCLA, 1993); Benjamin Marquez, *LULAC: The Evolution of a Mexican American Political Organization* (Austin: University Texas, 1993); Carl Allsup, *The American G.I. Forum: Origins and Evolution* (Austin: CMAS, University of Texas, 1982).

The issue of Hispanic Brokers is discussed in Rodolfo Acuña, *Occupied America: A History of Chicanos* 3d ed. (New York: Harper & Row, 1988); Ignacio M. Garcia, "Backward From Aztlan: Politics in the Age of Hispanics"; and Ignacio M. Garcia, *Chicanismo: The Forging of A Militant Ethos Among Mexican Americans* (Tucson: University of Arizona Press, 1997).

9. *Intellectual History.* Chicano intellectual history has been influenced by studies in folklore, literature, and political history. Key influences include Americo Paredes, Luis Leal, Juan Gómez-Quiñones, and Francisco Lomeli. Key works include Americo Paredes, "The Folk Base of Chicano Literature," in *Modern Chicano Writers,* Joseph Sommers, ed. (Englewood Cliffs, N.J.: Prentice Hall, 1979), 4–17; Luis Leal, "Mexican American Literature: A Historical Perspective," in

Modern Chicano Writers, Joseph Sommers, ed. (Englewood Cliffs, N.J.: Prentice Hall, 1979), 18–30; Francisco A. Lomeli, "An Overview of Chicano Letters: From Origins to Resurgence," in *Chicano Studies: A Multidisciplinary Approach,* Eugene E. Garcia, ed. (New York: Teachers College, Columbia University, 1984); and Juan Gómez-Quiñones, "Toward a Concept of Culture" in *Modern Chicano Writers,* Joseph Sommers, ed. (Englewood Cliffs, N.J.: Prentice Hall, 1979).

Mario Garcia has examined the role of intellectuals in the 1930s and 1940s in *Memories of Chicano History: The Life and Narrative of Bert Corona* (Berkeley: University of California Press, 1994); *Mexican Americans, Leadership, Ideology, and Identity, 1930–1960* (Berkeley: University of California Press, 1989); and *Ruben Salazar: Border Correspondent* (Berkeley: University of California, 1995). See also Richard Garcia, *Rise of the Mexican American Middle Class, San Antonio, 1929–1941* (College Station: Texas A & M University, 1991).

Postmodern cultural studies are an important influence on intellectual history, and include such works as Jose David Saldivar, "The Limits of Chicano Cultural Studies" (1990); and Ramon Saldivar, *Chicano Narrative: The Dialectics of Difference* (Madison: University of Wisconsin Press, 1990).

10. *Gender and Family History.* Chicano family history, which began with a demographic, social, and economic focus, has broadened to a concern with the history of patriarchy, gender relations and identity-stimulated gender history during the 1980s. The work of Richard Griswold Del Castillo has been key. See Richard Griswold Del Castillo, *La Familia: Chicano Families in the Urban Southwest, l848 to Present* (Notre Dame, Ind.: University of Notre Dame Press, 1984); idem, "Neither Activists Nor Victims: Mexican Women's Historical Discourse—The Case of San Diego, 1820–1850," *California History* (fall 1995); idem, "Patriarchy and the Status of Women in the Late Nineteenth-Century Southwest," in *The Mexican and Mexican American Experience in the Nineteenth Century,* Jaime E. Rodriguez O., ed. (Tempe, Ariz.: Bilingual Press, 1989); and Alex Saragoza, "The Conceptualization of the History of the Chicano Family," in *On the State of Chicano Research in Family, Labor and Migration Studies,* Armando Valdez et al. eds. (Stanford, Calif.: Stanford Center for Chicano Research, Stanford University, 1983).

Other key works include Adelaida Del Castillo, *Between Borders: Essays on Mexicana/Chicana History* (Encino, Calif.: Floricanto Press, 1990); Ramón Gutiérrez, "Community, Patriarchy and Individualism:

The Politics of Chicano History and the Dream of Equality," *American Quarterly* 45, no. 1 (March 1993); and Ramón Gutiérrez, *When Jesus Came the Corn Mothers Went Away* (Stanford, Calif.: Stanford University Press: 1991).

11. *Postmodern and Cultural Studies.* The postmodernist critique reexamines gender, patriarchal, and national components that can be integrated into a new synthesis for Chicano/a historiography. An excellent basic introduction is Frederic Jameson, *Postmodernism or the Cultural Logic of Late Capitalism* (Durham, N.C.: Duke University Press, 1991). Other key works include Jose David Saldivar, *The Dialectics of Our America* (Durham, N.C.: Duke University Press, 1991); Jose David Saldivar, "The Limits of Chicano Cultural Studies," *American Literary History* 2, (summer 1990); Hector Calderon, *Criticism in the Borderlands* (Durham, N.C.: Duke University Press, 1991); Ramón Gutiérrez, "Community, Patriarchy and Individualism: The Politics of Chicano History and the Dream of Equality." *American Quarterly* 45, no. 1 (March 1993): 44–72; Richard Garcia, "Turning Points: Mexican Americans in California History: Introduction to Special Issue," *California History* (fall 1995); Richard Garcia, "The Origins of Chicano Cultural Thought: Visions and Paradigms—Romano's Culturalism, Alurista's Aesthetics, and Acuna's Communalism," *California History* 74, no. 3 (fall 1995): 226–29.

12. *Public History.* "Public" and "applied" history are historical programs, media, publications with an impact in society outside of the university. Public history includes "local history" or "popular history" and history museums, historical societies, and their public programs. Mexican-American public history programs have been gradually increasing as scholars, museums, historical societies, and government agencies begin to produce Latino programs.

Mexican-American public history programs are described in Antonio Ríos-Bustamante, "El Orgullo de Ser: Latino Public History and Museum Programs." working paper (Tucson: Mexican American Studies and Research Center, University of Arizona, 1992); and Antonio Ríos-Bustamante and Christine Marin eds., *Latinos in Museums: A Heritage Reclaimed* (Malabar, Flor.: Krieger Press, 1997). A study of Latino representation in museums is Antonio Ríos-Bustamante, *Latinos and Native Americans in the Museum: The National Survey and Directory of Historical and Art Museum Professional Personnel* (Tucson: Mexican American Studies and Research Center, University of Arizona, 1997).

13. *Oral History.* Important Chicano/a oral history studies include Vicki L. Ruiz, "Oral History and la Mujer: The Rosa Guerrero Story," in *Women on the on the United States-Mexico Border: Responses to Change,* Vicki L. Ruiz and Susan Tiano eds. (Boston: Unwin & Allen, 1987): 219–231; Oscar Martinez, *Border People* (Tucson: University of Arizona Press, 1994); Raquel Rubio Goldsmith, "Oral History: Considerations and Problems for its Use in the History of Mexicanos in the United States," in *Regions of the La Raza: Changing Perspectives of Mexican American Regional History and Culture,* Antonio Ríos-Bustamante, ed. (Encino, Calif.: Floricanto Press, 1993); Devra Ann Weber, "The Organizing of Mexicano Agricultural Workers: Imperial Valley and Los Angeles, 1928–34, An Oral History Approach." *Aztlán* (1972); Carlos Vasquez, *The Oral History Program* (Albuquerque: The University of New Mexico Press, 1996). Important Oral History programs for Chicanos exist at the University of California, Berkeley and Los Angeles and at the University of New Mexico. The University of New Mexico, Albuquerque, has begun "Impact Los Alamos: Traditional New Mexico in a High-Tech World, 1945–1995," which will examine the impact of the federal laboratories at Los Alamos on native New Mexicans.

14. *Family History and Genealogy.* Family history and genealogy has developed from the research of genealogists and historians in California, New Mexico, and Texas. During the 1960s and 1970s, stimulated by the state genealogical societies, an increasing number of people were attracted to family history research. Major reference works include George R. Ryskamp, *Tracing Your Hispanic Heritage* (Riverside, Calif.: Hispanic Family History Research, 1984); George R. Ryskamp, *Finding Your Hispanic Family Roots* (Baltimore: Genealogical Publishing Co., 1997). The *SHHAR,* a journal, is published by the Society of Hispanic Historical and Ancestral Research, Fullerton, California, which also publishes a membership bulletin, *Somos Primos.*

15. *Religious History.* Religion has been a central factor in Mexican-American history, but studies of Mexican Catholicism and Protestantism is new. Important works dealing with Mexican Catholicism include Jay P. Dolan and Gilberto M. Hinojosa, *Mexican Americans and the Catholic Church, 1900–1965* (Notre Dame, Ind.: University of Notre Dame Press, 1994); and Cliford L. Holland, *The Hispanic Dimension* (Pasadena, Calif.: William Carey Library, 1974).

16. *Educational History.* The study of Mexican Americans and the educational system is central to interpretations of the identity, segrega-

tion, politics, and civil rights struggles of Mexican Americans in the twentieth century. Early twentieth-century Americanization educational reform programs tracked Mexican children into remedial and industrial arts programs. Studies that examine these themes are Gilberto G. Gonzalez, *Chicano Education in the Era of Segregation* (Philadelphia: Balch Institute Press, 1990). Mexican organizations had to fight school segregation, often in cooperation with African Americans. See Guadalupe San Miguel Jr., *Let All of Them Take Heed: Mexican Americans and the Campaign for Educational Equality in Texas, 1910–1981* (Austin: University of Texas Press, 1987).

17. *Psychohistory.* Psychohistory studies is an underdeveloped area with great potential, major works in this area include Rodolfo Alvarez, "The Psycho-Historical and Socioeconomic Development of the Chicano Community in the United States," *Social Science Quarterly* 53 (March 1973): 920–42; Mauricio Mazon, *Zoot Suits Riots* (Austin: University of Texas Press, 1984).

18. *Ethnohistory.* Enthnohistory, anthropology, and folklore all have influenced historical conceptions of the development of Mexican culture. An important work is Eric Wolf's *Sons of the Shaking Earth* (Chicago: University of Chicago Press, 1959). Folklorist Americo Paredes exercised a major influence on views of the development of Mexican-American folk identity and culture though his landmark studies. See Americo Paredes, *With a Pistol in His Hand* (Austin: University of Texas Press, 1958). Essays by Americo Paredes particularly influential for Chicano historians include "The Folk Base of Chicano Literature" and "The Problem of Identity in a Changing Culture: Popular Expressions of Culture Conflict Along the Lower Río Grande Border," which form part of a series of works now collected in Americo Paredes, *Folklore and Culture of the Texas Mexican Border* (Austin: University of Texas Press, 1994).

19. *Film.* Histories of Mexicans and Latinos have moved from images, and stereotypes to studies of playwrights, filmmakers, actors, and cinematographers, including Eustasio Montoya, Ramon Novarro, Dolores Del Rio, and Chicano dramatic and documentary filmmaking. Key works include Luis Reyes and Pater Rubie, *Hispanics in Hollywood: An Encyclopedia of Film and Television* (New York: Garland Press, 1994); Gary D. Keller, *Hispanics and United States Film: An Overview and Handbook* (Tempe, Ariz.: Bilingual Press, 1994); David Maciel, *El Norte: The U.S.-Mexican Border in Contemporary Cinema* (Institute for

Regional Studies of the Californias, San Diego State University, 1990); Antonio Ríos-Bustamante, Latino Participation in the Hollywood Film Industry, 1911–1945," in *Representation and Resistance,* Chon A. Noriega (Minneapolis: University of Minnesota, 1992); Antonio Ríos-Bustamante, "Mary Murillo: Early Anglo Latina Scenarist," in *Romance Languages Annual 1995* (West Lafayette, Ind.: Purdue University Press, 1995); Fernado Del Moral Gonzalez, "El Rescate de un Camarografo: Las Imagenas Perdidas de Eustasio Montoya," Renato Rosaldo Lecture Series (Tucson: Mexican American Studies and Research Center, University of Arizona, 10, 1992–93); Rosa Linda Fregoso, *The Bronze Screen: Chicana and Chicano Film Culture* (Minneapolis: University of Minnesota, 1995).

20. *Chicano/a Art History.* Chicano art history has antecedents in the art literature of Hispanic folk art in the Southwest, Spanish colonial revival architecture, and Santeros. This earlier literature was conditioned on the premise that southwestern folk art was primarily Spanish colonial and had a relation to Mexico as a conduit to Spanish art traditions. Until the 1960s few if any Mexican Americans held degrees in art history, and fewer still held professional positions as professors, curators, or critics of art in the United States. This is as opposed to Mexican-American artists and journalists writing in Spanish language newspapers on art produced by Mexicans in the United States. The first major work on the topic, *Mexican American Artists* (Austin: University of Texas Press, 1973), was authored by Jacinto Quirarte, one of the first Mexican Americans to hold a Ph.D. in art history. Since then the field has expanded in relation to the tremendous advance in recognition of Chicano art, and the work of Chicano Artists. Major sources include Tomas Ybarra Frausto and Shifra Goldman, eds., *Arte Chicano A Comprehensive Bibliography of Chicano Art, 1965–1981*. (Berkeley: Chicano Studies Library Publications Unit, University of California, 1985.); Richard Griswold Del Castillo, Teresa McKenna, and Yvonne Yarbro-Bejarano *Chicano Art: Resistance and Affirmation, 1965–1985* (Los Angeles: Wight Gallery, University of California, 1991), which contains a comprehensive and authoritative series of essays. An important work by a Mexican art historian is Sylvia Gorodezky, *Arte Chicano como cultura de protesta* (Mexico D.F.: Universidad Nacional de Mexico, 1993).

An especially important source are the catalog of exhibitions published by museums including those of the Mexican Fine Arts Center

Museum in Chicago, the Mexican Museum of San Francisco, and other institutions. These publications include Victor A. Sorell, *The Barrio Murals/Murales del Barrio* (Chicago: Mexican Fine Arts Center Museum, 1987); Amalia Mesa-Bains, *Ceremony of Memory : New Expressions in Spirituality among Contemporary Hispanic Artists,* (Santa Fe, N.M.: Center for Contemporary Arts of Santa Fe, 1988); Rene Yanez, *Gronk! A Living Survey, 1973–1993* (San Francisco: Mexican Museum, 1993). Other works include Chon Noriega, *From the West: Chicano Narrative Photography* (Seattle: Mexican Museum, University of Washington Press, 1995); Antonio Ríos-Bustamante and Cristine Marin, eds. *Latinos in Museums: A Heritage Reclaimed* (Melbourne: Krieger Press, 1997), contains essays on the Mexican Fine Arts Center Museum in Chicago, Chicano graphic art in East Los Angeles, and performance art.

Chicano Historiographic Paradigms

Several powerful paradigms have emerged within Chicano historiography. The first of these are "Mexican Americans as natives of the land" and "Mexican Americans as twentieth-century immigrants." While often presented as opposites, the two perspectives can be integrated in a new synthesis combining and recognizing both processes. Developing paradigms include world systems, gender, and postmodernism. These include critiques of gender, patriarchal, and nationalist components of the first two decades of Chicano historiography.

Natives of the Land Paradigm

The "natives of the land" paradigm includes several subperspectives: [30]

1. Indigenous Meso-American perspective. Ethnohistorians and anthropologists David Carrasco and James Diego Vigil have provided support for the continuing importance of the Meso-American origins of Chicanos (Carrasco, *Religions of MesoAmerica,* 1990; Vigil, *From Indians to Chicanos: The Dynamics of Mexican American Culture,* 1980). Historian John R. Chavez examines the influence of the Chichimec concept of Aztlan in *The Lost Land: The Image of the Southwest* (1984).

2. Spanish Myth perspective. The oldest section of the community, Spanish colonials, and their history are separated from that of other Mexican Americans on the basis of a unique "Spanish heritage."

3. Resistance perspective. This emphasizes the violent, nonviolent, and passive resistance to conquest and the imposition of a dominant Anglo-American society (See Rodolfo Acuña, *Occupied America*). Emphasis is placed upon resistance to colonization, internal colonization, and other forms of domination.

4. Internal colonial perspective. This emphasizes the initial conquest and colonization of Mexican Americans and the development and imposition of internal colonialization within which Mexican communities are subordinate enclaves with inferior status. The internal colonial perspective is too static and does not account for post-1970 demographic and political change and the rise of a Mexican-American middle class and brokers.

5. Resistance, persistence, and accommodation model. This integrates elements of the other models with an emphasis on the persistence of the Mexican community. It allows for a more complex dynamic process, which can be defined as postcolonial rather than internal colonial.

6. Social change and world systems perspective. Historical sociologists Mario Barrera, David Montejano, and Tomas Almaguer have developed critiques of race and class within larger and smaller systems, such as the world economy or the state of Texas.

Immigrant Paradigms

The "Mexican Americans as twentieth-century immigrants" perspective often denies continuity with the eighteenth and nineteenth centuries and holds that no significant influence survived except in New Mexico. The immigrant perspective includes the following submodels:

1. Assimilation perspective. Mexican Americans are an immigrant community, and despite unique features, can be understood within the immigration historiographic perspective developed for European immigrant groups.

2. Cultural persistence/racial exclusion perspective. Mexican Americans are immigrants, but because most are viewed as nonwhite by society, they face racial discrimination.

3. Immigration labor perspective. Within the process of labor immigration Mexican immigrants assimilate over time through formal and informal Americanization. Mario T. Garcia's *Desert Immigrants: The Mexicans of El Paso, 1880–1920* (New Haven, Conn.: Yale University,

1981) is viewed as a classic statement of this approach as applied to Mexican Americans.

4. Ethnic assimilation perspective. George J. Sanchez (*Becoming Mexican American* [New York: Oxford University Press, 1993]) views Mexican Americans as assimilating as working ethnics in a similar manner to Central Europeans in the upper Midwest.

5. Pluralist/multicultural model. This model views the United States fundamentally as multicultural society, within which many different ethnic groups, including Mexican Americans, have maintained or may be able to maintain cultural diversity while moving toward the achievement of increased social and economic parity. [31]

Mexicana/Chicana Paradigms

Chicana scholars were stimulated by advances in European, American, and Latin American women's history. Nonhistorians took the lead because there were few historians researching Chicana history. An early history was Martha P. Cotera's *Diosa y Hembra: The History and Heritage of Chicanas in the U.S.* (Austin, Tex.: Information and Development, 1976). Early collections of essays included Rosaura Sanchez, ed., *Essays on La Mujer* (1977), and Adelaida del Castillo, ed., *Between Borders: Essays on Mexicana/Chicana History* (1990).[32]

A primary concern of Chicana history is the centrality of women in the reproduction of culture and society. Major themes include the role of women in the reproduction of culture; changing female-male relationships; women's work and labor organization; changing female and male gender roles and images; biographical studies; Chicana literary history; politics, culture, and ideology in Mexican-American history. Important works include Rosaura Sanchez's "The History of Chicanas: Proposal for a Materialist Perspective" (1990); Ramón A. Gutiérrez's "Marriage and Seduction in Colonial New Mexico"(1990); Antonia Castañeda's "The Political Economy of Nineteenth Century Stereotypes of Californianas" (1990) and "Women of Color and the Rewriting of Western History: The Discourse, Politics, and Decolonization of History" (1992); Cynthia E. Orozco's "Sexism in Chicano Studies and the Community" (1986) and "Beyond Machismo, La Familia, and Ladies Auxiliaries: A Historiography of Mexican Origin Women's Participation in Voluntary Associations and Politics in the United States, 1870–1990" (1995); Alma Garcia's "The Development of Chicana Feminist Discourse, 1970–1980" (1990); and Vicki L. Ruiz's *Cannery Women/Cannery Lives* (1987) and *From Out of the Shadows Mexican American Women in the Twentieth Century* (1998).[33]

Postmodernist Paradigm

Postmodernist and cultural studies reexamine gender, patriarchal, and national components of the first phase of Chicano historiography. Gender analysis and postmodern theories of despair and social decomposition are critical of earlier historiography. Major perspectives, especially the critique of patriarchy, can be integrated into a new synthesis for Chicano/a historiography. Ramón A. Gutiérrez may be viewed as a precursor of Chicano/a postmodernist historiography.

Major works include Ramón A. Gutiérrez's "Community, Patriarchy and Individualism: The Politics of Chicano History and the Dream of Equality" (1993); Richard Garcia's "Turning Points: Mexican Americans in California History" (1995) and "The Origins of Chicano Cultural Thought: Visions and Paradigms—Romano's Culturalism, Alurista's Aesthetics, and Acuña's Communalism" (1995); and Jose David Saldivar's "The Limits of Chicano Cultural Studies" (1990). [34]

General Histories

Comprehensive general histories, as opposed to regional works, begin with Carey McWilliams's *North from Mexico* (1949). In 1990, a revised version appeared with an update by Matt S. Meier. The master text remains Rodolfo Acuña's seminal *Occupied America: The Chicanos Struggle Toward Liberation* (1972), which has gone through two complete rewrites: *Occupied America: A History of Chicanos*, second edition (1981) and third edition (1988). *Occupied America* reflects changes in the various subperspectives of the "natives of the land" model. The other major general works are Matt S. Meier and Feliciano Rivera's *The Chicanos: A History of Mexican Americans* (1972) and F. Arturo Rosales's *Chicano: The History of the Mexican American Civil Rights Movement* (1996). Other works are more general, less comprehensive, or written as secondary-school survey texts.[35]

Development of a Historiographic Literature

Key contributors to Chicano/a historiography include Manuel Servin, Americo Paredes, Rodolfo Acuña, Juan Gómez-Quiñones, Luis Leobardo Arroyo, Mario T. Garcia, Albert Camarillo, Richard Griswold del Castillo, Vicki L. Ruiz, Carlos E. Cortes, Louis Año Nuevo Kerr, Arnoldo de Leon, Antonia Castañeda, David Weber, Cynthia E. Orozco, Alex Saragoza, Ramón A. Gutiérrez, Jorge Klor de Alva, and Richard Garcia.[36]

Journals publishing major historiographic essays have included *The Journal of Mexican American History; Aztlan; Pacific Historical Review; Western Historical Review; Ethnic Affairs; Journal of Ethnic Studies; Journal of American Studies; Fronteras/Frontiers; American Quarterly; Latin American Studies Perspectives; Annals of the Association of American Geographers;* and *The New Scholar.*[37]

Important centers for research and graduate training include or have included the University of California (Los Angeles, San Diego, Berkeley, and Santa Barbara campuses); Stanford University; the University of Southern California; the University of Texas at Austin; the University of Michigan; the University of New Mexico; the University of Arizona; and Arizona State University. Many other universities offer graduate courses but have produced few Ph.D.s in Chicano/a history.

Key historiographic works include the early precursorial literature, previously mentioned, by Carey McWilliams, Manuel P. Servin, Americo Paredes, and Carlos Castañeda. The important exchange between Arthur Corwin Jr. and Rodolfo Acuña is included in Norris Hundley Jr.'s *The Chicano* (1975). The historiographic essays of Juan Gómez-Quiñones form a canonal source for the initiation of Chicano historiographic writing, especially his "Toward a Perspective on Chicano History" (1971) and, with Arroyo, "On the State of Chicano History: Observations on Its Development, Interpretations, and Theory, 1970–1974" (1976).

Essays by Carlos E. Cortes, Albert Camarillo, Luis Leobardo Arroyo, Alex Saragoza, Richard Griswold del Castillo, and David G. Gutierrez provide critical snapshot assessments of each of the three decades of ongoing development of the field: Albert Camarillo, "The 'New' Chicano History: Historiography of Chicanos of the 1970s" (1983); Luis Leobardo Arroyo, "Notes on Past, Present and Future

Directions of Chicano Labor Studies" (1975); Carlos E. Cortes, "Mexicans" (1980); Alex Saragoza, "The Significance of Recent Chicano-Related Historical Writings: An Appraisal" (1987) and "Recent Chicano Historiography: An Interpretive Essay" (1988–90); David G. Gutierrez, "The Third Generation: Recent Trends in Chicano/Mexican American Historiography" (1989); and Richard Griswold del Castillo, "Chicano Historical Discourse in the 1980s: An Overview and Evaluation" (1993).[39]

The essays of Vicki L. Ruiz and Cynthia E. Orozco are critical in developing Chicana historiography. These include Ruiz's "Mascaras y Muros: Chicana Feminism and the Teaching of U.S. Women's History" (1994) and "Star Struck: Acculturation, Adolescence, and Mexican American Women, 1920–40" (1992) and Orozco's "Beyond Machismo, La Familia, and Ladies Auxiliaries: A Historiography of Mexican Origin Women's Participation in Voluntary Associations and Politics in the United States, 1870–1990" (1995).[40]

Important for regional historiography are the essays of Richard Griswold del Castillo and Arnoldo de Leon: Richard Griswold del Castillo, "Southern California's Chicano History: Regional Origins and National Critique" (1988–90) and "Tejanos and California Chicanos: Regional Variations in Mexican American History" (1985); Arnoldo de Leon, "Tejano History Scholarship: A Review of the Recent Literature" (1985) and "Texas Mexicans: Twentieth Century Interpretations" (1991).[41]

Reflecting the shift from internal colonial to postmodern and post-colonial perspectives are the essays of Tomas Almaguer: "Interpreting Chicano History: The World System Approach to nineteenth Century California" (1977) and "Ideological Distortions in Recent Chicano Historiography: The Internal Colonial Model and the Chicano Historical Interpretation" (1989).[42]

Seminal postmodern critiques of identities are found in the essays of Ramón A. Gutiérrez, including "Community, Patriarchy and Individualism: The Politics of Chicano History and the Dream of Equality" (1993); "Unraveling America's Hispanic Past: Internal Stratification and Class Boundaries" (1987); and "Historiography and a New Vision for Chicana/o Studies" (1996).[43]

Future Complexity of Chicano/a History

The Chicano history field is part of the great wave of social and ethnic history that impacted the U.S. historical profession beginning in the late 1960s. The establishment of social, women's, and ethnic histories occurred in the face of skepticism, inertia, and resistance. Despite the difficulties, women's history and ethnic histories, including Chicano/a, achieved formal professional recognition in the 1990s.

The field of Chicano/a history was established, underwent, and is undergoing great intellectual change. An academic cadre of Chicano/a historians can be found in many American universities and colleges; courses in Chicano/a history now exist; and undergraduate and graduate degrees are being granted. The development of Chicana history, Chicana historiography, and a Chicana critique of patriarchy mark a fundamental change in the field. Today much more remains to be accomplished in introducing new historiographic interpretations where teaching occurs, not only in the universities and community colleges but especially in the secondary and elementary schools.[44]

The increasing size and complexity of Mexican-American/Chicano/a history reflects the intellectual vitality of the field. Multiple perspectives, theories, periodizations, methodologies, and proliferating texts contribute to a richer dialogue and promise exciting debates.[45]

Notes

1. The terms of identity used by Mexican Americans have changed over time. I use the terms used in the periods by the people of that time. The terms *México Americano* and *México Texano* were used by Texano resistance leader Catarino Garza in his 1888 memoirs, "La Logica de los Hechos." (reproduced in Celso Garza Guajardo, *Universidad Autonoma de Nuevo Leon* [Monterrey: 1989]). The term *Mexican American* was used in the Dillingham Commission Report on Immigration. See Senate Documents, Vol. 85, Part 3, 61st Congress, 2nd Session, 1909–1910, Report of the Immigration Commission, Immigrants in Industries, Part 25, p. 157: "the Mexican-Americans...are hardly distinguishable from the immigrant Mexicans." The use of the term Mexican American in this report is as a synthetic, formal official category similar to that of the term Italian American and clearly precedes group use of the term. In the 1930s and 1940s (including the 1930 census), many publications and the U.S. government referred

to *Mexicans,* not *Mexican Americans.* The term *Chicano* was used by Manuel Gamio in the 1920s and by Ernesto Galarza in his autobiography, *Barrio Boy* (Notre Dame, Ind.: Universty of Notre Dame Press, 1971).

2. The "Recovering the U.S. Hispanic Literary Heritage Program," located at the University of Houston, is directed by Nicolas Kanellos. The program was created for the purpose of recovery and publication of mainly Spanish-language literature. See Ramón A. Gutiérrez and Genaro Padilla, eds., *Recovering the U.S. Hispanic Literary Heritage* (Houston: Arte Publico, 1993). Works discussing Californio memoirs are Rosaura Sanchez, *Telling Identities: The Californio Testimonies* (Minneapolis: University of Minnesota Press, 1995); and Rosaura Sanchez, ed., "Nineteenth-Century Californio Testimonios," *Critical Monograph Series* (San Diego: UCSD Ethnic Studies/Third World Studies, 1994). Nineteenth- and early twentieth-century regional histories included Hubert Howe Bancroft, *History of California* (San Francisco: The History Company, 1884–1890); Ralph E. Twitchell, *The Leading Facts of New Mexico History* (Cedar Rapids: The Torch Press, 1911–17). Other regional amateur historians also made extensive use of these documentary collections. They, however, heavily edited the views of Mexican authors, informants who were rarely cited in full. For a discussion of this literature see Juan Gómez-Quiñones, "Toward a Perspective on Chicano History," *Aztlán,* 2, no. 2 (fall 1971): 1–49.
3. These authors included Mexican Americans such as Benjamin Read, George I. Sanchez, Jovita Gonzales de Mireles, and Adelina Otero Warren, and Anglo-Americans such as Nellie Van de Grift de Sanchez. Many of these authors, including Charles F. Lummis, were contributors to the development of the "Spanish Myth, " which divided earlier Mexican settlers from later, post-1900 immigrants. See Ramón A. Gutiérrez, "Nationalism and Literary Production: The Hispanic and Chicano Experiences," in *Recovering the U.S. Hispanic Literary Heritage,* Ramón A. Gutiérrez, ed. (Houston: Arte Publico Press, 1993); Genaro Padilla, *My History Not Yours* (Madison: University of Wisconsin Press, 1993); and A. Gabriel Melendez, *So All Is Not Lost: The Poetics of Print in Nuevo Mexicano Communities, 1834–1958* (Albuquerque: University of New Mexico Press, 1997). See also Felix D. Almaraz Jr., "Carlos Eduardo Castañeda, Mexican American Historian: The Formative Years, 1896–1927" *Pacific Historical Review* 42 no. 3 (August 1973): 319–34; Luis Leal, "El Paso y la Huella: The Reconstruction of Chicano Cultural History," in *Estudios Chicanos and the Politics of Community,* Mary Romero, ed. (Houston: National Association for Chicano Studies, 1989); Felix D. Almaraz Jr., "Carlos Eduardo Castañeda, Mexican American Historian: The Formative Years, 1896–1927," in *The Chicano,* Norris Hundley Jr., ed. (Santa Barbara: Clio Books, 1975): 57–72. Folklorist Jovita Gonzalez de Mireles contributed a short chapter on "Latin Americans" in *Our Racial and National Minorities: Their History,*

Contributions, and Present Problems, Francis Brown, ed. (New York: Prentice Hall, 1937).

4. Corwin's thesis inspired a major debate in history journals with Rodolfo Acuña. See Arthur Corwin Jr., "Mexican-American History: An Assessment," *Pacific Historical Review,* "Chicano Issue," 42, no. 3 (August 1973); Rodolfo Acuña, "Mexican American History: A Reply," in *The Chicano,* Norris Hundley Jr., ed. (Santa Barbara: Clio Books, 1975): 41–46.
5. Ramón Eduardo Ruiz, ed., *The Mexican War: Was It Manifest Destiny?* (New York: Holt, Rinehart and Winston, 1963); and Neil Foley, *The White Scourge: Mexicans, Blacks and Poor Whites in Texas Cotton Culture* (Berkeley: University of California, 1997).
6. Leonard Pitt, *The Decline of the Californios* (Berkeley: University of California Press, 1966); Alan C. Hutchinson, *Mexican Settlement in Frontier California* (New Haven, Conn.: Yale University Press, 1969); David J. Weber, ed., *Foreigners in Their Native Land: Historical Roots of Mexican Americans* (Albuquerque: University of New Mexico, 1973); idem, *New Spain's Far Northern Frontier* (Albuquerque: University of New Mexico Press, 1979); idem, *The Mexican Frontier, 1821–1846: The American Southwest under Mexico* (Albuquerque: University of New Mexico Press, 1982).
7. Guides to this literature include John Francis Bannon, *The Spanish Borderlands Frontier* (New York: Holt, Rinehart and Winston, 1970); David Weber, *The Spanish Frontier in North America* (New Haven, Conn.: Yale University Press, 1992); Henry Putney Beers, *Spanish and Mexican Records of the American Southwest* (Tucson: University of Arizona Press, 1979). Late-nineteenth-century Mexican visitors such as Guillermo Prieto briefly described Mexican communities in their works. For example, see Guillermo Prieto, *Viaje a Los Estados Unidos, 1877–1878* (San Francisco: 1934) for a discription of the San Francisco Mexican community.
8. Mercedes de Carreras de Velesco, *Los Mexicanos que devolvio la crisis, 1929–1932* (México D.F.: Secretaria de Relaciones Exteriores, 1974). Rodolfo Acuña has identified the M.A. thesis of Stella L. Carrillo, "Importancia Economica y Social de la Poblacion Mexicana en Estados Unidos de Norteamerica" (Universidad Nacional Autonoma de México, 1963), as the first Mexican scholarly work marking the new shift in interest.
9. Herbert Eugene Bolton was the founder of the history of the Americas and Spanish Borderlands schools of history. The term Spanish Borderlands was coined by Bolton and employed as the title of his seminal work, *The Spanish Borderlands* (New Haven, Conn.: Yale University Press, 1921). Bolton's work was continued by his many students including John Francis Bannon, *The Spanish Borderlands Frontier* (New York: Holt, Rinehart and Winston, 1974).
10. In the 1980s a revisionist historiography of the West developed that incorporated much of the critiques of Rodolfo Acuña, Vine Deloria, and other Chicano, Native, African, and Asian Americans. Among these works were

Patricia Nelson Limerick, *The Legacy of Conquest: The Unbroken Past of the American West* (New York: Norton, 1987); Richard White, *A New History of the American West* (Norman: University of Oklahoma, 1991); Clyde A. Milner et al, eds., *The Oxford History of the American West* (New York: Oxford University Press, 1994).

11. See Manuel P. Servin, "California's Hispanic Heritage: A View into the Spanish Myth" *Journal of San Diego History* 19 (1973): 1–9.
12. Luis Leal, "Americo Paredes and Modern Mexican American Scholarship," *Ethnic Affairs* 1 (fall 1987): 1–11; Matt S. Meier and Feliciano Rivera, *The Chicanos: A History of Mexican Americans* (New York: Hill & Wang, 1972); idem, *Mexican Americans/American Mexicans* (New York: Hill & Wang, 1992). Manuel P. Servin is credited with a 1965 address to the Western Historical Association on Mexican Americans in western history. Lyle Saunders presented a paper titled "The Social History of Spanish Speaking People in the Southwestern United States Since 1846" at the First Conference of Historians of Mexico and the United States, in 1950.
13. This tiny senior group includes scholars such as Ramón Eduardo Ruiz and the late Manuel P. Servin, whose career was tragically ended by serious illness.
14. For a discussion of the social and political influence and perspectives of these scholars, see Mario T. Garcia, *Mexican Americans: Leadership, Ideology, & Identity, 1930–1960* (New Haven, Conn.: Yale University Press, 1989).
15. For example, in the 1930s and 1940s the work of Mexican scholars Jose Vasconcelos, through works such as *La Raza Cosmica: Mision de la Raza Iberoamericana* (Barcelona: Agencia Mundial de Libererias, 1925), and Ulises Criollo influenced some Mexican-American intellectuals, while the writings of American scholars such as John Dewey and Charles Beard influenced educators and teachers. Exiled Mexican clergy and other conservatives also exercised an important influence.
16. Rodolfo Acuña has identified progressive historian Carl Becker as an early influence on him. Acuña was also trained under Manuel P. Servin at the University of Southern California.
17. Arthur Corwin Jr., writing in 1972, characterized Mexican-American historians as then being divided into a "Mexican-American" or "establishment school" and a radical Chicano, or "La Raza school" of historiography; see Corwin Jr., "Mexican American History: An Assessment," in Norris Hundley Jr., ed., *The Chicano* (Santa Barbara: Clio Books, 1975). See also Manuel A. Machado. *Listen Chicano!* (Chicago: Nelson Hall, 1978); E. C. Orozco, *Protestant Republicanism in Aztlan* (Glendale, Ariz.: Peterins Press, 1980). A thematic history of all Hispanic groups, including Mexican Americans, from neoliberal and conservative perspectives is L. H. Gann and Peter J. Duignan, *The Hispanics in the United States* (Boulder, Col.: Westview, 1986.)

18. Mexican-American women historians prior to the 1970s were frequently discouraged from continuing beyond the master's degree level. Louise Año Nuevo Kerr was probably the first Chicana Ph.D. in history to actually teach and research the history of Mexican-American women. Several Chicana history professors recall being discouraged in the 1960s from continuing, and having their programs terminated with the M.A. because of the unwillingness of faculty to mentor them. A small but significant number of Mexican-American women apparently graduated with master's degrees in history during the period from the 1920s to the 1950s, from the Universities of California and Texas. Some were apparently directed into high school teaching.
19. The younger members of these clusters were still graduate students or recent Ph.D.s. As late as the end of the 1980s, the number of Chicana history Ph.D.s could be counted on the fingers of one hand.
20. Much of Paredes's work was conditioned by Texas historian perspectives of the cultural conflict between Anglos and Tejanos. Paredes's research on the *corrido* (the Norteno Mexican folk ballad, which evolved from the earlier cancion and decima song forms) led to a perspective that prefigured colonial and postcolonial perspectives and influenced Chicano postmodernism.
21. Other Chicano/a historians in the first phase who were still graduate students included Vicki Ruiz, Shirlene Soto, Antonia Castañeda, Raquel Rubio Goldsmith, and Guadalupe Castillo. A larger second phase included Ramón A.Gutiérrez, Deena J. Gonzalez, George Sanchez, and other scholars.
22. Fred A. Cervantes, "Chicanos as a Post Colonial Minority: Some Questions Concerning the Adequacy of the Paradigm of Internal Colonialism," in *Perspectivas en Chicano Studies,* Reynaldo Flores Macias, ed. (Los Angeles: UCLA, Chicano Studies Research Center, 1977): 123–35.
23. This parallels the movement of Democratic Party liberals, including President Clinton, to a centrist or neoliberal position on social issues.
24. Richard A. Garcia, "The Origins of Chicano Cultural Thought: Visions and Paradigms—Romano's Culturalism, Alurista's Aesthetics, and Acuña's Communalism" *California History*, Mexican Americans in California Issue 74, no. 3 (fall 1995): 290–305. For a discussion of neoliberalism and neoconservatism in the United States, Britain, and Europe, see Anthony Giddens, *Beyond Left and Right: The Future of Radical Politics* (Stanford, Calif.: Stanford University Press, 1994).
25. Ramón A. Gutiérrez, *When Jesus Came, the Corn Mothers Went Away: Marriage, Sexuality, and Power in New Mexico, 1500–1846* (Stanford, Calif.: Stanford University Press, 1991).
26. *Occupied America: A History of Chicanos* (New York: Harper and Row, 1981) has developed through three completely different editions. From the first edition in 1973, which adopted the perspective of internal colonization, it has evolved to a more complex interpretation of domination.

27. Albert Camarillo, *Chicanos in a Changing Society* (Cambridge, Mass.: Harvard University Press, 1979).
28. Jaime Rodriguez, ed., *The Mexican and Mexican American Experience in the Nineteenth Century* (Tempe, Ariz.: Bilingual Press, 1989); Ray Padilla, "Apuentes Para Documentacion de la Cultura Chicana," *El Grito* 5, no. 2 (winter 1971–72): 1–46; Antonio Ríos-Bustamante, *Mexican Los Angeles: A Narrative and Pictorial History* (Encino, Calif.: Floricanto Press, 1992).
29. In a forthcoming essay, I plan to discuss the development of each of the twenty theoretical thematic approaches identified here, along with their key literature.
30. For the Meso-American perspective, see David Carrasco, *Religions of MesoAmerica* (New York: Harper & Row, 1990); James Diego Vigil, *From Indians to Chicanos: The Dynamics of Mexican American Culture* (Prospect Heights, Ill.: Waveland Press, 1980); Jack Forbes, *Aztecas del Norte* (New York: Fawcett, 1973). John R. Chavez examines the influence of the Chichimec concept of Aztlan in *The Lost Land: The Image of the Southwest* (Albuquerque: University of New Mexico Press, 1984). A secondary school text by Carlos M. Jimenez, *The Mexican American Heritage* (Berkeley: TQS Publications, 1994), also supports indigenous origins. Also see Ramon D. Chacon, "Quetzalcoatl in San Jose: Conflict Over a Commemoration," *California History* 74, no. 3 (fall 1995): 328–39.

    For the Spanish Myth perspective, see Richard D. Nostrand, *The Hispano Homeland* (Norman: University of Oklahoma Press, 1992); Jim Blaut and Antonio Ríos-Bustamante, "A Commentary on Nostrand's 'Hispanos' and Their 'Homeland,'" in *Regions of la Raza: Changing Perspectives of Mexican American History and Culture,* Antonio Ríos-Bustamante, ed. (Encino, Calif.: Floricanto Press, 1993): 153–67; Jose R. Lopez-Gaston, *Tradicion Hispanica De Nuevo México* (México S. A.: Editorial Progreso, 1985); Antonio S. Blanco, *La Lengua Espanola en la historia de California* (Madrid: Espasa-Calpe, 1965); and Angelico Chavez, *My Penitent Land* (Albuquerque: University of New Mexico Press, 1974).

    For the resistance perspective, see Robert J. Rosenbloom, *Mexicano Resistance in the Southwest* (Austin: University of Texas Press, 1981); and Albert Camarillo and Pedro Castillo, *Los Bandidos Chicanos* (Los Angeles: UCLA, CSRC, 1975).

    For the internal colonial perspective, see Mario Barrera and Carlos Ornelas, "The Barrio as an Internal Colony," in *People and Politics in Urban Society,* Harlan Hahn, ed. (Los Angeles: Sage Publications, 1972); Robert Blaunner, *Racial Oppression in America* (New York: Harper & Row, 1972); Tomas Almaguer, "Towards the Study of Chicano Colonialism" *Aztlán* 2, no. 1 (spring 1971): 7–21; Tacho Mendiola, ed., *Occupied America: A Chicano History Symposium* (University of Houston, Mexican American Studies, 1982); and Fred A. Cervantes, "Chicanos as a Post-Colonial Minority: Some

Questions Concerning the Adequacy of the Paradigm of Internal Colonialism," in *Perspectivas en Chicano Studies,* Reynaldo Flores Macias, ed. (Los Angeles: UCLA, CSRC, 1977): 123–135.

For the resistance, persistence, and accommodation perspective, see Juan Gómez-Quiñones, "Toward a Concept of Culture," in *Modern Chicano Writers,* Joseph Sommers, ed. (Englewood Cliffs, N.J.: Prentice Hall, 1979); and Rodolfo Acuña, "The Age of the Brokers: The New Hispanics" and "The Age of the Brokers: The Rambo Years," in *Occupied America*, 3d ed. (New York: Harper & Row, 1988).

For the world system perspective, see Thomas D. Hall, Social *Change in the Southwest 1350–1880* (Lawrence: University of Kansas Press, 1992); Tomas Almaguer, "Interpreting Chicano History: The 'World System' Approach to Nineteenth-Century California," *Review* 4 (winter 1981); Mario Barrera, *Beyond Aztlan: Ethnic Autonomy in Comparative Perspective* (Notre Dame, Ind.: University of Notre Dame Press, 1988); and David Montejano, "Anglos and Mexicans in the Twenty-First Century," JSRI Occasional Paper no. 3 (East Lansing, Mich.: Michigan State University, Julian Samora Center, 1992).

31. For the assimilation perspective (Mexican Americans are an immigrant community and despite unique features can be understood within the immigration historiographic model developed for European immigrant groups), see Arthur Corwin Jr., "Mexican American History: An Assessment," and Rodolfo Acuña, "Mexican American History: A Reply," in Norris Hundley Jr., ed., *The Chicano*. George Sanchez finds that Mexican Americans have assimilated but as a working ethnic group; see George Sanchez, *Becoming Mexican American* (New York: Oxford University Press, 1993). Also see Ricardo Romo, "Mexican Americans in the New West," in *The Twentieth Century West: Historical Interpretations,* Gerald D. Nash and Richard W. Etulain, eds. (Albuquerque: University of New Mexico Press, 1989).

For the cultural persistence/racial exclusion perspective (Mexican Americans are immigrants, but because most are viewed as nonwhite by society, face class, racial, and cultural discrimination), see Juan Gómez-Quiñones, "Mexican Immigration to the United States, 1948–1980: An Overview," in *Chicano Studies: A Multidisciplinary Approach,* Eugene E. Garcia, ed. (New York: Columbia University, Teachers College, 1984); Antonio Ríos-Bustamante (ed.), *Mexican Immigrant Workers in the United States* (Los Angeles: UCLA, CSRC, 1981); and David G. Gutierrez, *Walls and Mirrors: Mexican Americans, Mexican Immigrants, and the Politics of Ethnicity* (Berkeley: University of California Press, 1995).

For the pluralist/multicultural perspective, see Ron Takaki, *Iron Cages* (New York: Alfred A. Knopf, 1979); Tomas Almaguer, *Racial Faultlines* (Berkeley: University of California Press, 1994); Douglas Monroy, *The Making of California Mexican Identity* (Berkeley: University of California

Press, 1994); and Ramón A. Gutiérrez, "Community, Patriarchy and Individualism: The Politics of Chicano History and the Dream of Equality," *American Quarterly* 45, no. 1 (March 1993): 44–72.

32. Particularly influential were Adelaida del Castillo, "Malinzin Tenepal: A Preliminary Look into a New Perspective," in *Essays on La Mujer,* Rosaura Sanchez, ed. (Los Angeles: UCLA, CSRC, 1977): 124–49; Vicki L. Ruiz, "Obreras y Madres: Labor Activism among Mexican Women and Its Impact on the Family," in *La Mexicana/Chicana,* Renato Rosaldo Lecture Series, vol. 1, series 1983–84 (Tucson: University of Arizona, Mexican American Studies and Research Center, 1983): 19–38; Douglas Monroy, "La Costura en Los Angeles, 1933–1939: The ILGWU and the Politics of Domination," in *Mexican Women in the United States,* Magdalena Mora and Adelaida del Castillo, eds. (Los Angeles: UCLA, CSRC, 1980); and Rosaura Sanchez, "The History of Chicanas: Proposal for a Materialist Perspective," in *Between Borders: Essays on Mexicana/Chicana History,* Adelaida del Castillo, ed. (Encino, Calif.: Floricanto Press, 1990), 1–29.

33. Rosaura Sanchez, "The History of Chicanas: Proposal for a Materialist Perspective," in *Between Borders: Essays on Mexicana/Chicana History,* Adelaida del Castillo, ed. (Encino, Calif.: Floricanto Press, 1990), 1–29; Antonia Castañeda, "The Political Economy of Nineteenth-Century Stereotypes of Californianas," in *Between Borders,* Del Castillo, ed.; Ramón A. Gutiérrez, "Marriage and Seduction in Colonial New Mexico," in *Between Borders,* Del Castillo, ed.; Cynthia E. Orozco, "Sexism in Chicano Studies and the Community," in *Chicana Voices,* Theresa Cordoba, ed. (Austin: University of Texas, CMAS, 1986); Orozco, "Beyond Machismo, La Familia, and Ladies Auxiliaries: A Historiography of Mexican Origin Women's Participation in Voluntary Associations and Politics in the United States, 1870–1990," *Perspectives* 5 (1995); Alma Garcia, "The Development of Chicana Feminist Discourse, 1970–1980," in *Unequal Sisters,* Ellen Carol DuBois and Vicki L. Ruiz, eds. (New York: Routledge, 1990), 418–437; Antonia Castañeda, "Women of Color and the Rewriting of Western History: The Discourse, Politics, and Decolonization of History," *Pacific Historical Review* 61, no. 4 (1992): 501–33; Vicki L. Ruiz, *Cannery Women/Cannery Lives* (Albuquerque: University of New Mexico Press, 1987); Vicki L. Ruiz, "Mascaras y Muros: Chicana Feminism and the Teaching of U.S. Women's History," in *New Viewpoints in U.S. Women's History,* Susan Ware, ed. (Cambridge, Mass.: Radcliffe College, Schleslinger Library Publications, 1994); Vicki L. Ruiz, "Star Struck: Acculturation, Adolescence, and Mexican American Women, 1920–1940," in *Small Worlds,* Elliot West and Paula Petrik, eds. (Lawrence: University of Kansas Press, 1992); Gilberto Garcia, "Beyond the Adelita Image: Women Scholars in the National Association for Chicano Studies, 1972–1992," *Perspectives* 5 (1995); George J. Sanchez, "'Go After the Women': Americanization and the

Mexican Immigrant Woman, 1915–1929," in *Unequal Sisters,* Ellen Carol DuBois and Vicki L. Ruiz, eds. (New York: Routledge, 1990), 250–63; and Vicki L. Ruiz, "Using Missionary Records in Mexican American Women's History," *Frontiers: A Journal of Women's Studies* 2 (1991).

34. See Ramón A. Gutiérrez, "Community, Patriarchy and Individualism: The Politics of Chicano History and the Dream of Equality," *American Quarterly* 45, no. 1 (March 1993): 44–72; Frederic Jameson, *Postmodernism or the Cultural Logic of Late Capitalism* (Durham, N.C.: Duke University Press, 1991); Benedict Anderson, *Imagined Communities: Reflections on the Origin and Spread of Nationalism*; Ramon Saldivar, *Chicano Narrative: The Dialectics of Difference* (Madison: University of Wisconsin Press, 1990); Jose David Saldivar, *The Dialectics of Our America* (Durham, N.C.: Duke University Press, 1991); Jose David Saldivar, "The Limits of Chicano Cultural Studies," *American Literary History* 2 (summer 1990); Hector Calderon, *Criticism in the Borderlands* (Durham, N.C.: Duke University Press, 1991); Richard Garcia, "Turning Points: Mexican Americans in California History: Introduction to Special Issue," *California History* 74, no. 3 (fall 1995): 226–29; Richard Garcia, "The Origins of Chicano Cultural Thought: Visions and Paradigms—Romano's Culturalism, Alurista's Aesthetics, and Acuña's Communalism," *California History* (fall 1995): 290–305; and Jorge Klor de Alba, "The Postcolonization of the (Latin) American Experience: A Reconsideration of 'Colonialism,' 'Postcolonialism,' and 'Mestizaje,'" in *After Colonialism: Imperial Histories and Postcolonial Displacements,* Gyan Prakash, ed. (Princeton, N.J.: Princeton University Press, 1995).

35. Carey McWilliams, *North from Mexico* (Philadelphia: J.B. Lippincott, 1949); Carey McWilliams with Matt S. Meier, *North from Mexico*, new edition, with update by Matt S. Meier (New York: Praeger, 1990); Rodolfo Acuña, *Occupied America: The Chicanos Struggle Toward Liberation* (San Francisco: Canfield Press, 1972); Acuña, *Occupied America: A History of Chicanos*, 2d ed. (New York: Harper & Row, 1981); Acuña, *Occupied America: A History of Chicanos*, 3d ed. (New York: Harper & Row, 1988); Matt S. Meier and Feliciano Rivera, *The Chicanos: A History of Mexican Americans* (New York: Hill and Wang, 1972); F. Arturo Rosales, *Chicano: The History of the Mexican American Civil Rights Movement* (Houston: Arte Publico Press, 1996). James Diego Vigil, *From Indians to Chicanos: The Dynamics of Mexican American Culture* (Prospect Heights, Ill: Waveland Press, 1980), is an ethnographic interpretation. A major Indigenista interpretation is Jack Forbes, *Aztecas del Norte* (New York: Fawcett, 1973). Histories written for secondary schools include Julian Samora and Patricia Vandel Simon, *A History of the Mexican-American People* (Notre Dame, Ind.: University of Notre Dame Press, 1977); Julian Nava, *Mexican Americans: Past Present and Future* (New York: American Book Company, 1978); Carlos M. Jimenez, *The Mexican American Heritage* (Berkeley: TQS Publications, 1994); Elizabeth Martinez,

ed., *500 Years of Chicano History* (Albuquerque: Southwest Community Organizing Project, 1991). A new popular work written to accompany the PBS series "Chicano" is F. Arturo Rosales, *Chicano: The History of the Mexican American Civil Rights Movement* (Houston: Arte Publico, 1996). A thematic work that treats all Hispanic groups including Mexican Americans from neoliberal and conservative perspective is L. H. Gann and Peter J. Duignan, *The Hispanics in the United States* (Boulder, Colo.: Westview, 1986).

The first and second editions of Acuña's *Occupied America* are critiqued in Tacho Mendiola, ed., *Occupied America: A Chicano History Symposium* (Houston: University of Houston Mexican American Studies Program, 1982). Other short works include Carey McWilliams, *The Mexicans in America* (Teachers College Press, 1968). Other early works by historians include Ruth S. Lamb, *Mexican Americans: Sons of the Southwest* (Claremont, Calif.: Ocelot Press, 1970); John Tebbel and Ramón E. Ruiz, *South by Southwest: The Mexican American and His Heritage* (Garden City, N.Y.: Zenith Books, 1969).

Other works for young readers in elementary to high school include Rodolfo Acuña, *The Story of the Mexican Americans: The Men and the Land* (New York: American Book Company, 1971); Rodolfo Acuña, *Cultures in Conflict* (New York: Charter School Books, 1970); and Julie Catalano, *The Mexican Americans* (New York: Chelsea House Publications, 1988). Pedro A. Caban, Barbara Cruz, Jose Carrasco, and Juan Garcia, *The Latino Experience in U.S. History* (Paramus, N.J.: Globe Fearon, 1994) is a high school level history of the major Latino groups, including Mexican Americans.

Since 1969 quite a number of other lesser "histories" have been produced for the elementary to high school level. Most simply provide a simplified, less informed version of the better works cited above.

36. The core Chicano/a historiographic literature includes the following: Carey McWilliams, *North From Mexico* (Philadelphia: J.B. Lippincott, 1949); McWilliams, *The Mexicans in America* (New York: Columbia University, Teacher College, 1968); McWilliams, "Once a Well Kept Secret," in *The Chicano,* Norris Hundley Jr., ed. (Santa Barbara, Calif.: Clio Books, 1975), 47–56; Manuel P. Servin, "The Post World War II Mexican American, 1925–1965: A Non-Achieving Minority," Paper presented to Conference of the Western History Association, 15 October 1965, Helena, Montana, in *The Mexican Americans: An Awakening Minority,* Manuel P. Servin, ed. (Beverly Hills: Glencoe Press, 1970), 144–60; Joseph Navarro, "The Condition of Mexican American History," *Journal of Mexican History* 1 (fall 1970); Jesus Chavarria, "A Precise and a Tentative Bibliography on Chicano History," *Aztlán* 1 (spring 1970); Juan Gómez-Quiñones, "Research Notes on the Twentieth Century," *Aztlán* 1 (spring 1970); Herminio Rios and Lupe Castillo, "Toward a True Chicano Bibliography: Mexican American

Newspapers: 1848–1942," *El Grito* 3, no. 4 (summer 1970); Carlos E. Cortes, "Chicop: A Response to the Challenge of Local Chicano History," *Aztlán* 1, no. 2 (fall 1970); Manuel A. Machado Jr., "Mexican American History: Problems and Prospects," *Western Review* 8, (winter 1971); Americo Paredes and John Womack Jr., "Who are the Chicanos?" in *Many Pasts: Readings in American Social History,* Herbert G. Gutman, ed. (Englewood Cliffs, N.J.: Prentice Hall, 1972); Abraham Hoffman, "Where are the Mexican Americans? A Textbook Omission Overdue for Revision," *The History Teacher* 6 (1972); Arthur Corwin Jr., "Mexican American History: An Assessment," *Pacific Historical Review,* "Chicano Issue" 42, no. 3 (August 1973); Rodolfo Acuña, "Mexican American History: A Reply," in *The Chicano,* Norris Hundley Jr., ed. (Santa Barbara, Calif.: Clio Books, 1975): 41–46; Acuña, "The Struggles of Class and Gender: Current Research in Chicano Studies," *Journal of Ethnic Studies* (spring 1990); Acuña, "An Essay on Truth and Objectivity in Chicano Scholarship," JSRI Occasional Papers (East Lansing, Mich.: Michigan State University, Julian Samora Research Institute, 1996); Juan Gómez-Quiñones, "The First Steps: Chicano Labor Conflict and Organizing 1900–1920," *Aztlán* 3, no. 1 (spring 1973); Gómez-Quiñones, "Questions within Women's Historiography," in *Between Borders,* Adelaida del Castillo, ed. (Encino, Calif.: Floricanto Press, 1990); Gómez-Quiñones, "Toward a Perspective on Chicano History," *Aztlán* 2, no. 2 (fall 1971); Gómez-Quiñones and Arroyo, "On the State of Chicano History: Observations on Its Development, Interpretations, and Theory, 1970–1974," *Western Historical Quarterly* 7, no. 2 (April 1976); Gómez-Quiñones, "Towards a Concept of Culture," *Revista Chicano-Riquena* 5, no. 2 (spring 1977); Gómez-Quiñones, "The Origins and Development of the Mexican Working Class in the United States: Laborers and Artisans North of the Rio Bravo, 1600–1900," Paper presented to the Fifth International Congress of Mexican Studies, 1977, in *El Trabajo y los Trabajadores en la Historia de México,* Elsa Cecilia Frost et al., eds. (México D.F.: El Colegio de México y University of Arizona Press, 1979); Gómez-Quiñones and Antonio Ríos-Bustamante, "La Comunidad Al Norte Del Río Bravo," in *La Otra Cara de México: El Pueblo Chicano,* David R. Maciel, ed. (México D.F.: El Caballito, 1977); Luis Leobardo Arroyo, Víctor Nelson Cisneros, Juan Gómez-Quiñones, and Antonio Ríos-Bustamante, "Preludio A Futuro: Pasado y Presente De Los Trabajadores Mexicanos Al Norte Del Río Bravo, 1600–1975," in Maciel, *La Otra Cara de México*; Luis Leobardo Arroyo, "Notes on Past, Present and Future Directions of Chicano Labor Studies," *Aztlán* 6, no. 2 (summer 1975): 137–49; Carlos E. Cortes, "Mexicans," in *Harvard Encyclopedia,* Stephen Therstrom, ed. (Cambridge, Mass.: Harvard University Press, 1980); Alex Saragoza, "Recent Chicano Historiography: An Interpretive Essay," *Aztlán* 19, no. 1 (spring 1988–90): 1–77; Raymond V. Padilla, "A Critique of Pittian History," *El Grito* 6, no. 1 (fall 1972); Alex

Saragoza, "The Significance of Recent Chicano-Related Historical Writings: An Appraisal," *Ethnic Affairs* no. 1 (fall 1987): 24–62; Albert Camarillo, "The 'New' Chicano History: Historiography of Chicanos of the 1970s," in *Chicanos and the Social Sciences: A Decade of Research and Development (1970–1980),* Isidro D. Ortiz, ed. (Santa Barbara: University of California, Center for Chicano Studies, 1983); Mario T. Garcia, "Americanization and the Mexican Immigrant, 1880–1930," *Ethnic Studies* 6 (summer 1978); J. Jorge Klor de Alva, "Chicana History and Historical Significance: Some Theoretical Considerations," in *Between Borders,* Adelaida del Castillo, ed. (Encino, Cal.: Floricanto Press, 1990): 61–86; Vicki L. Ruiz, "Texture, Text, and Context: New Approaches in Chicano Historiography," *Mexican Studies/Estudios Mexicanos* 2, no. 1 (winter 1986); Ruiz, "Mascaras y Muros: Chicana Feminism and the Teaching of U. S. Women's History," in *New Viewpoints in U. S. Women's History,* Susan Ware, ed. (Cambridge, Mass.: Radcliffe College, Schleslinger Library Publications, 1994); Ruiz, "Star Struck: Acculturation, Adolescence, and Mexican American Women, 1920–1940," in *Small Worlds,* Elliot West and Paula Petrik, eds. (Lawrence: University of Kansas Press, 1992); Cynthia E. Orozco, "Chicano Labor History: A Critique of Male Consciousness in Historical Writing," *La Red/The Net* 77 (February 1994): 2–5; Orozco, "Beyond Machismo, La Familia, and Ladies Auxiliaries: A Historiography of Mexican Origin Women's Participation in Voluntary Associations and Politics in the United States, 1870–1990," *Perspectives* 5 (1995): 1–34; Alma Garcia, "The Development of Chicana Feminist Discourse, 1970–1980," in *Unequal Sisters,* Ellen Carol DuBois and Vicki L. Ruiz, eds. (New York: Routledge, 1990), 418–31; Antonia Castañeda, "Women of Color and the Rewriting of Western History: The Discourse, Politics, and Decolonization of History," *Pacific Historical Review* 61, no. 4 (1992); Richard Griswold del Castillo, "New Perspectives on the Mexican and American Borderlands," *Latin American Research Review* 19, no. 1 (1984); Griswold del Castillo, "Tejanos and California Chicanos: Regional Variations in Mexican American History," *Mexican Studies/Estudios Mexicanos* 1, no. 1 (winter 1985); Griswold del Castillo, "Southern California's Chicano History: Regional Origins and National Critique," *Aztlán* 19, no. 1 (spring 1988–90): 109–124; Griswold del Castillo, "Chicano Historical Discourse in the 1980s: An Overview and Evaluation," *Perspectives* 4 (1993); Arnoldo de Leon, "Tejano History Scholarship: A Review of the Recent Literature," *West Texas Historical Association Year Book* 59 (1985); De Leon, "Texas Mexicans: Twentieth-Century Interpretations," in *Texas Through Time: Evolving Interpretations,* Walter L. Buenger and Robert A. Calvert, eds. (College Station: Texas A&M University Press, 1991); Richard Garcia, "Turning Points: Mexican Americans in California History: Introduction to Special Issue," *California History* (fall 1995): 226–29; Richard Garcia, "The Origins of Chicano

Cultural Thought: Visions and Paradigms—Romano's Culturalism, Alurista's Aesthetics, and Acuña's Communalism," *California History* (fall 1995); 290–305; Ramón A. Gutiérrez, "Community, Patriarchy and Individualism: The Politics of Chicano History and the Dream of Equality," *American Quarterly* 45, no. 1 (March 1993): 44–72; Ramón A. Gutiérrez, "Unraveling America's Hispanic Past: Internal Stratification and Class Boundaries," *Aztlan* 17, no. 1 (1986): 79–101; Ramón A. Gutiérrez, "Historiography and A New Vision for Chicana/o Studies," JSRI Occasional Papers (East Lansing, Mich.: Michigan State University, Julian Samora Research Institute, 1996); David G. Gutierrez, "The Third Generation: Recent Trends in Chicano/Mexican American Historiography," *Mexican Studies/Estudios Mexicanos* 5, no. 1 (summer 1989); Tacho Mendiola, ed., *Occupied America: A Chicano History Symposium* (Houston: University of Houston, Mexican American Studies, 1982); Antonio Ríos-Bustamante, "A Contribution to the Historiography of the Greater Mexican North in the Eighteenth Century," *Aztlán* 7, no. 3 (fall 1976): 347–356; Tomas Almaguer, "Towards the Study of Chicano Colonialism," *Aztlán* 2, no. 1 (spring 1971); Almaguer, "Interpreting Chicano History: The World System Approach to Nineteenth Century California," Working Paper No. 101 (Berkeley: University of California, Institute for the Study of Social Change, 1977); Almaguer, "Ideological Distortions in Recent Chicano Historiography: The Internal Colonial Model and the Chicano Historical Interpretation," *Aztlán* 18, no. 1 (1987): 7–28; and Louise Año Nuevo Kerr, "State of the Literature: Chicano History," JSRI Occasional Papers (East Lansing, Mich.: Michigan State University, Julian Samora Research Institute, 1996).

37. The *Journal of Mexican American History* and *Ethnic Affairs* no longer exist.
38. Albert Camarillo, "The 'New' Chicano History: Historiography of Chicanos of the 1970s," in *Chicanos and the Social Sciences: A Decade of Research and Development (1970–1980)*, Isidro D. Ortiz, ed. (Santa Barbara: University of California, Center for Chicano Studies, 1983); Luis Leobardo Arroyo, "Notes on Past, Present and Future Directions of Chicano Labor Studies," *Aztlán* 6, no. 2 (summer 1975): 137–149; Carlos E. Cortes, "Mexicans," in *Harvard Encyclopedia,* Stephen Therstrom, ed. (Cambridge, Mass.: Harvard University Press, 1980); Alex Saragoza, "The Significance of Recent Chicano-Related Historical Writings: An Appraisal," *Ethnic Affairs* 1 (fall 1987); Saragoza, "Recent Chicano Historiography: An Interpretive Essay," *Aztlán* 19, no. 1 (spring 1988–90): 1–77; David G. Gutierrez, "The Third Generation: Recent Trends in Chicano/Mexican American Historiography," *Mexican Studies/Estudios Mexicanos* 5, no. 1 (summer 1989); Richard Griswold del Castillo, "Chicano Historical Discourse in the 1980s: An Overview and Evaluation," *Perspectives* 4 (1993).
39. Vicki L. Ruiz, "Mascaras y Muros: Chicana Feminism and the Teaching of U.S. Women's History," in *New Viewpoints in U. S. Women's History,* Susan

Ware, ed. (Cambridge, Mass.: Radcliffe College, Schleslinger Library Publications, 1994); Ruiz, "Star Struck: Acculturation, Adolescence, and Mexican American Women, 1920–1940," in *Small Worlds,* Elliot West and Paula Petrik, eds. (Lawrence: University of Kansas Press, 1992); Ruiz, "Texture, Text, and Context: New Approaches in Chicano Historiography," *Mexican Studies/Estudios Mexicanos* 12 (winter 1986); Ruiz, "Teaching Chicano/American History: Goals and Methods," *History Teacher* 20, no. 2 (February 1987); Cynthia E. Orozco. "Beyond Machismo, La Familia, and Ladies Auxiliaries: A Historiography of Mexican Origin Women's Participation in Voluntary Associations and Politics in the United States, 1870–1990," *Perspectives* 5 (1995): 1–34.

Other key essays include Alma Garcia, "The Development of Chicana Feminist Discourse, 1970–1980," in *Unequal Sisters,* Ellen Carol DuBois and Vicki L. Ruiz, eds. (New York: Routledge, 1990): 418–431; and Antonia Castañeda, "Women of Color and the Rewriting of Western History: The Discourse, Politics, and Decolonization of History," *Pacific Historical Review* 61, no. 4 (1992)501–533.

40. Richard Griswold del Castillo, "Southern California's Chicano History: Regional Origins and National Critique," *Aztlán* 19, no. 1 (spring 1988–90): 105–124; Griswold del Castillo, "Tejanos and California Chicanos: Regional Variations in Mexican American History," *Mexican Studies/Estudios Mexicanos* 1, no. 1 (winter 1985); Arnoldo de Leon, "Tejano History Scholarship: A Review of the Recent Literature," *West Texas Historical Association Year Book* 59 (1985); de Leon, "Texas Mexicans: Twentieth Century Interpretations," in *Texas Through Time: Evolving Interpretations,* Walter L. Buenger and Robert A. Calvert, eds. (College Station: Texas A&M University Press, 1991).

41. Tomas Almaguer, "Interpreting Chicano History: The World System Approach to nineteenth Century California," Working Paper No. 101 (Berkeley: University of California, Institute for the Study of Social Change, 1977); Almaguer, "Ideological Distortions in Recent Chicano Historiography: The Internal Colonial Model and the Chicano Historical Interpretation," *Aztlán* 18, no. 1 (1987): 7–28.

42. Ramón A. Gutiérrez, "Community, Patriarchy and Individualism: The Politics of Chicano History and the Dream of Equality," *American Quarterly* 45, no. 1 (March 1993): 44–72; Ramón A. Gutiérrez, "Unraveling America's Hispanic Past: Internal Stratification and Class Boundaries," *Aztlan* 17, no. 1 (1986): 79–101; Ramón A. Gutiérrez, "Historiography and A New Vision for Chicana/o Studies," JSRI Occasional Papers (East Lansing, Mich.: Michigan State University, Julian Samora Research Institute, 1996).

43. Abraham Hoffman, "Where are the Mexican Americans? A Textbook Omission Overdue for Revision," *History Teacher* 6 (1972); Roger W. Lochin and David J. West, "The New Chicano History: Two Perspectives, Three

Recent Books and Two Analytical and Bibliographical Essays," *History Teacher* 16, no. 2 (February 1983); and Vicki L. Ruiz, "Teaching Chicano/American History: Goals and Methods," *History Teacher* 20, no. 2 (February 1987).

44. Among asessments of the direction of the field are Rodolfo F. Acuña, "An Essay on Truth and Objectivity in Chicano Scholarship," JSRI Occasional Papers (East Lansing, Mich.: Michigan State University, Julian Samora Research Institute, 1996); and Ramón A. Gutiérrez. "Chicano History: Paradigm Shifts and Shifting Boundaries," JSRI Occasional Papers (East Lansing, Mich.: Michigan State University, Julian Samora Research Institute, 1996).

CHAPTER 14

THE ORIGINS AND HISTORY OF THE CHICANO MOVEMENT

Roberto Rodríguez

The Origins and History of the Chicano Movement

SOME MARK THE BEGINNING OF the Chicano resistance movement when Columbus was met by a fusillade of arrows in his first attempt to land in the Americas. Others set its beginning at the time of the defense of Tenochtitlán (now Mexico City) in 1521—pitting the Cuauhtemoc-led forces against the Spanish invaders. Others set it at the end of the Mexican-American War in 1848, when Mexico lost half of its territory to the United States and its Mexican residents became "strangers in their own lands."

The modern Chicano political movement, most scholars agree, began during the mid-1960s—a time coinciding with the Black Power Movement.

"It was a time of de-colonization struggles around the world and global revolution," says educator Elizabeth Martinez, author of various books, including "500 Years of Chicano History."[1]

In the 1960s, the Chicano Movement was both a civil and human rights struggle, and a movement for liberation. In this realm, universities became one of the focal points of protest in the movement. Some of the principal demands were to open up universities to people of color and the establishment of Chicano studies, which was envisioned—through "El Plan de Santa Barbara"—as a place where the intellectual work of the movement could take place, at the service of the Chicano community.

Ada Sosa-Riddell, director of the Chicana/Latina Center, University of California at Davis, says that Movimiento Estudiantil Chicano de

Aztlán (MEChA) and Chicano studies represent two of the long-lasting legacies of the Chicano Movement. However, with the advent of the anti-affirmative action mood of the country, we may well see the death of ethnic studies, she says.

"But you can't destroy Chicano studies" she continues, "You would have to burn the literature."

Chicano and Chicana Movements

In terms of the Chicano Movement, perhaps it's more appropriate to speak of movements in the plurality because the struggles in the different parts of the country were many, with separate goals and visions and unique histories. Some of them included: the struggle to improve the lives of farmworkers, the effort to end Jim Crow–style segregation and police repression, the land-grant struggles to recoup land lost as a result of the Mexican-American War, the struggle to improve educational opportunities, and the struggle for political representation and self-determination.

In time, other movements blossomed, specifically, the struggle for gender equality, access to higher education and immigrant rights, and a literary and artistic revolution that spoke to cultural rebirth and a rediscovery of mestizo/indigenous roots and self-definition.

This was brown power. It was also the building of Aztlán. For some, building Aztlán (the U.S. Southwest—or the lands stolen from Mexico during the Mexican-American War) literally meant fighting for a sovereign nation, while for others, it was the spiritual building of a people.

Each of these movements spawned hundreds of organizations, such as the United Farm Worker's Union, La Raza Unida Party, La Alianza de Pueblos Libres, the Brown Berets, the National Chicano Moratorium, CASA—Hermandad General de Trabajadores, the Crusade For Justice, the Mexican American Youth Organization, MEChA, the August 29th Movement, and Comision Femenil Nacional Mexicana. This succeeded a period in history in which the Mexican community was perceived by society as politically dormant.

During this time of great social upheaval, political fervor, and cultural rebirth, the Chicano Movement was hardly unified. The reasons: lack of historical memory, regionalism and sectarianism, but also government and law enforcement efforts to destroy this nascent movement, which was viewed as divisive and separatist.

The 1960s and 1970s were an exciting time, says Lea Ybarra, associate provost for academic affairs at California State University at Fresno. "We felt we could make a difference."

At Fresno State, where she began her studies, there was only a handful of Chicano and Chicana students. Today, there are more than four thousand. Now, students take things for granted: "We are witnessing a new phenomenon: the professors are more radical than the students," she states.

Luis Arroyo, professor and chair of Chicano and Latino studies at California State University at Long Beach, says that the Chicano Movement began as a movement for dignity and self-respect. During that phase—of struggling to be recognized as a people—there was a sense of unity. Yet, once an attempt was made to define the movement and give it an ideology, "We began to develop competing definitions as to what the movement was," says Arroyo.

To this day, those competing definitions continue to shape how scholars define what the movement was or wasn't, when it started, when and if it ended, and what it should be. A spillover of that conflict included what to call people of Mexican-origin and whether the words Chicano and Chicana included people with origins other than Mexico.

Teresa Cordova, a feminist Chicana scholar at the University of New Mexico, says that an analysis of the Chicano Movement cannot be reduced to a European "great men in history" model (or great women), because it was a social movement. Those who say the Chicano Movement is dead, she adds, reveal their own disconnection: "Anyone saying the movement is dead means he's dead!"

A number of the past activists—many of whom were students—are today part of the environmental justice movement, work with youth, work in health or legal clinics, or teach in schools, she says. Many are also now senior scholars. "When we focus on the big names, we're missing the point. It didn't function that way," says Cordova. "There were lots of soldiers."

To the thesis that the Chicano Movement is dead, Ada Sosa-Riddell replies: "No, but there's a lot of people trying to kill it."

Precursors and the Missing Generation

What differentiates the Chicano Movement from earlier Mexican civil rights struggles is its national character, its mass nature, and its strong student base at colleges and universities.

Indeed, the role of students was unique in the 1960s and 1970s. The university became both a political battleground and a focal point of protest regarding its elitist nature in keeping people of color and working-class students outside of its doors.

While there had been political resistance ever since the Mexican-American War, and while there had been student activism on a smaller scale during the 1930s and 1940s, it was not until after World War II that Mexican Americans began to be visible on college campuses. However, it was not until the 1960s—as a result of educational opportunity programs—that Chicanos/Chicanas streamed onto campuses in unprecedented numbers. The exception, particularly in the nineteenth century, were the children of landed elites.

Their prior absence was generally due to segregation/discrimination in the educational system, says Carlos Muñoz, professor at UC Berkeley and author of "Youth, Identity and Power," a book that chronicles the Chicano Movement.[2]

As such, there was no intellectual tradition in the Mexican-American community in higher education similar to that which has existed in the African-American community. The reason, says Muñoz, is that after the Mexican-American War, Whites did not feel a responsibility to educate Mexican Americans. Thus, there was never a push to create Mexican-American colleges similar to the Black colleges.

Absent a large presence in higher education, Mexican-American public scholars debated the issues of the day in newspapers, as opposed to lecture halls. As an example, *El Clamor Público,* published by Francisco P. Ramirez in Los Angeles in the 1850s, provided a forum for the discontented Mexican community in the United States.

Arturo Madrid, the Murchison Distinguished Professor of Humanities at Trinity University, says that contrary to popular belief, there is an untapped wealth of literature in Mexico about the Mexican-origin population in the United States prior to 1960. This was the era of McArthyism and large-scale deportations of Mexicans that were both indiscriminate and also selectively targeted against Mexican political, labor, and community leaders—"against anyone that was suspect," he says. With a few exceptions, the effect was to leave in place a less combative Mexican-American intellectual leadership, says Madrid.

Luis Arroyo agrees, saying that in his research he has uncovered a wealth of information regarding writings, books, and writers by immigrants prior to the 1960s. One such writer was Ramon Welch, he says, who wrote political commentaries and was a social activist in the 1950s prior to being deported.

Felix Gutierrez, director of the Freedom Forum's Pacific Media Center and whose parents were journalists and student activists during the 1930s–50s, says that political activism has always been a part of the Mexican-American community. "What people were talking about in the 1960s, we were living in the 1950s," he says.

Gutierrez himself represents a link between the "Mexican-American Movement" of the 1930s–50s, whose motto was "Progress through Education," and the 1960s movement. He, along with Ralph Guzman, were the faculty advisors for the first United Mexican American Student organization at California State University at Los Angeles.

Incidentally, Gutierrez followed in his parents' footsteps, obtaining a masters degree in journalism from Northwestern University. Yet at a time when Whites could obtain jobs in newsrooms without degrees, Gutierrez could not obtain a job in mainstream media. After a career in academe, he is now considered one of the nation's top media experts.

While Gutierrez sees the birth of the Chicano Movement as a resurgence of the earlier 1930s–50s movement, he distinguishes the 1960s as "a period of turbulence."

One of the principal parts of the country where that turbulence manifested was in Crystal City, Texas, where in 1963, Chicanos took over the city council in a part of the country that had long been dominated by agricultural patrons. The program of activists there, which is documented in the book "Avant-garde of the Chicano Movement in Texas," by UC Riverside professor Armando Navarro, [3] "was to eliminate and replace the gringo," says Jose Angel Gutierrez, a professor at the University of Texas at Arlington

Struggling against Jim Crow institutions, Chicano activists also won school board elections in South Texas but found out that Anglos remained embedded in power, as power brokers, teachers, and administrators. This knowledge, says Angel Gutierrez, is what triggered the creation of La Raza Unida Party—the first and only political party for Chicanos: "We became the electoral arm of the Chicano Movement."

Links to the Black Civil Rights Movement

Elizabeth Martinez, a past director of the New York chapter of the Student Nonviolent Coordinating Committee (SNCC) and affiliated with the organization since 1960, says that the Chicano Movement had not simply symbolic links with the civil rights movement, but actual ties. Martinez, who is of Oaxacan indigenous ancestry, grew up riding the back of the bus in the nation's capital. That experience is what created a bond with her to the civil rights movement.

SNCC was one of the principal groups involved in sit-ins at lunch counters and voter education in efforts to desegregate the South. In 1963, after four little girls were killed by a Ku Klux Klan bomb in Birmingham, Alabama, Martinez was enraged to the point where she joined the organization as a full-time member. In the Freedom Summer of 1964, shortly after the bodies of three murdered civil rights workers were found, Martinez recalls driving through the Mississippi Delta, thinking that the place was "stained with so much blood of so many black people who just tried to register people to vote."

Martinez notes that in 1965, as a member of SNCC, she delivered a speech at the historic farmworker march from Delano, California to Sacramento, in solidarity with the United Farm Worker's Union. In 1968, on behalf of SNCC, she traveled to Albuquerque, to connect with the Chicano land struggle associated with New Mexico and to help found *El Grito del Norte* newspaper. "I went for two weeks and I stayed for eight years," she says.

New Mexico had drawn the attention of SNCC because in 1967, members of the Alianza land grant organization had staged an armed raid on a courthouse, protesting the Anglo theft of New Mexican land grants. Prior to the courthouse raid, the farmworker's movement—begun in 1963—had drawn the support of Martin Luther King Jr.

In 1966, aware of the uneasy race relations within the civil rights movement, Martinez began writing articles about being neither Black or White. Even then, she pointed to a problem that Latinos today often observe: when it comes to race, Latinos don't matter.

Many other Chicanos and Chicano organizations, such as Denver's Crusade for Justice and the National Brown Berets, were involved with the Black civil rights movement. Many of them later became instrumental in forming linkages between the Chicano, the Black Power, and the American Indian Movements.

The Development of Chicano Studies

In the late 1960s, as the struggle over access to higher education became increasingly important, high schools, colleges, and universities became not simply focal points of protest but also recruitment grounds for the different movements.

Carlos Muñoz, one of the many principals involved in the political development of the 1960s movement, says that the relatively large influx of Chicano students into universities unleashed both a political movement focused on civil and human rights, and an intellectual movement that both challenged historical knowledge and created the discipline of Chicano studies.

UCLA professor Juan Gómez-Quiñonez, author of various books including "Roots of Chicano Politics, 1600–1940" and "Chicano Politics: Reality and Promise, 1940–1990," says that while resistance has always been present in the Chicano community, "Something different did happen in the 1960s that wasn't there before. It was an attitude."

That attitude was reflected in the concepts of Chicanos belonging to a community and that they were not foreigners, but indigenous to the Southwest. Gómez-Quiñonez notes that the placard, "This is our Land," first appeared at a rally at UCLA in 1967. Prior to the Chicano Movement, many people of Mexican origin privately spoke of the Southwest as Mexican/indigenous land, but it was not until the Chicano movement that this was done in a public or political manner.

Books such as *Occupied America,* by CSU Northridge professor, Rodolfo Acuña[4]—which was widely used in Chicano studies classes—created the intellectual underpinnings that rejected the notions, accepted by previous generations, that Chicanos were immigrants or foreigners, that they wanted to assimilate, and that they were docile.

When Chicano studies was created, its purpose was to give intellectual support to the movement and to listen to the voices of both men and women and the community organizations. The community produced the ideas and Chicano studies provided the intellectual support, says Gómez-Quiñonez.

Prior to the development of Chicano studies as a discipline, very little knowledge existed about the Chicano, says Refugio Rochín, former director of the Julian Samora Research Institute (JSRI) at Michigan State University. Neither was there a Chicano studies curriculum, and there were very few Chicano professors.

Julian Samora, who taught at Notre Dame from 1959–85, along with folklorist Americo Paredes and scholar labor activist Ernesto Galarza, was one of the few scholars who studied Mexican Americans and the Mexican-American community. Today, the JSRI, founded in 1989, carries on the work that Samora pioneered, the study of Latinos in the Midwest.

In the 1950s and early 1960s, because the scholarship of those three and a few others was not widely known, students like Rochín who were interested in studying Mexicans had to rely on Anglo scholars. After a stint with the Peace Corps in Colombia in the early 1960s, Rochín says his experience in Latin America reaffirmed his interest in his roots. Yet there was nowhere to study Mexican Americans except in the Latin American departments, he says. "Anglos were teaching us about ourselves," he says. It was the same mentality that Peter Skerry, author of *Mexican Americans: The Ambivalent Minority* writes about today: "the Anglo model of wanting us to assimilate," says Rochín. [5]

With the advent of Chicano studies programs, for the first time, Chicano and Chicana scholars began to produce knowledge about their own community.

"Chicano studies changed the way we viewed the land we lived on," and it also allowed Chicanos to see U.S. imperialism, says Rochín. It also connected Chicanos to their indigenous roots and to Native American studies, he says.

The movement also created the idea of "sin fronteras"—"the concept of no borders," says Rochín.

Rochín notes also that while there are a few Chicano research centers or departments in the Midwest, such as at Michigan State University, Wayne State University, the University of Minnesota, and the University of Wisconsin, most were developed in California, where Chicanos were numerous, but still in the minority. This contrasts with a general lack of Chicano studies programs along the U.S./Mexico border, where Chicanos are in the majority.

The body of knowledge, and the resultant vast and growing literature, produced and recovered by a generation of Chicano and Chicana scholars, has proved that Chicano studies is a discipline, not a subdiscipline, adds Rochín. "Chicano studies has its own merit and its literature is unique."

Chicano and Chicana studies has pioneered immigrant studies and the study of the family, bilingual issues, and mestizaje, or cultural and racial mixture, says Rochín. The study of living and dealing with duality can be helpful to societies that are now having to deal with similar populations and ethnic tensions, he says.

Despite this, Chicano and Chicana studies is not on safe ground, and the reason for this has more to do with political attacks and back door attacks against their budgets than it does with scholarship.

Rochín says that multiculturalism has actually "killed interest [on the part of universities] in Chicano studies." Additionally, the notion of grouping all Latinos under the rubric "Hispanic" has also weakened and diluted the intent of Chicano studies and Puerto Rican studies, he says. Now, professors with little or no connection to Chicano studies get hired simply by the fact that they are from Spain or South America. "We're still suffering from that," he says.

Jose Angel Gutierrez, of the University of Texas at Arlington, whose Mexican-American studies center was recently created, says that Chicano studies centers and departments have stopped being advocates. The exception, he says, are campuses such as CSU Northridge. Unlike other departments around the country, CSUN's Chicano studies department has historically been connected to political action, not simply quaint and disconnected ideological theories that focus on the self, he says. His center's contribution to the discipline, he says, will be to teach how to win an election and how to take community control. With his long experience in organizing, he says he will also contribute advice on how not to make mistakes. "I'm not a footnote."

Arturo Madrid states that after the initial phase of Chicano studies, Chicano and Chicana scholars—not by their choosing—generally confined their studies to the university. This is what motivated a number of scholars, including himself, to create the Tomas Rivera Center (TRC) think tank in 1984.

"It [TRC] was the first place where on a sustained basis, the intellectual research on the Chicano/Latino community was connected with persons who shape and influence public policy," says Madrid. As opposed to leaving the research on a university shelf, the idea was "to bring intellectual firepower [to public policy debates]," he says.

Maria Herrera Sobek, a professor at UC Santa Barbara is the kind of scholar who was both a product of and a participant in the Chicano Movement. Born of farmworker immigrant parents, Sobek grew up in a shack, attended segregated schools in Texas, and also picked cotton. Today a renowned scholar and poet, she says her background helped shape her academic studies. Her work on folklore and *corridos*—or ballads—comes directly from her upbringing, she says.

She says that while Chicano studies has been great for the university and the community, she agrees that Chicano scholars have not been successful at presenting their research to the public. This is particularly true on the issue of bilingual education. Despite the fact that all major research shows that bilingual education works, "The opposition has shaped the debate," she says.

Antonia Castañeda, a history professor at St. Mary's University in Texas, says that Chicano studies challenged the structure of the university. Yet because it is relatively a new field, it has historically been engaged in a struggle for survival. That's part of the reason why many scholars did not take part in public policy debates outside of the academy. "Linkages [still] need to be made," she says.

"The issues of housing, health, education, and child welfare have not gone away," says Castañeda. "Some of us have made it, but power will always make room for individuals."

The Rise of Chicana Feminist Scholars

Lea Ybarra was present when the National Association of Chicana and Chicano Scholars (NACCS) was formed. "By the time NACCS was created in 1974, women had to be taken into account," she says. For example, as an undergraduate, she had been the chair of the Third World Coalition at UC Berkeley, where women were in many leadership positions.

Despite this, men had to be constantly challenged for their lack of attention to women's issues. The women of NACCS did not allow themselves to be walked upon, she says: "There were so few of us, we were assertive. We had to be."

However, NACCS did not have a conference dedicated to women until 1983. Castañeda says that the Chicano Movement—which was a movement for liberation—was fraught with internal contradictions: "It was male-defined. It was sexist, misogynistic, and homophobic. The movement was about economic, educational and political equality, but fundamentally, it was not about gender equality."

Contrary to the picture of the ideal Mexican family—promoted by Chicano scholars—in which the woman stays at home to raise the children, Mexican women have always worked, at both waged and unwaged labor, says Castañeda. The challenge for Chicana scholars is not only to dispel such myths, but also to continue to examine the intersection of class, race, and gender, she adds. "For instance, Chicano scholars have examined police brutality, but not internal [domestic] violence directed at women."

Just as importantly, the anti–affirmative action mood of the country has Castañeda "terrified," because she fears it will shut off the pipeline of Chicana and Chicano scholars currently being trained at universities. "That is their [foes'] intent."

Chicana feminist scholars are exploring issues ignored by Chicanos, such as the role of women and gender in colonial society; early labor organizing efforts by Chicanas; and the role of women in community, civil, and human rights organizations. Chicana lesbians are also at the forefront of literature and other critical issues that affect all of the Chicano/Chicana community, says Castañeda.

At the end of the 1970s, Ada Sosa-Ridell, who was part of the early Chicana Caucus within NACCS, helped confound Mujeres Activas en Letras en Cambio Social (Active Women in Letters for Social Change [MALCS]), to deal with specific Chicana feminist issues. Prior to the time when Chicana feminists stepped forward, dealing with feminist issues had been "seen as White women stuff," she says.

This emphasis on examining women's issues caused a big conflict. "The biggest conflict was internal—among Chicanas," says Sosa-Riddell. "We were passionate." When Chicanas debated Chicanos, Chicanas didn't take their male counterpart's arguments seriously. "What do you expect, they're men," was the attitude Chicana scholars had.

Some of the issues that created heavy conflicts were lesbian concerns. "At stake was what it meant to be woman-centered," says Sosa-Riddell. Yet, to this day, many of the same issues continue to cause intense conflict, she adds.

MALCS has allowed for a full articulation of feminism, says Sosa-Ridell. For instance, Cynthia Orozco, a professor at the University of New Mexico, has challenged the 1969 "El Plan de Santa Barbara," the document that laid the foundation for Chicano studies, as excluding women.

A Resurgence of the Chicano/Chicana Movement

Many scholars maintain that ever since the death of farm labor leader Cesar Chávez in 1993, there has been a resurgence in the Chicano Movement, particularly at colleges and universities nationwide.

This new activism peaked in 1994 when hundreds of thousands of junior and senior high and college students across the country walked out of schools and held marches and rallies in opposition to California's anti-immigrant Proposition 187. "The mass mobilization against 187 reaffirmed the need to be unified," says Angela Acosta, an organizer with the Willie Valesquez Research Institute in Los Angeles. "The Chicano Movement shaped my life," says Acosta. Yet as someone who worked against 187, she believes the new movement isn't limited to Chicanos, but includes Latinos and other immigrants as well.

This new activism is also being manifested in the current multiracial movement to defend affirmative action, in which men and women and members of all races are struggling jointly to fight off the anti-affirmative movement.

Lea Ybarra says that despite the continuing attacks against Latinos and other people of color, "We [the 60s generation] have to be proud. There's still a lot to do, but we have to remember that we did accomplish a lot." Ybarra concludes: "There will always be a need for Chicano studies. It is a discipline, it's not taught in high schools, and our color's not going to change."

Genevieve Aguilar, a student at Stanford, says that the Chicano Movement is definitely not dead—that it lives in students like herself who battle against those who believe that racism no longer exists and who don't see a need for Chicano or Latino programs. When students ask Aguilar, who has been in a number of Chicano and Chicana education organizations since she was in the ninth grade, why there isn't an institute for Whites, she responds: "There is: It's called government."

Maria Jimenez, a long-time human rights activist and director of the Immigration and Law Enforcement Monitoring Project with the American Friends Service Committee in Houston, says that the October 12, 1996, Latino march on Washington was the culmination of twenty-five to thirty years of struggle of the Chicano Movement: "It was the culmination of a historical experience," she says.

She views the march as "a maturation of political forces." While acknowledging that there have been thousands of Raza marches throughout the country, none had ever been staged in Washington. Latinos and Latinas have always had local marches because they've responded to the local conditions in which they live. The march demonstrated a national presence, she says. The message the marchers delivered, she says, is: "We're here, we've always been here, and we're not going away."

References

Acuña, Rodolfo. *Occupied America: A History of Chicanos,* 2d ed. (New York: Harper & Row, 1981).

Martinez, Elizabeth Sutherland. *Viva La Causa!; 500 Years of Chicano History* (Collision Course Video Productions, 1995).

Muñoz, Carlos. *Youth, Identity, Power: The Chicano Movement* (London: Verso, 1989).

Navarro, Armando. *Mexican American Youth Organization: Avant-garde of the Chicano Movement in Texas* (Austin: University of Texas Press, 1995).

Skerry, Peter. *Mexican Americans: The Ambivalent Minority* (New York: Free Press; Maxwell Macmillan Canada; Maxwell Macmillan International, 1993).

Notes

1. Elizabeth Sutherland Martinez, *Viva La Causa!; 500 Years of Chicano History* (Collision Course Video Productions, 1995).
2. Carlos Muñoz, *Youth, Identity, Power: The Chicano Movement* (London: Verso, 1989).
3. Armando Navarro, *Mexican American Youth Organization: Avant-garde of the Chicano Movement in Texas* (Austin: University of Texas Press, 1995).
4. Rodolfo Acuña, *Occupied America: A History of Chicanos,* 2d ed. (New York: Harper & Row, 1981).
5. Peter Skerry, *Mexican Americans: The Ambivalent Minority* (New York: Free Press; Maxwell Macmillan Canada; Maxwell Macmillan International, 1993).